THE WINTER
OF THE WORLD

INTRODUCTION

I

War – the 'Great War', as it was already being called – had been prophesied and feared in Britain long before August 1914. Late nineteenth-century literature is full of imagery of last sunsets, mass slaughter and apocalypse. Unexpected disasters in the South African war and the worrying rise of German militarism led to a long-running national debate, as well as a vociferous campaign for rearmament and conscription, strongly supported by a number of writers, including Rudyard Kipling and other poets.[1] Novels, as well as two long poems by Charles Doughty, *The Cliffs* (1909) and *The Clouds* (1912), warned of a German invasion, Doughty denouncing Britain as 'Petticoat Island', inexcusably weak and unprepared. Liberals and radicals replied that such 'alarmism' would only make conflict more likely. Public opinion was divided, although nearly everyone could agree that a modern war would be immense and terrible. Alfred Noyes's 1913 poem, *The Wine Press*, described young men on a Somme-like battlefield:

Mown down! Mown down! Mown down! Mown down!
　　They staggered in sheets of fire,
They reeled like ships in a sudden blast,
　　And shreds of flesh went spattering past ...

INTRODUCTION

In the weeks before August 1914 many poems and articles expressed dread and revulsion at the growing threat, but when the crisis came the overwhelming majority of British people accepted that the German invasion of Belgium could not be allowed to go unchallenged. The Liberal government's eventual declaration of war was generally applauded, and Noyes was typical of many poets in putting doubts and disagreements aside: the only answer to Germany now had to be 'Unity and Scorn' ('The United Front', *Daily Mail*, 6 August). Anthologies of old patriotic poems were hurried into print, and in the introduction to one of them, *Our Glorious Heritage / A Book of Patriotic Verse for Boys and Girls*, the Dean of Norwich explained what he and many others believed to be the task of the war poet:

> he can give articulate voice to the love of country and the love of freedom and any other special idea that animates either combatant, such as respect for a nation's pledged word, or the protection of the weak against the strong; and also he can celebrate the heroic exploits of armies and individuals which every war calls forth.

The 'special ideas' in Britain — seen as inescapable moral imperatives for war — were sympathy for Belgium and outrage at Germany's violation of the treaty, the 'pledged word', by which both Britain and Germany had guaranteed Belgian neutrality. 'Brave little Belgium' had to be rescued from the Prussian monster. Prussia was thought of as the source of German militarism — professional, highly specialized, pitiless — and against it there would be gallant British amateurs, sportsmen, gentlemen players, who would 'take the Kaiser's middle wicket / And smash it by clean British Cricket', as Jessie Pope was to assure the *Daily Mail*'s readers in May 1915.[2] Soon the war was being referred to as 'the Greater Game', 'the Great Adventure', 'the Last Crusade'.

Established poets took up the challenge with enthusiasm, often waiving copyright or donating fees to new wartime charities. On 2 September 1914 *The Times* published a letter from the Poet Laureate, Robert Bridges, declaring that the war was between Christ and the Devil, and a poem, 'For all we have and are', by Kipling, who warned that the old world was dead – as in ancient Rome, the 'Hun' was at the gate (7). On the same day, the government's new propaganda department held a secret conference for at least twenty-five senior 'men of letters', including Bridges, Laurence Binyon, G. K. Chesterton, Arthur Conan Doyle, Thomas Hardy, John Masefield and Owen Seaman. One result was Hardy's 'Men Who March Away' (8). The main task was to support the recruiting drive, but ministers also wanted help in exerting discreet influence on neutral countries, especially the United States. It is worth remembering that many 1914–16 poems by leading writers were intended, though never explicitly, to show American readers how united and honourable Britain was. New poems appeared daily in newspapers and magazines, and many were reproduced as postcards and broadsheets, sold in aid of Belgian refugees. The first two anthologies of wartime verse, *Poems of the Great War* and *Songs and Sonnets for England in War Time*, were in print by the end of 1914.

Some older poets were astonishingly prolific: by May 1915, for instance, Canon H. D. Rawnsley – now mainly remembered as a co–founder of the National Trust – had published no fewer than 148 war poems, mostly sonnets. William Watson had published sixteen poems by mid-September 1914, with ten more ready to be sent off to newspapers. Watson had been a fierce opponent of the Boer War, but now, like many other Liberals, he rallied to the cause (later earning a knighthood for a poem that heaped praise on Lloyd George), and he hoped to become the leading poet of the war. 'I am giving my brain, I am giving my heart', he declared in August (4). No one seems to have pointed out that soldiers were making such sacrifices rather more literally.

Watson and many other writers were convinced that poetry had to be patriotic and that the only language for it was traditional nineteenth-century rhetoric. One newspaper even claimed that 'the literary appeal, and nothing else, has saved this country from conscription'.[3] 'The demand is for the crude, for what everybody is saying or thinking,' Edward Thomas commented in a December article, adding that when thoughts become ready for true poetry they 'may recede far from their original resemblance to all the world's, and may seem to have little to do with daily events'.[4] He might have been describing his own poems, few of which refer directly to the war although all were written during it. As the war went on, the chorus of 'what everybody is saying' began to break down into individual voices, as the more talented poets worked out what they wanted to say and how to say it. Even by the end of 1914, plenty of critics would have agreed with the left-wing publisher C. W. Daniel that the old language was proving to be hopelessly inadequate:

The farther you get with this dam' nonsense the more difficult
    it becomes,
And instead of trying to write intelligently you find yourself
    talking of 'drums'
For no other reason than because 'drums' and 'becomes' rhymes,
Which seems to be the main idea of all the war poetry I have
    read in *The Times*.[5]

Satire directed at the war and its supporters did not begin with
Siegfried Sassoon, Wilfred Owen or any other poet who had seen
the trenches. The strength of radical politics in Victorian and
Edwardian Britain, as well as a literary tradition inherited from
Swift, Byron, Shelley, Southey and others, meant that there was
some political opposition to the conflict from August 1914
onwards.[6] A handful of civilian writers on left-wing newspapers
scorned official motives and excuses from the beginning (*18*), (*19*),
(*20*); but – as in other European countries – radicals disagreed
about the war. The well-known socialist, H. G. Wells, supported
the government with his famous assertion that this would be a
'war that will end war'. The dissenting voices were therefore
relatively few and scarcely heard: if there was to be a new language
for war poetry it would have to come from elsewhere.

***

II

One of the first poems with any depth to it was by John Masefield (11), a leading 'Georgian' poet. *Georgian Poetry 1911–1912*, an anthology of new verse by younger writers, edited by Edward Marsh, had been published by Harold Monro's Poetry Bookshop in December 1912.[7] Four more volumes were to follow, two during the war in 1915 and 1917, and two after, in 1919 and 1922. The project had been agreed on by Marsh and four poets, Monro, Wilfrid Gibson, Rupert Brooke and John Drinkwater, three of whom were to make crucial contributions to war poetry in 1914. The typical Georgian style was deliberately anti-Victorian, replacing nineteenth-century rhetoric and vagueness with plain language, simplicity and realistic, occasionally even violent, detail – a way of writing that had been pioneered by Gibson, who in 1905 had become the first twentieth-century poet to decide that poets should concern themselves with the lives and troubles of ordinary, contemporary people. Gibson's verse earned him the title of 'People's Poet', and by 1912 he was easily the best known of the four founder-Georgians.

Until 1919, *Georgian Poetry* was seen by many as the brightest hope for the future of English verse, and some of the war's most original poets were either contributors to the anthology or closely associated with them. Gibson, Monro and Drinkwater contributed to all five volumes, as did Walter de la Mare. The 1917 edition featured three of the most promising young soldier-poets, Sassoon, Robert Graves and Robert Nichols, as well as a lyric by Isaac Rosenberg. Edmund Blunden came in after the war. Edward

Thomas was friendly with several Georgians, Owen was proud to call himself a Georgian in 1918, Charles Sorley thought highly of Masefield, and Ivor Gurney admired the work of both Masefield and Gibson. The 1919 volume was a sad disappointment, however, reviled by critics – and some contributors – as a feeble response to the war. 'Georgianism', which had never had any organization or agreed aims, was swept aside by the movement now known as Modernism – and as a result the Georgian achievement has been seriously undervalued. No other group of writers made a greater contribution to First World War poetry.

Modernism had taken root in the arts across Europe before 1914. In Britain a handful of poets, led by T. E. Hulme, F. S. Flint and the American Ezra Pound, had begun meeting in 1908–09 to hammer out new ideas. Hulme wanted poetry to be 'impressionist', precise, direct, 'hard' and 'dry', free, as Pound put it in 1912, from 'emotional slither'. These early Modernists had much in common with the future Georgians, and for a while they worked together, but in 1912 Pound broke away to set up a short-lived school of his own, announcing that Hulme, Richard Aldington and a few others were 'Imagists'. His anthology, *Des imagistes* (April 1914), was a counterblast to *Georgian Poetry*, even though it, too, was published by Monro. It found few readers; most of the public and even many poets were scarcely aware of Modernism in literature until the 1920s. Among the soldier-poets, several, notably Rosenberg and Pound's friend Frederic Manning, were influenced by the new way of writing, but perhaps only Hulme, Aldington and Herbert Read can be seen as fully committed Modernists – although the civilian John Rodker took the style to extremes, beyond anything they might have attempted (*228*).

Most older poets were unaffected by either Georgianism or Modernism. The two most celebrated poets of the age, still at the height of their powers, were Hardy and Kipling: Hardy had few imitators, and Kipling was detested by many younger writers for his political views, but both men need to be counted among the leading 'war poets', writing in support of the war yet showing that they were well aware of the suffering and loss that it caused. Kipling's loathing of Germany emerged in some deeply unattractive work (*212*): when it was rumoured in 1914 that he might be sent to lecture in America, the Liberal Foreign Secretary, Sir Edward Grey, actually threatened to resign. Moderate voices were more useful, and Hardy was one of many senior writers who did their best to turn out poems when government departments asked for them.

IIII

It has been usual for at least the last forty years to imagine that most civilian poets in 1914–18 tended to write in an elevated, idealistic style like William Watson's, whereas most poetry by soldiers was more or less 'Sassoonish': angry, often satirical protests on behalf of ordinary soldiers, intended to make civilians recognize the truth about life and death in the trenches. At the start there were Rupert Brooke and Julian Grenfell, patriotic, naïve, deluded; later, mostly after the Somme, there were Sassoon, Owen and many more, writing in savage indignation from the bitterness of front-line experience. So runs the myth. But First World War poetry is more complex and interesting than that. Where did Sassoonish, supposedly 'typical', Great War poetry come from? Who first set aside the language of patriotism and sacrifice, trying instead to write in simple, direct words about front-line realities?

The first attempts came from civilians, not soldiers, and very early in the war. In the September 1914 editorial of his influential periodical *Poetry and Drama*, Monro commented that most war poems so far had been 'in the nature either of music-hall songs or rhymed leading articles' – but the conflict might in due course encourage the 'tendency of pre-war poets to strip verse of romantic ornament and sentimental detail, and to expose the raw material of thought and the elementary facts of experience'. The most appropriate style might be that of military despatches (he was probably thinking of newspaper reports, which were not yet censored), a plain, direct language that laid bare 'the plain facts of the human psychology of the moment'.

This was radical advice, both Georgian and Modernist, and Monro put it into practice in a quartet of poems, 'Youth in Arms' (*14*). Two of these are known to have been finished by 22 October, and all four may well have been written as early as September. They are remarkable for their date, especially 'Retreat', which is based on reports of the August retreat from Mons. Monro uses elements of the Modernist style to convey the 'plain facts', with no regard for patriotic sentiments or high-flown diction. He is the first 1914–18 poet to focus on the likely front-line experience and mental state of the ordinary soldier.

Monro's ideas would have been known to his fellow poet and former lodger, Wilfrid Gibson. Gibson could not think of war in terms of national values or movements of armies: to him it was always a matter of 'innumerable personal tragedies'.[8] His pre-war poems had been about the lives of the industrial and rural poor, and it was a natural step from there to writing about ordinary soldiers at the front. His first war poems, 'Breakfast' and 'The Messages', were published in *The Nation* on 17 October 1914 (*15*), (*16*). They deserve to be recognized as two of the most significant works in the development of First World War poetry. Their extraordinarily early date had been forgotten by the 1960s, when anthologists assumed that Gibson had been writing later in the war as a soldier who had been in the fighting. In fact, he didn't join the army until 1917, and never got nearer the front than south London. Even so, like 'Retreat', 'Breakfast' is about actual front-line experience: it derives from a soldier's anecdote that Gibson had read in *The Nation*.

Gibson continued to produce poems of this kind for nearly a year, publishing them as a little book, *Battle*, in September 1915. All but one of the *Battle* poems are very short, and many of them are probably drawn from stories he had read in the press or heard from returning soldiers. He told Marsh he wanted the book to 'get at' people. Marsh sent copies to several poets in the army, including Graves, Sassoon and Rosenberg, and *Battle* was also read by Owen and Gurney. It was a seminal work: most obviously, it provided models for Sassoon in 1916–17, when – with the same aim as Gibson – he started writing short, ironic poems about the real experiences of ordinary Tommies.

Both Monro and Gibson were friends of Rupert Brooke, but they started writing war poems before he did. His famous '1914' sonnets, written at the end of the year after his return from the Antwerp expedition, were perhaps the earliest poems to emerge from a poet's first-hand knowledge of the Western Front (*32*). Brooke was in action only very briefly, but he saw enough to know something of the reality, and in particular he saw the long lines of Belgian refugees. It was the human misery of war that convinced him of the rightness of the Allied cause, driving him to write as he did. In the surge of feeling and propaganda that followed his death, the pioneering work of Gibson and Monro was forgotten.

IV

Brooke's sonnets were not published until February 1915.[9] In the opinion of *The Times Literary Supplement* on 11 March, 'No passion for glory is here, no bitterness, no gloom, only a happy, clear-sighted, all-surrendering love'.[10] Brooke's death on St George's Day, 23 April, and a propagandizing obituary by Winston Churchill, made him an instant hero. Protests from his friends, including Monro, went unheeded: the dead poet, who had been an atheist, socialist and iconoclast, himself became an icon. His message was a seductive one, making no mention of horrors: volunteering was a willing sacrifice, with the power to redeem not only individual soldiers but also the nation they were fighting for. The sonnets attracted innumerable answers and imitations, some ironic (*80*), (*81*), some serious (*82*). One of the most influential was John McCrae's 'In Flanders Fields', with its call to those still fighting not to 'break faith' with the dead (*47*).

As a non-believer, Brooke could hardly make the obvious link between sacrifice and Christianity, but other poets were less reluctant. From the spring of 1915 onwards, war poetry's most frequent image was of the soldier as a Christ-figure, motivated by 'greater love', carrying his own and the world's sins and atoning for them by his death. In one remarkable instance, Christ is shown as a soldier dead in a trench (46), and in another he actually picks up a rifle and starts shooting Germans.[11] The image could be given many different implications, but it lent itself all too easily to propaganda, making sense of passive suffering and distracting attention from the fact that soldiers had to kill as well as be killed. If death in this war was a martyrdom, there was less need to dwell on its hideousness: as G. K. Chesterton said as late as 1918, to 'allow the horrors of the martyrdom to eclipse the halo of the martyr is simply a very stupid confusion of thought'.[12] John Oxenham, whose little books sold in hundreds of thousands, repeatedly assured soldiers they were 'Christs All!' (71), while the jingoistic journalist Horatio Bottomley, editor of the savagely anti-German newspaper *John Bull*, told them again and again that anyone who died in battle would certainly go to heaven. Evangelicals objected that such imagery was heretical, if not blasphemous – according to orthodox doctrine, Christ's death was an all-sufficient sacrifice, making further blood sacrifices pointless – but some poets remained convinced that blood would have to be shed in great quantities.

Another frequent, related, theme was that the war generation, like Christ, had been born to suffer and die: only through sacrifice could a corrupted world renew itself. Many poets would have been aware of *The Golden Bough*, James Frazer's recent, exhaustive study of pagan vegetation rituals, in which the king or his substitute had to be killed in winter to ensure the return of spring. Owen's earliest poem about the war describes the conflict as 'the Winter of the world', needing 'sowings for new Spring, and blood for seed' (*29*). There were many variations: 'There are crocuses at Nottingham! ... / Because we're here in Hell!';[13] 'Not till thousands have been slain / Shall the green wood be green again' (*65*). Natural cycles took on a new significance: a soldier could no longer look 'with uncomprehending eyes' at the daily 'fresh and sanguine sacrifice' of sunset (*89*). Sorley imagined the earth gladly accepting soldiers' songs and in due course their bodies (*30*), and Julian Grenfell, in a famous poem, saw battle as entirely consistent with the natural order (*44*).

Poets often thought of nature as some kind of guarantee that the war had to be fought. The German military expert Friedrich von Bernhardi had horrified British readers before 1914 by arguing that war was a 'biological necessity', but in fact John Ruskin had said much the same: nations sometimes needed to strengthen and cleanse themselves by fighting. It was all part of the natural pattern of life, death and renewal – and the survival of the fittest, a phrase J. C. Squire used for the title of his 1916 collection of satires.

V

The sort of patriotic verse that had appeared in such quantities in 1914 became less conspicuous as the war continued. This can be misleading: recruiting verse ceased to be needed after January 1916, when conscription was introduced, but in general both civilians and soldiers were still determined to carry on. It is true, however, that as more and more men marched away, an ever-widening gulf opened up between them and the civilians they left behind.

Fortunately, not all civilian versifiers were as insensitive as Jessie Pope (*34*) or Katharine Tynan ('They shot Flynn's eyes out. That was good. / Eyes that saw God are better blind'). Tynan's numerous war poems, published in many periodicals, often stressed the youth of soldiers and turned them into angels, 'little Knights of Paradise of eighteen and nineteen'.[14] Soldiers regarded such nonsense with increasing contempt. Comradeship and suffering at the front became an exclusive experience, often expressed in the language of love poetry, an intense bond between men that civilians could neither share nor understand. Ironically, pacifists who were working to end the fighting were often fiercely denounced by soldiers: 'You thrive by virtue of our agony ... / Lapping the spilt blood of the crucified'.[15]

It can also be misleading to assume that the Somme campaign, which began on 1 July 1916, was a turning point for poetry by soldiers. Sassoon's first sceptical poem, 'In the Pink' (*78*), was written in February of that year, and T. P. C. Wilson's cry of horror, 'A Soldier', in June (*91*). Arthur Graeme West was losing faith in the cause well before July, yet Gilbert Frankau continued to believe in it for the rest of his life. Robert Graves, who saw horrors on the Somme in July, was still sure later in the year that the army would eventually drive the barbarians out of France (*102*). In February R. E. Vernède prayed: 'Not in our time, not now, Lord, we beseech thee / To grant us peace. The sword has bit too deep' – and in November, by which time the disaster on the Somme had become obvious, he finished his poem, insisting the fight must go on (*132*).

One soldier who had no illusions to lose and who wrote many of his best poems in France was Isaac Rosenberg, whose 'Break of

Day in the Trenches' was composed on the Somme front in June (*105*). Some critics, notably the late Jon Silkin, have made a strong case for Rosenberg as the greatest of all the war's poets. He was certainly one of the most original and imaginative, coming closer than any poet until David Jones in the 1930s to shaping a myth of his own that would embody his vision of the conflict. Unlike many soldier-poets, he served as a private, with none of the privileges enjoyed by officers, and he was in France for twenty-one gruelling months with only one brief period of home leave. He regarded most of his 'trench poems' as a digression from his most ambitious work on the war, a verse play called *The Unicorn* that he was never able to finish. The poems are sometimes obscure, and occasionally no more than what he himself described as 'patriotic gush', but the best of them are magnificently written, rich with imagery and vivid detail.

VI

Veneration for soldiers grew with the casualty lists. The first anthology of poems exclusively by members of the armed services appeared in September 1916 to favourable reviews: *Soldier Poets: Songs of the Fighting Men*, edited by Galloway Kyle and published by Erskine Macdonald, was aimed at a new market and sold very well.

Kyle was an enterprising man. He had founded the Poetry Society not long before the war, taking advantage of – and perhaps contributing to – an increasing public enthusiasm for poetry. 'Erskine Macdonald' was his creation, too, not a real person as the public was led to believe, but a profitable device for publishing slim volumes at their authors' expense. In 1912 Kyle had helped Monro start *The Poetry Review*, but when Monro proved too progressive for Kyle's purposes he was replaced as editor by Stephen Phillips until the latter's death in 1915. From then on, Kyle took full control and was able to perfect an ingenious racket: young soldiers, keen to publish before they were killed, and grieving parents, anxious to bring out memorial volumes, could be drawn in by the magazine; they were recommended by the editor to 'Mr Macdonald', and the resulting books were warmly praised in the *Review*. Royalties were elusive, but Kyle knew well that his authors, if still alive, would be more interested in getting into print than in being paid.

Originality and new ideas were now out of fashion; as Gibson pointed out in January 1917, so many young writers were dead or caught up in the war that criticism and reviewing had fallen into the hands of 'old men' and 'maiden aunts'. Most of Kyle's poets wrote the kind of verse that was wanted. J. W. Streets was often singled out for special mention: he was a former coal miner, a fine example of working-class patriotism at a time when miners had been horrifying the middle classes by going on strike ('lepers in a paradise of health', one officer-poet called them). Kyle frequently plugged his own authors, and he described *Soldier Poets* with absurd bombast: 'No literary work of our day has possessed so much genetic force or been of greater influence'. Yet he did some good. 'The "Poetry Review" may start me writing again', Gurney wrote in a 1917 letter: 'such imperfection in print is most encouraging.'[16] Dozens of young aspirants owed their first – and in some cases their last – appearances in print to Kyle's enterprises, among them Streets, Leslie Coulson, R. C. G. Dartford, Geoffrey

Howard, R. Watson Kerr, P. H. B. Lyon, J. E. Stewart, and even Vera Brittain and Edmund Blunden.

VII

If there had been a poll in late 1917 to identify the war's most distinguished soldier-poets, Brooke, Grenfell and Sorley would almost certainly have headed the list, together with Robert Nichols (whose book, *Ardours and Endurances*, had been the sensation of the year) and a few others, including Vernède and W. N. Hodgson. Sassoon was beginning to be well known, admired not only by opponents of the war but also by some of its most ardent supporters, including Churchill and Newbolt. Very few people were as yet aware of Edward Thomas as a poet, not many had noticed Gurney, and no one had even heard of Blunden, Owen or Rosenberg.

November 1917 brought the publication of *Georgian Poetry 1916–1917*, the third volume of the anthology, giving prominence to Nichols, Sassoon and Graves. Nichols wrote about battle in what seemed a bold, modern style:

Ha! ha! Bunched figures waiting.
Revolver levelled quick!
Flick! Flick!
Red as blood.
Germans. Germans.
Good! O good!
Cool madness.[17]

'It was characteristic of our war-time criticism that this masterpiece of drivel … was hailed as a work of genius', Douglas Goldring commented acidly in 1920, and in the same year J. B. Morton parodied Sassoon as well as Nichols:

Flash, crump, flick, and whirr,
General's singing – 'Give 'em Hell!'
Bill's dead and Joe's dead
Dick's gone west, and Alf's gone mad,
General's wife eating quail at the Ritz …[18]

During the war, though, Nichols's work was widely admired, by Sassoon and Graves among others, and the hysteria underlying his writing found a ready response.

If any generalization about soldier-poets in 1917 holds true, it is probably that the most talented among them were in revolt against false language, the incessant, optimistic rhetoric of politicians, newspapers and armchair patriots. As Osbert Sitwell declared, 'we are poets, / And shall tell the truth' (*169*). Nevertheless, truth meant different things to different people. E. A. Mackintosh was motivated by duty and the intense loyalty that many officers felt towards their men. Gilbert Frankau, perhaps more than any other wartime poet, even his master Kipling, was driven by hatred of Germany, yet his poems describe the trenches in gruesome detail, a reminder that 'realism' in First World War poetry is not always evidence of opposition to the war. He was scornful of officers who were still using the old language, writing about battle as 'a kind of Military Tournament': future generations would have to know that their forebears had endured the front with all its horrors because they had understood 'that thus, / *And only thus*, by sacrifice, might they / Secure a world worth living in – *for you*' (172).

Graves and Sassoon are often written about together as though they shared the same view of the war, but in fact the two friends held very different opinions. Graves detested false language, being a superb and strictly honest craftsman in words, but he never seriously doubted that the war was being fought in an honourable cause. He told Sassoon to 'cheer up' and stop writing 'corpse poems', believing that an officer's first duty was to keep up the troops' morale. At the end of 1917 he told Owen to 'cheer up', too, because Owen's new work had become 'too Sassoonish'.

Sassoon's 1917 protest against the war seems to have been without parallel.[19] On 6 July 1917 he sent a statement to his commanding officer 'as an act of wilful defiance of military authority, because I believe the War is being deliberately prolonged'. He claimed that what had begun as 'a war of defence and liberation' had become 'a war of aggression and conquest': the original aims could now be resolved by negotiation. Up to that point the statement is closely based on advice Sassoon had received from Bertrand Russell and other leading civilian pacifists, who were convinced that Lloyd George's government had secretly changed its aims, and that had it not done so the war could now be ended through peace talks. Sassoon added that he could no longer assist in prolonging the sufferings of the troops and that he was speaking on their behalf; that he was protesting against politicians, not generals; and that he hoped his action might help to destroy the 'callous complacence' of civilians. The authorities responded –

ingeniously and not altogether unkindly – that this 'gallant officer' was under severe nervous strain. Instead of being court-martialled, as he had expected, he was put away in Craiglockhart Hospital as a shellshock patient and told unofficially that he would stay there until he agreed to keep quiet.

During the next few months Sassoon wrote some of his harshest poems against the war, showing many of them to his fellow-patient, Wilfred Owen. Had Owen and Sassoon not happened to be in the same hospital at the same time, Owen's war poems might never have been written. He had been through appalling experiences in France, but until he met Sassoon in August 1917 he had believed the fighting had to go on. Sassoon explained the pacifists' case for negotiations and protest: the politicians would never alter course unless public opinion forced them to, and the public had to be told the truth. By early October Owen was writing 'Dulce et Decorum Est', attacking the 'callous complacence' of Jessie Pope and writers like her.

One woman poet who might have escaped Owen's anger in 1917 was Mary Borden, an American heiress who had taken British nationality and married an Englishman. She had volunteered to finance her own mobile hospital behind the French lines, and had been working in it as director and nurse; she could write from experience, and, like Owen and Sassoon, she seems to have read that bitter anti-war novel, Henri Barbusse's *Le Feu* (1916). Her furious diatribe on behalf of the archetypal 'Unidentified' soldier, published in December 1917, is one of the war's most powerful – and least known – poems (*184*).

VIII

Through the 'pale, cold days', as Rosenberg called them, of early 1918, there was relatively little activity on the Western Front. The Germans were busy pacifying their Eastern Front, taking huge swathes of territory, but it was obvious that once they had completed victory there they would launch an offensive in the west.

The attack began in enormous strength on 21 March, rapidly overwhelming the British line and putting an end at last to stalemate and trench warfare. Ground that had been gained during months and years of hard fighting was lost in days. Among the poets, Rosenberg, Wilson and Stewart were killed, Read and Claude Penrose were in the retreat, and Sassoon was one of many soldiers hurriedly brought back to France. At home, men on sick leave and light duties were being sent for fitness training, Owen among them. For the first time, civilians began to face the possibility of an Allied defeat, although many soldiers remained resolute, convinced the tide would turn (*199*). The rhetoric of 1914 was heard again (*193*), (*194*), to the disgust of the war's opponents (*196*), (*197*). Nichols hailed the first signs of British recovery with grand, heroic imagery, in a poem approved by Sassoon (*200*).

There was no chance now for peace negotiations (many modern historians would say there never had been, even in 1917). Now only war could end war, and there was no longer any point in writing Sassoonish satire. Owen, realizing he would soon be sent back to France, hired a room in a cottage near the training camp at

Ripon so that he could work undisturbed in his free evenings. In little more than two months he wrote many of his greatest poems, including 'Strange Meeting', an elegy for himself and all poets lost in war (*203*). His fragmentary preface for a book of poems ('My subject is War, and the pity of War...'), and its accompanying list of contents, show him working towards a Shelleyan definition of the task of a 'true War Poet'. The key was 'pity', the imaginative feeling with and for other people that would lead to right thinking and practical action. It is this programme and the Ripon poems that make Owen unique: no one else thought and wrote so profoundly about the relationship between poetry and war. 'Strange Meeting' is perhaps the only wartime poem in which the poet meets an 'enemy' he has killed, speaks, listens, learns the truth, and joins the other man, now a 'friend', in death.

Unlike Owen, Sassoon was unable to go beyond protest. In his little-known poem, 'Testament', which he sent to Owen, he accepted that he had done all he could: 'O my heart, / Be still; you have cried your cry; you have played your part' (*207*). His satires were never likely to be forgotten, however. In July 1918 five of them were included in *Poems Written During the Great War*, the first anthology to be aimed against the war: the editor, Bertram Lloyd, also selected work by W. N. Ewer, Margaret Sackville, Eliot Crawshay-Williams, Osbert Sitwell, Squire and Gibson among others, commenting in his preface that all his chosen poets shared a 'hatred of the cant and idealization and false glamour' that still overlaid notions of war 'in the minds of numbers of otherwise reasonable people'. Lloyd noted, too, that 'Youth' had come to feel 'disgust and revulsion' at being driven by 'Age', usually under the 'traditional catchwords of Glory and Duty', into 'utter disillusionment and cynicism'. Even 'the Man in the Street' was beginning to grow restive. But Lloyd did not say, nor did most of his poets, that the war itself was futile: even in 1918, and ever afterwards among the war generation, that was a view held only by a small minority.

The tide did turn at last: by August 1918 the Germans were in retreat, and by October it was clear that the war was drawing to an end. If the earliest work by a soldier-poet who had seen action had been Brooke's sonnets, with their promise of 'an English heaven', the last may well have been the closing stanza of Owen's 'Spring Offensive', his final recognition that soldiers, however heroic, were destined to end in hell (*215*).

IX

The war ended with an overwhelming Allied victory, although both sides were almost equally exhausted. The Armistice was greeted with excitement in the streets, but not in poetry. The 'men of letters' who had led the poetic response in 1914 again came to the fore, with verses by the Poet Laureate and others in *The Times*. Binyon's 'For the Fallen', originally published in 1914, provided lines for many war memorials, and Kipling was commissioned to compose epitaphs for the great cemeteries overseas. Conventional patriotic verse was still being written, but, as had been predicted, its language was tired and unconvincing. For the more original poets, relief at victory was mingled with sorrow and disillusion – and dismay that the old social order seemed to be scarcely shaken:

Two bleeding years I fought in France, for Squire:
I suffered anguish that he's never guessed.
Once I came home on leave: and then went west...
What greater glory could a man desire? (*226*)

Most soldiers were sure the war had been won by military victory, and that it had been fought, as Godfrey Elton said later, 'to prevent Prussian militarism and materialism from dominating Europe. And this tremendous object it had very palpably achieved'.[20] Some poets, including Sassoon, hoped for a while that socialism would bring in a brave new world. Others remembered the trenches with increasing bitterness as they discovered that the civilians who had prospered in wartime now seemed to have no use for them (*223*), (*246*). Many ex-soldiers failed to find jobs, and some were reduced to begging. Meanwhile, the politicians, led by Woodrow Wilson but dominated by the French premier, Georges Clemenceau, imposed hard terms on Germany, to the horror of some observers (*236*).

Women poets wrote some of their best work in the years immediately after the Armistice, reflecting on their own and their men's states of mind, and on the losses and silence that could never be made good. May Wedderburn Cannan, who had written poems in support of Kipling well before 1914, still held to her opinion, but she understood the price that had to be paid:

Now must we go again back to the world
Full of grey ghosts and voices of men dying,
And in the rain the sounding of Last Posts,

And Lovers' crying –

Back to the old, back to the empty world. (*238*)

Vera Brittain, too, felt the war had been necessary, although she had suffered agonizing losses; she was quick to sympathize with unemployed ex-servicemen (*237*), but she did not become a pacifist until years later. Lady Margaret Sackville, on the other hand, had been implacably opposed to the war from 1914; before then she had written lightweight, romantic verse, but the war made her a passionate advocate of peace. She condemned women, 'We mothers and we murderers of mankind' (*113*), as strongly as men, and her 1920 poem, 'The Women to the Men Returned', is a rare and revealing study of the lasting gap that the war had opened up between women and soldiers (*241*).

Three former soldiers did not find their mature voices until the 1920s. Edgell Rickword and Edmund Blunden recalled the front line with a meticulous, literary irony that no one could have mastered during the chaos of the war years; and Ivor Gurney recorded memories of the often unsoldierly comrades who had helped to keep him sane. Gurney's strange, rough-hewn style is in striking contrast to the polished elegance of Rickword and Blunden, but in its own way it is just as impressive. Like Rosenberg, he wrote from the point of view of a private, and his post-war poems vividly evoke life among the Other Ranks. Compared to Owen and Sassoon, he and Blunden have long been undervalued, yet their work in the 1920s puts them among the best of the 'war poets' – and it demonstrates how the conflict kept its hold on the memories of men who had endured it.

In November 1920 Hardy was asked for the last time to produce a poem on the war. He concluded that pity was the truest response:

> Some could, some could not, shake off misery:
> The Sinister Spirit sneered: 'It had to be!'
> And again the Spirit of Pity whispered, 'Why?' (247)

Ten years later, and equally in character, Kipling denounced the Labour government for what he saw as attempts to eradicate memories of the dead (273). That those memories have in fact been kept alive is in no small measure due to the war's poets. If there is any one message that they have in common it is that the aims and sufferings of the war generation should be remembered with what both Hardy and Owen called pity, in the hope that a full understanding of past events might ensure that no 'Great War' could ever happen again.

X

For most readers, First World War poetry will always have to be approached through anthologies, if only because there is so much of it. Critics often say that this was a very literary war, a poets' war, but it could as well be described as a mechanics' or a bank clerks' war – for the first time in British history, enormous numbers of young civilians suddenly became soldiers, poets along with the rest. Catherine Reilly's invaluable bibliography (1978) lists 2,225 British writers who experienced the war and published poems about it. Many more names could be added, and other countries were no less productive. Over thirty British anthologies were published between 1914 and 1918: one, probably the largest ever, had over two hundred contributors, all of them now forgotten, and one consisted exclusively of poems by women, the only book of its kind until Reilly's *Scars Upon My Heart* (1981).

The market collapsed rapidly after 1918, and only two anthologies came out in the next ten years. Bertram Lloyd produced a second selection, *The Paths of Glory* (1919), aiming to expose war as 'an execrable blot upon civilization'. Jacqueline Trotter's *Valour and Vision* (1920) was very different, intended to recall 'the honour of our Nation's purpose'. The poems were treated as history and arranged in a supposedly chronological order to tell a heroic story, although many were in fact misplaced and at least one had actually been written before 1914.[21] Trotter included one Sassoon poem, and her enlarged edition in 1923 added two more, as well as one by Blunden and two by Owen, 'Anthem for Doomed Youth' and 'Greater Love'.

Interest in the war revived in the late 1920s, with a spate of novels and prose memoirs by, among others, Sassoon, Aldington, Graves, Blunden, Manning and Mary Borden, but even then Frederick Brereton's *Anthology of War Poems* (1930) was the only book of its kind. Brereton's selection marks the beginning of the modern canon: the introduction – by Blunden – proclaimed Sassoon and Owen as the greatest poets of the war, and three poems by Rosenberg were included, his first appearance in an anthology. Thirteen years later, during the Second World War, Robert Nichols published a shorter selection, with an immensely long but thoughtful preface. He chose work by fourteen poets, all but one of whom were to figure regularly in later anthologies. Sassoon was represented by twelve poems, Blunden by nine, Graves by eight, Brooke by his five sonnets – but Owen, though highly praised in the preface, was allowed only four poems, while Rosenberg and Gurney were omitted altogether.

Again there was a long gap. First World War poetry was largely ignored by literary critics, and although Brooke remained famous not many people knew much about the other poets – even Owen. Then, half a century on from 1914, the 1960s changed everything. Theatre Workshop's play, *Oh! What a Lovely War* (1963), caught the public mood, with its portrayal of the Great War as a game played by ambitious profiteers and generals at the expense of common soldiers, who suffer helplessly as exploited victims. Brian Gardner's anthology, *Up the Line to Death* (1964), helped to establish the new myth, arranging poems to tell a story of idealism turning to realism, satire, protest and pity. It was no coincidence that the Vietnam War would soon come to be understood by many people in much the same terms. Several similar anthologies followed, none of them making much attempt to date or annotate poems, but organizing their material to fit the myth. The results were often highly misleading: early poems by civilians were mistaken for late ones by soldiers, seriousness was presented as irony, flippancy as satire, militarism as pity. Women poets were almost entirely overlooked.

Our own *Poetry of the Great War* (1986) attempted to correct many of these failings, ranging much more widely among the poets and giving a more balanced view of the war's poetry as a whole. Martin Stephen's *Never Such Innocence* (1988) also ranged widely, although some of the old mistakes were repeated.

INTRODUCTION

Numerous other anthologies followed, including volumes by David
Roberts (1996, 1998) and Robert Giddings (1998); two more
collections of women's poetry, edited by Nora Jones and Liz Ward
(*The Forgotten Army*, 1991) and Nosheen Khan (*Not with Loud
Grieving*, 1994); Martin Taylor's *Lads: Love Poetry of the Trenches*
(1989); and, more recently, a new Penguin edited by George Walter
(2006). The most original new anthology is *Voices of Silence: The
Alternative Book of First World War Poetry*, edited by Vivien Noakes
(2006), a selection of the war's unknown verse.

The present book is the first anthology of Great War poetry to
make a serious attempt to present poems in chronological order.
There are six sections, one for each year from 1914 to 1918 and
one for the post-war decade, each prefaced by a brief historical
outline to give a context for the poems. Inevitably, not all dates are
known, so we have not always kept strictly to chronology within
each year: civilians are sometimes separated from soldiers, because
their experiences of the war were necessarily very different, and
sometimes poems by the same author are grouped together.
Nevertheless, we believe our chronology to be generally reliable –
and it is certainly more accurate than in most previous anthologies.

But poetry must never be mistaken for history. Ever since the
1960s, historians have objected to the way in which 'war poetry',
especially the work of Sassoon and Owen, has distorted the
public's view of the Great War. 'Revisionist' scholars have pointed
out that the generals were not all 'donkeys' (nor all the troops
'lions'), and that tactics and technology improved rapidly after the
Somme, making the British army more than a match for its
opponent. Owen and Sassoon were not in the least representative

or typical: the fact that they wanted the war stopped in 1917, for instance, does not mean that most soldiers – or even most poets – would have agreed with them. But that does not diminish the value of their testimony: military historians, like generals, often have to think of nothing much smaller than a division (very roughly, ten thousand men – over fifty divisions took part in the Somme), but poets, the best of them, write about individual feelings and experience, and in that sense the war's verse forms a record both unique and true.

1. The campaign for national service produced an unknown number of poetry books, such as Frank Taylor, *The Gallant Way* (1913) – in effect pre-war First World War poetry.

2. 'Cricket – 1915', *Daily Mail*, 18 May 1915.

3. 'Can Poets Help?' and a further article, *Evening News*, 11 and 17 December 1914.

4. Thomas, 'War Poetry', *Poetry and Drama*, December 1914.

5. Undated cutting, *Poems Relating to the European War*, VI, 42 (Birmingham Public Reference Library).

6. For anti-war literature before 1914, see *All in a Maze*, ed. Daniel George and Rose Macaulay (1938); *War Songs*, ed. C. Stonefield (1908); *An Anthology of War Poetry*, ed. Julian Symons (1942).

7. 'Georgian' for the new king, George V, crowned in 1911.

8. See D. Hibberd, *Harold Monro and Wilfrid Gibson: The Pioneers*, War Poets series (2006).

9. C. Hassall, *Rupert Brooke* (1964), 486, 503. The sonnets were published on about 27 February in the 'December 1914' issue of *New Numbers*, edited by Gibson and Lascelles Abercrombie.

10. The reviewer was de la Mare.

11. A. St J. Adcock, 'Christ in the Trenches', *Songs of the World War* (1916).

12. Chesterton, 'The Case for the War Song', *New Witness*, 17 May 1918, 48–9.

13. Maud Anna Bell, 'From a Trench', *A Treasury of War Poetry*, ed. G. H. Clarke (1917 edn).

14. Tynan, 'The Vision', *New Witness*, 27 January 1916; 'The Short Road to Heaven', *Herb o' Grace* (1918).

15. Geoffrey Fyson, 'To a Pacifist', *The Survivors* (1919).

16. Gibson, interview, *New York Times Magazine*, 4 January 1917. Ivan Firth ('lepers'), 'To Strikers in Wartime', *Bellicosities* (1915). Kyle, preface, *More Songs by the Fighting Men* (1917). Gurney, *War Letters*, 159.

17. 'The Assault', *Ardours and Endurances* (1917).

18. Goldring, *Reputations* (1920), 111; 'JBM', *Gorgeous Poetry* 1911–1920.

19. But see biographical notes on van Beek, Plowman and West.

20. Lord Elton, *Among Others* (1938), 259.

21. Herbert Asquith's 'The Volunteer' was probably written in 1912: he sent it to the *Spectator* in 1913, but it was shelved until 8 August 1914, when the war made it suddenly topical. Several modern anthologists have repeated Trotter's mistake.

1914

On 28 June 1914 a Bosnian Serb nationalist assassinated the heir to the Austro-Hungarian empire, and within a month Austria declared war on Serbia. Serbia appealed to Russia, which mobilized, and Germany, fearing encirclement, joined Austria, launching pre-emptive strikes against France and Russia. A highly efficient German army crashed through Belgium on its way to northern France. It was this unprovoked invasion of Belgium that convinced British public opinion, wavering until then, that Germany had to be resisted. The Liberal government under the Prime Minister, H. H. Asquith, had striven for peace, but on 4 August Britain declared war. Many poets, led by Robert Bridges, the Poet Laureate, rallied to the cause.

The British Expeditionary Force (BEF) was soon in the line, but the army was small by European standards and its loss could not be risked. In late August the BEF had to make a long, exhausting retreat from Mons, journalists vividly describing a 'broken army'. The generals hastily imposed strict censorship – from then on newspapers had to be vague and relentlessly optimistic – but the Mons stories led paradoxically both to a surge in recruiting and to the first attempts, actually by civilians, at realistic verse about life in the front line. Unlike other major powers, Britain had always relied on volunteers: within a month an intensive recruiting campaign inspired by Lord Kitchener, the Minister for War, had pulled in the first hundred thousand men. Leading poets joined in the call for volunteers.

After years of internal dissension – constitutional crises, labour unrest, looming civil war in Ireland – most British people took pride in their new-found unity. Liberal poets who had opposed the South African war now put aside their doubts, hoping like many others that fighting would rejuvenate the world and sweep away decadence, idleness and false values.

Nevertheless, pacifists and some socialists opposed the war from the start. As early as September 1914 Bertrand Russell was arguing that Britain's true motives were to grab colonies and smash Germany as a trade rival. The first satirical poems were equally early, and they came from civilians, not from soldiers. Among the 'war poets' who are famous today, Isaac Rosenberg, Wilfred Owen and Charles Sorley all happened to be abroad at the beginning of August, so they missed the initial fervour. Rupert Brooke, who was in England, joined up without much enthusiasm – but he became passionately committed to the war when he saw its effects in Belgium, and his sonnets were to provide a new language for patriotic poetry.

While the Eastern Front remained fluid, with the Russians suffering enormous losses, the Western Front stabilized in October as a line of trenches stretching from the Belgian coast to Switzerland. The BEF held its ground at Ypres, volunteers continued to pour into recruiting offices – and the nation began to realize that it was facing the largest, costliest task it had ever set itself.

(1) 'Wake Up, England!'

Thou careless, awake!
   Thou peacemaker, fight!
Stand England for honour
   And God guard the Right!

Thy mirth lay aside,
   Thy cavil and play;
The fiend is upon thee
   And grave is the day.

Through fire, air and water
   Thy trial must be;
But they that love life best
   Die gladly for thee.

Much suffering shall cleanse thee
   But thou through the flood
Shalt win to salvation,
   To beauty through blood.

Up, careless, awake!
   Ye peacemakers, fight!
Stand England for honour,
   And God guard the Right!

ROBERT BRIDGES

The Times, 8 August 1914. *October and Other Poems* (1920). Bridges got down promptly to his duty as Poet Laureate, borrowing his title from 'the King's well-known call to the country in 1901' (a speech by the future George V at the Guildhall). Bridges wanted the poem to be simple and 'universally approved'. A Modernist reviewer, John Gould Fletcher (*Egoist*, 2 November), suggested it might stop the war: if the Germans saw it, they would 'explode' with laughter.

   The fiend: Bridges was persuaded by friends to alter this to 'Thy foe' in the 1914 version, but he restored his original wording in the 1920 text given here; he also omitted three stanzas and altered the last lines, which were originally 'England Stands for Honour / God Defend the Right', printed in capitals and 'purposely set out of metre'.

(2) War

The serpent-horror writhing in her hair,
   And crowning cruel brows bent o'er the ground
   That she would crimson now from many a wound,
Medusa-like, I seem to see her there –
War! with her petrifying eyes astare –
   And can no longer listen to the sound
   Of song-birds in the harvest fields around;
Such prophecies do her mute lips declare.

Evils? Can any greater be than they
   That troop licentious in her brutal train?
     Unvindicated honour? She brings shame –
     Shame more appalling than men dare to name,
Betraying them that die and them that slay,
   And making of the earth a hell of pain!

FLORENCE EARLE COATES

Athenaeum, 8 August 1914. A comment by a visiting American, possibly written in the last apprehensive days before the war.

(3) The Call to Arms in Our Street

There's a woman sobs her heart out,
   With her head against the door,
For the man that's called to leave her,
   – God have pity on the poor!
     But it's beat, drums, beat,
     While the lads march down the street,
     And it's blow, trumpets, blow,
     Keep your tears until they go.

1914

There's a crowd of little children
  Who march along and shout,
For it's fine to play at soldiers
  Now their fathers are called out.
    So it's beat, drums, beat;
    But who'll find them food to eat?
    And it's blow, trumpets, blow,
    Ah! the children little know.

There's a mother who stands watching
  For the last look of her son,
A worn poor widow woman,
  And he her only one.
    But it's beat, drums, beat,
    Though God knows when we shall meet;
    And it's blow, trumpets, blow:
    We must smile and cheer them so.

There's a young girl who stands laughing,
  For she thinks a war is grand,
And it's fine to see the lads pass,
  And it's fine to hear the band.
    So it's beat, drums, beat,
    To the fall of many feet;
    And it's blow, trumpets, blow,
    God go with you where you go!

WINIFRED M. LETTS

Saturday Westminster Gazette, 15 August 1914. *Hallow-E'en and Poems of the War* (1916). Originally entitled 'The Call to Arms'.

(4) Duty

Give gladly, you rich − 'tis no more than you owe −
For the weal of your Country, your wealth's overflow!
Even I that am poor am performing my part;
I am giving my brain, I am giving my heart.

WILLIAM WATSON

Westminster Gazette, 26 August 1914. Reprinted as the epigraph to the first of the many wartime anthologies, *Poems of the Great War* (1914), sold in aid of the Prince of Wales's National Relief Fund, a charity set up to help those whose earnings were reduced by the war.

(5) The Shirker

He moors the skiff within the cooler gloom
Of river-branches, unaware of doom;
Cushioned he lolls, and looks in faces fair,
Nursing with placid hand anointed hair.
It seems he scarcely can uplift the weight
Of summer afternoon, far less of fate.
So the young Briton, sprawling in his strength,
Supports a heavy Sabbath at full length,
Till sinks the sun on more than that sweet river,
Perhaps upon our day goes down for ever.
But though that orb may on an Empire set,
Tomlinson lights another cigarette.

STEPHEN PHILLIPS

Daily Mail, 30 August 1914. Composed 'evidently [by] a foreigner who is desperately trying to write English', Fletcher commented (*Egoist*, 16 November). But Phillips intends the ornate style to be taken seriously: the contrasting simplicity of the last line implies that Tomlinson, like Brooke's 'half-men' (*32*), is impervious to noble poetic values.

(6) Fall In

What will you lack, sonny, what will you lack
  When the girls line up the street,
Shouting their love to the lads come back
  From the foe they rushed to beat?
Will you send a strangled cheer to the sky
  And grin till your cheeks are red?
But what will you lack when your mate goes by
  With a girl who cuts you dead?

Where will you look, sonny, where will you look
  When your children yet to be
Clamour to learn of the part you took
  In the War that kept men free?
Will you say it was naught to you if France
  Stood up to her foe or bunked?
But where will you look when they give the glance
  That tells you they know you funked?

How will you fare, sonny, how will you fare
  In the far-off winter night,
When you sit by the fire in an old man's chair
  And your neighbours talk of the fight?
Will you slink away, as it were from a blow,
  Your old head shamed and bent?
Or say – I was not with the first to go,
  But I went, thank God, I went?

Why do they call, sonny, why do they call
   For men who are brave and strong?
Is it naught to you if your country fall,
   And Right is smashed by Wrong?
Is it football still and the picture show,
   The pub and the betting odds,
When your brothers stand to the tyrant's blow
   And Britain's call is God's?

HAROLD BEGBIE

Daily Chronicle, 31 August 1914. *Fighting Lines* (1914). The public loved this rallying call. Begbie waived copyright, and the War Office distributed the poem. A song-sheet, with 'a swinging and contagious march melody' by Sir Frederic Cowen, was sold in aid of the National Relief Fund and performed at eleven London theatres. Other publicity included gramophone recordings, posters, cards and a badge: 'Sing the Song! Wear the Badge! Play the March!'

   The Times (3 October) disliked the appeal to shame, and J. C. Squire thought Begbie's war verse 'positively nauseating' (*New Statesman*, 14 November). *TP's Weekly* (January 1915) said the song was 'balderdash', whereupon someone wrote in to say it had persuaded him to enlist.

(7) 'For all we have and are'

For all we have and are,
For all our children's fate,
Stand up and take the war,
The Hun is at the gate!
Our world has passed away,
In wantonness o'erthrown.
There is nothing left today
But steel and fire and stone!
  Though all we knew depart,
  The old Commandments stand:–
  'In courage keep your heart,
  In strength lift up your hand.'

1914

Once more we hear the word
That sickened earth of old:–
'No law except the Sword
Unsheathed and uncontrolled.'
Once more it knits mankind,
Once more the nations go
To meet and break and bind
A crazed and driven foe.

Comfort, content, delight,
The ages' slow-bought gain,
They shrivelled in a night.
Only ourselves remain
To face the naked days
In silent fortitude,
Through perils and dismays
Renewed and re-renewed.
   Though all we made depart,
   The old Commandments stand:–
   'In patience keep your heart,
   In strength lift up your hand.'

No easy hopes or lies
Shall bring us to our goal,
But iron sacrifice
Of body, will, and soul.
There is but one task for all –
One life for each to give.
Who stands if Freedom fall?
Who dies if England live?

RUDYARD KIPLING

The Times, 2 September 1914. The Years Between (1919). 'I'm thankful to see Kipling
hasn't written a poem yet', Charles Sorley said in August, but Kipling was the nation's
unofficial poet laureate and his many admirers expected him to give a lead.
   courage ... strength ... patience ... heart: Psalms 27:14.
   No ... Sword: the alleged German doctrine was 'Might is Right'.

(8) Men Who March Away

What of the faith and fire within us
    Men who march away
    Ere the barn-cocks say
    Night is growing gray,
Leaving all that here can win us;
What of the faith and fire within us
    Men who march away?

Is it a purblind prank, O think you,
    Friend with the musing eye,
    Who watch us stepping by
    With doubt and dolorous sigh?
Can much pondering so hoodwink you!
Is it a purblind prank, O think you,
    Friend with the musing eye?

Nay. We well see what we are doing,
    Though some may not see −
    Dalliers as they be −
    England's need are we;
Her distress would leave us rueing:
Nay. We well see what we are doing,
    Though some may not see!

In our heart of hearts believing
    Victory crowns the just,
    And that braggarts must
    Surely bite the dust,
Press we to the field ungrieving,
In our heart of hearts believing
    Victory crowns the just.

Hence the faith and fire within us
Men who march away
Ere the barn-cocks say
Night is growing gray,
Leaving all that here can win us;
Hence the faith and fire within us
Men who march away.

THOMAS HARDY

The Times, 9 September 1914. *Satires of Circumstance* (1914). Original title: 'The Song of the Soldiers'. A product of the secret 'men of letters' conference (see Introduction), written after 'church and a bad sermon'. Hardy waived copyright, so the poem was widely reproduced and set to music by several composers.

We ... doing: 'We know what we are fighting for, and we love what we know' (Cromwell, quoted by Andrew Bonar Law, leader of the opposition, in a Guildhall speech, 4 September).

Victory ... just: 'the worst line he ever wrote – filched from a leading article in the *Morning Post*' (Sorley, in a 1914 letter).

(9) Forty Men from Simpson's

Forty men from Simpson's!
'Will you 'ave it rare?
Try a bit of pudding, sir;
Yes, the cheddar's fair.'

Forty men from Simpson's!
Quitting in a group,
Marching off in khaki for
To fix the Kaiser's soup.

Forty men from Simpson's!
'Will you take it 'ot ?
'Ere's your Hell served in the shell,
Piping from the pot!'

Forty men from Simpson's!
 Hurry, turn 'em loose,
They're the sort we need in front
 To cook the German goose.

Forty men from Simpson's!
 What a thing to read:
Forty humble serving men
 Serving Britain's need!

Forty men from Simpson's!
 Don't you blush with shame,
While they play the soldier's part
 And you, the *waiting* game?

HERBERT KAUFMAN

The Song of the Guns (October 1914).
  Simpson's: London restaurant, famous for its roast beef.

(10) The Poets are Waiting

To what God
Shall we chant
Our songs of Battle?

The professional poets
Are measuring their thoughts
For felicitous sonnets;
They try them and fit them
Like honest tailors
Cutting materials
For fashion-plate suits.

1914

The unprofessional
Little singers,
Most intellectual,
Merry with gossip,
Heavy with cunning,
Whose tedious brains are draped
In sultry palls of hair,
Reclining as usual
On armchairs and sofas,
Are grinning and gossiping,
Cake at their elbows –
They will not write us verses for the time;
Their storms are brewed in teacups and their wars
Are fought in sneers or little blots of ink.

To what God
Shall we chant
Our songs of Battle?

Hefty barbarians,
Roaring for war,
Are breaking upon us;
Clouds of their cavalry,
Waves of their infantry,
Mountains of guns.
Winged they are coming,
Plated and mailed,
Snorting their jargon.
Oh, to whom shall a song of battle be chanted?
Not to our lord of the hosts on his ancient throne,
Drowsing the ages out in Heaven alone.
The celestial choirs are mute, the angels have fled:
Word is gone forth abroad that our lord is dead.

To what God
Shall we chant
Our songs of battle?

HAROLD MONRO

Probably written late August 1914. *Children of Love* (1914). Monro was one of the first to recognize that the early response to the war by poets – and churchmen – was sadly inadequate.

Little singers: especially Ezra Pound, notorious for his long hair and literary quarrels – Monro had recently had tea with him.

(11) August, 1914

How still this quiet cornfield is tonight!
By an intenser glow the evening falls,
Bringing, not darkness, but a deeper light;
Among the stooks a partridge covey calls.

The windows glitter on the distant hill;
Beyond the hedge the sheep-bells in the fold
Stumble on sudden music and are still;
The forlorn pinewoods droop above the wold.

An endless quiet valley reaches out
Past the blue hills into the evening sky;
Over the stubble, cawing, goes a rout
Of rooks from harvest, flagging as they fly.

So beautiful it is, I never saw
So great a beauty on these English fields,
Touched by the twilight's coming into awe,
Ripe to the soul and rich with summer's yields.

1914

***

These homes, this valley spread below me here,
The rooks, the tilted stacks, the beasts in pen,
Have been the heartfelt things, past-speaking dear
To unknown generations of dead men,

Who, century after century, held these farms,
And, looking out to watch the changing sky,
Heard, as we hear, the rumours and alarms
Of war at hand and danger pressing nigh.

And knew, as we know, that the message meant
The breaking off of ties, the loss of friends,
Death, like a miser getting in his rent,
And no new stones laid where the trackway ends.

The harvest not yet won, the empty bin,
The friendly horses taken from the stalls,
The fallow on the hill not yet brought in,
The cracks unplastered in the leaking walls.

Yet heard the news, and went discouraged home,
And brooded by the fire with heavy mind,
With such dumb loving of the Berkshire loam
As breaks the dumb hearts of the English kind,

Then sadly rose and left the well-loved Downs,
And so by ship to sea, and knew no more
The fields of home, the byres, the market towns,
Nor the dear outline of the English shore,

But knew the misery of the soaking trench,
The freezing in the rigging, the despair
In the revolting second of the wrench
When the blind soul is flung upon the air,

And died (uncouthly, most) in foreign lands
For some idea but dimly understood
Of an English city never built by hands
 Which love of England prompted and made good.

* * *

If there be any life beyond the grave,
It must be near the men and things we love,
Some power of quick suggestion how to save,
Touching the living soul as from above.

An influence from the Earth from those dead hearts
So passionate once, so deep, so truly kind,
That in the living child the spirit starts,
Feeling companioned still, not left behind.

Surely above these fields a spirit broods
A sense of many watchers muttering near
Of the lone Downland with the forlorn woods
Loved to the death, inestimably dear.

A muttering from beyond the veils of Death
From long-dead men, to whom this quiet scene
Came among blinding tears with the last breath,
The dying soldier's vision of his queen.

All the unspoken worship of those lives
Spent in forgotten wars at other calls
Glimmers upon these fields where evening drives
Beauty like breath, so gently darkness falls.

Darkness that makes the meadows holier still,
The elm-trees sadden in the hedge, a sigh
Moves in the beech-clump on the haunted hill,
The rising planets deepen in the sky,

And silence broods like spirit on the brae,
A glimmering moon begins, the moonlight runs
Over the grasses of the ancient way
Rutted this morning by the passing guns.

JOHN MASEFIELD

English Review, September 1914. *Philip the King* (1914). One of the first thoughtful,
literary responses to the war, with echoes of Gray, Wordsworth, Tennyson and Arnold:
the crisis is considered in terms of the great Romantic elegies and nature poems of the
past. The landscape is the Thames valley near Wallingford, where the poem was written.
An acknowledged leader of the Georgians, Masefield tried to write more war poems
but could finish very few of them, silenced, perhaps, by the horrors he soon saw in
military hospitals.

(12) Summer in England, 1914

On London fell a clearer light;
   Caressing pencils of the sun
Defined the distances, the white
   Houses transfigured one by one,
The 'long, unlovely street' impearled.
O what a sky has walked the world!

Most happy year! And out of town
   The hay was prosperous, and the wheat;
The silken harvest climbed the down:
   Moon after moon was heavenly-sweet,
Stroking the bread within the sheaves,
Looking 'twixt apples and their leaves.

And while this rose made round her cup,
   The armies died convulsed. And when
This chaste young silver sun went up
   Softly, a thousand shattered men,
One wet corruption, heaped the plain,
After a league-long throb of pain.

Flower following tender flower; and birds,
   And berries; and benignant skies
Made thrive the serried flocks and herds. –
   Yonder are men shot through the eyes.
      Love, hide thy face
From man's unpardonable race.

         * * *

Who said 'No man hath greater love than this,
   To die to serve his friend'?
So these have loved us all unto the end.
   Chide thou no more, O thou unsacrificed!
The soldier dying dies upon a kiss,
   The very kiss of Christ.

ALICE MEYNELL

A Father of Women and Other Poems (1917). Probably written in 1914, this poem is one of the first to begin turning that year's famous golden summer into myth.

   long unlovely street: Tennyson, *In Memoriam*, VII.

   No man … his friend: Christ's saying, 'Greater love hath no man than this, that a man lay down his life for his friends' (John 15:13), was referred to again and again during the war – cf. (*202*).

(13) August, 1914

God said, 'Men have forgotten Me:
  The souls that sleep shall wake again,
And blinded eyes be taught to see.'

So since redemption comes through pain
  He smote the earth with chastening rod,
And brought destruction's lurid reign;

But where His desolation trod
  The people in their agony
Despairing cried, 'There is no God.'

VERA BRITTAIN

Written at Somerville College, Oxford, where Brittain was a student from October 1914 to June 1915. *Verses of a VAD and Other Poems* (1918).

(14) Youth in Arms

I

Happy boy, happy boy,
David the immortal willed,
Youth a thousand thousand times
Slain, but not once killed,
Swaggering again today
In the old contemptuous way;

Leaning backward from your thigh
Up against the tinselled bar –
Dust and ashes! is it you?
Laughing, boasting, there you are!
First we hardly recognised you
In your modern avatar.

Soldier, rifle, brown khaki –
Is your blood as happy so?
Where's your sling, or painted shield,
Helmet, pike, or bow?
Well, you're going to the wars –
That is all you need to know.

Greybeards plotted. They were sad.
Death was in their wrinkled eyes.
At their tables, with their maps
Plans and calculations, wise
They all seemed; for well they knew
How ungrudgingly Youth dies.

At their green official baize
They debated all the night
Plans for your adventurous days
Which you followed with delight,
Youth in all your wanderings,
David of a thousand slings.

II Soldier

Are you going? Tonight we must all hear your laughter;
We shall need to remember it in the quiet days after.
Lift your rough hands, grained like unpolished oak.
Drink, call, lean forward, tell us some happy joke.
Let us know every whim of your brain and innocent soul.
Your speech is let loose; your great loafing words roll
Like hill-waters. But every syllable said
Brings you nearer the time you'll be found lying dead
In a ditch, or rolled stiff on the stones of a plain.

(Thought! Thought go back into your kennel again:
Hound, back!) Drink your glass, happy soldier, tonight.
Death is quick; you will laugh as you march to the fight.
We are wrong. Dreaming ever, we falter and pause:
You go forward unharmed without Why or Because.
Spring does not question. The war is like rain;
You will fall in the field like a flower without pain;
And who shall have noticed one sweet flower that dies?
The rain comes; the leaves open, and other flowers rise,
The old clock tolls. Now all our words are said.
We drift apart and wander away to bed.
We dream of War. *Your* closing eyelids keep
Quiet watch upon your heavy dreamless sleep.
You do not wonder if you shall, nor why,
If you must, by whom, for whom, you will die.
You are snoring. (The hound of thought by every breath
Brings you nearer for us to your foreign death.)

Are you going? Good-bye, then, to that last word you spoke
We must try to remember you best by some happy joke.

III Retreat

That is not war – oh it hurts! I am lame.
A thorn is burning me.
We are going back to the place from which we came.
I remember the old song now:

> *Soldier, soldier, going to war,*
> *When will you come back?*

Mind that rut. It is very deep.
All these ways are parched and raw.
Where are we going? How we creep!
Are you there? I never saw –

Damn this jingle in my brain.
I'm full of old songs – Have you ever heard this?

All the roads to victory
Are flooded as we go.
There's so much blood to paddle through,
That's why we're marching slow.

Yes sir; I'm here. Are you an officer?
I can't see. Are we running away?
How long have we done it? One whole year,
A month, a week, or since yesterday?

Damn the jingle. My brain
Is scragged and banged –

Fellows, these are happy times;
Tramp and tramp with open eyes.
Yet, try however much you will,
You cannot see a tree, a hill,
Moon, stars, or even skies.

I won't be quiet. Sing too, you fool.
I had a dog I used to beat.
Don't try it on me. Say that again.
Who said it? *Halt!* Why? Who can halt?
We're marching now. Who fired? Well. Well.
I'll lie down too. I'm tired enough.

IV Carrion

It is plain now what you are. Your head has dropped
Into a furrow. And the lovely curve
Of your strong leg has wasted and is propped
Against a ridge of the ploughed land's watery swerve.

You are swayed on waves of the silent ground;
You clutch and claim with passionate grasp of your fingers
The dip of earth in which your body lingers;
If you are not found,
In a little while your limbs will fall apart;
The birds will take some, but the earth will take most of your
    heart.

You are fuel for a coming spring if they leave you here;
The crop that will rise from your bones is healthy bread.
You died – we know you – without a word of fear,
And as they loved you living I love you dead.

No girl would kiss you. But then
No girls would ever kiss the earth
In the manner they hug the lips of men:
You are not known to them in this, your second birth.

No coffin-cover now will cram
Your body in a shell of lead;
Earth will not fall on you from the spade with a slam,
But will fold and enclose you slowly, you living dead.

Hush, I hear the guns. Are you still asleep?
Surely I saw you a little heave to reply.
I can hardly think you will not turn over and creep
Along the furrows trenchward as if to die.

HAROLD MONRO

Children of Love (December 1914). 'Soldier': published alone, *Saturday Westminster Gazette*, 7 November. 'Retreat': based on newspaper reports of the retreat from Mons in late August. All four poems probably written between early September and mid-October. Owen quoted from the first poem in 1915 after Monro had 'smiled sadly' at his new uniform.

(15) Breakfast

We ate our breakfast lying on our backs,
Because the shells were screeching overhead.
I bet a rasher to a loaf of bread
That Hull United would beat Halifax
When Jimmy Stainthorp played full-back instead
Of Billy Bradford. Ginger raised his head
And cursed, and took the bet; and dropt back dead.
We ate our breakfast lying on our backs,
Because the shells were screeching overhead.

W. W. GIBSON

Nation, 17 October 1914. *Battle* (September 1915). Original title: 'Under Fire'. This and
the next poem, with Monro's 'Retreat' and 'Carrion', seem to be the earliest attempts
to imagine the realities of life and death at the front. Monro and Gibson were both
civilians until 1916–17, and neither served abroad. Both make use of press reports:
'Breakfast' is based on a soldier's anecdote quoted in the *Nation*, 3 October.

(16) The Messages

'I cannot quite remember ... There were five
Dropt dead beside me in the trench – and three
Whispered their dying messages to me ...'

Back from the trenches, more dead than alive,
Stone-deaf and dazed, and with a broken knee,
He hobbled slowly, muttering vacantly:

'I cannot quite remember ... There were five
Dropt dead beside me in the trench – and three
Whispered their dying messages to me ...

'Their friends are waiting, wondering how they thrive –
Waiting a word in silence patiently ...
But what they said, or who their friends may be

'I cannot quite remember ... There were five
Dropt dead beside me in the trench – and three
Whispered their dying messages to me ...'

W. W. GIBSON

Nation, 17 October 1914. *Battle* (1915). Perhaps the first 1914–18 poem to refer to shellshock.

(17) On the Belgian Expatriation

I dreamt that people from the Land of Chimes
Arrived one autumn morning with their bells,
To hoist them on the towers and citadels
Of my own country, that the musical rhymes

Rung by them into space at meted times
Amid the market's daily stir and stress,
And the night's empty star-lit silentness,
Might solace souls of this and kindred climes.

Then I awoke; and lo, before me stood
The visioned ones, but pale and full of fear;
From Bruges they came, and Antwerp, and Ostend,

No carillons in their train. Foes of mad mood
Had shattered these to shards amid the gear
Of ravaged roof, and smouldering gable-end.

THOMAS HARDY

Written 18 October 1914. *King Albert's Book* (1914). The plight of Belgian refugees
had enormous media coverage in 1914; like many people, Hardy was deeply moved by
their suffering.

(18) Five Souls

First Soul

I was a peasant of the Polish plain;
I left my plough because the message ran:–
Russia, in danger, needed every man
To save her from the Teuton; and was slain.
I gave my life for freedom – This I know
For those who bade me fight had told me so.

Second Soul

I was a Tyrolese, a mountaineer;
I gladly left my mountain home to fight
Against the brutal, treacherous Muscovite;
And died in Poland on a Cossack spear.
I gave my life for freedom – This I know
For those who bade me fight had told me so.

Third Soul

I worked in Lyons at my weaver's loom,
When suddenly the Prussian despot hurled
His felon blow at France and at the world;
Then I went forth to Belgium and my doom.
I gave my life for freedom – This I know
For those who bade me fight had told me so.

Fourth Soul

I owned a vineyard by the wooded Main,
Until the Fatherland, begirt by foes
Lusting her downfall, called me, and I rose
Swift to the call – and died in far Lorraine.
I gave my life for freedom – This I know
For those who bade me fight had told me so.

Fifth Soul

I worked in a great shipyard by the Clyde;
There came a sudden word of wars declared,
Of Belgium, peaceful, helpless, unprepared,
Asking our aid: I joined the ranks, and died.
I gave my life for freedom – This I know
For those who bade me fight had told me so.

W. N. Ewer

Nation, 3 October 1914. *Five Souls and Other War-Time Verses* (1917). The first wartime satires were not by soldiers. Ewer, a committed socialist and in due course conscientious objector, was sceptical from the start about the war's many aims and motives.

(19) 1814–1914

On reading The Dynasts

Read here the tale of how England fought for freedom
Under Pitt and Castlereagh;
Gave unstintingly of her blood and treasure
To break a tyrant's sway.

'Europe in danger – her liberties imperilled.'
So the statesmen cried.
Stern, stupid Englishmen, foolishly believing them,
Marched and fought and died.

When the Corsican was broken and the pale suffering peoples
Thought their freedom due;
France got – her Bourbons back; Italy – her Bomba,
England – Peterloo.

A hundred years passed – once again: – 'The liberties
Of Europe are at stake!'
Once again the statesmen bid the silent Englishmen
Die for freedom's sake.

Stern, stupid Englishmen, nowise disbelieving them,
March cheerfully away,
Heedless of the story of their fathers' 'War for Freedom'
Under Pitt and Castlereagh.

W. N. EWER

Dated November 1914. *Herald*, 20 March 1915. *Five Souls and Other War-Time Verses* (1917).

   The Dynasts: Hardy's epic-drama about the Napoleonic wars. Ewer reads it as a grim warning of how history repeats itself: after the defeat of the Corsican (Napoleon), reactionary monarchs were restored in Europe and protesters at home were brutally repressed (Peterloo, 1819).

   March cheerfully away: an ironic allusion to Hardy's 'Men Who March Away'.

(20) The Climax

In this strange world in which we live,
　　Great marvels never cease:
But, lo! a wonder passing all, –
　　Wells preaches War for peace!

T. W. MERCER

Labour Leader, 29 October 1914. In August, at the request of Lloyd George, the Fabian socialist H. G. Wells had written some influential essays arguing that this was the 'war that will end war' – an idea scorned by those on the far left such as Mercer, the Independent Labour Party and its organ, *The Labour Leader*.

(21) Casus Belli

War for the end of War,
　　Fighting that Fighting cease;
Why do our cannon roar?
　　For a thousand years of Peace.

HAROLD BEGBIE

Fighting Lines (1914). Despite left-wing objections, Wells's notion of 'war that will end war' was widely – often eagerly – accepted.

(22) War Exalts

War exalts and cleanses: it lifts man from the mud!
Ask God what He thinks of a bayonet dripping blood.

By War the brave are tested, and cowards are disgraced!
Show God His own image shrapnel'd into paste.

Fight till tyrants perish, slay till brutes are mild!
Then go wash the blood off and try to face your child.

HAROLD BEGBIE

Fighting Lines (1914). The final, unexpected poem in Begbie's book.

(23) Gheluvelt

Epitaph on the Worcesters. October 31, 1914

Askest thou of these graves? They'll tell thee, O stranger, in
  England
How we Worcesters lie where we redeem'd the battle.

ROBERT BRIDGES

October and Other Poems (1920). One of many wartime imitations of Simonides' ancient epitaph on Thermopylae: 'Go tell the Spartans, you who pass by, / That here obedient to their laws we lie' – cf. (*35*), (*158*), (*262*). Probably written soon after 31 October 1914, when members of the Worcester Regiment turned the tide of the first Battle of Ypres by closing a gap in the line at Gheluvelt, losing a hundred men as they did so. For the last time in British history, officers charged with swords drawn. The battle was considered to have 'saved England': poets were to return to it – see (*158*).

(24) Pro Patria

In bowler hats, top coats,
With woollen mufflers round their throats,
   They played at war,
These men I watched today.
Weary with office work, pinched-faced, depressed,
About the field they marched and counter-marched,
Halting and marking time and all the rest –
Meanwhile the world went on its way
To see the football heroes play.

No music, no applause,
No splendour for them but a Cause
   Hid deep at heart.
They drilled there soberly,

Their one half-holiday – the various show
Of theatres all resisted, home renounced;
The Picture Palace with its kindly glow
Forgotten now, that they may be
Worthy of England's chivalry.

WINIFRED M. LETTS

Westminster Gazette, 7 December 1914. *Hallow-E'en* (1916). The war is not going to be 'over by Christmas' after all, but the true heroes are still the volunteers. Newspapers had been attacking footballers for weeks.

(25) The Two Mothers

'Poor woman, weeping as they pass,
  Yon brave recruits, the nation's pride,
You mourn some gallant boy, alas!
  Like mine who lately fought and died?'

'Kind stranger, not for soldier son,
  Of shame, not grief, my heart will break,
Three stalwarts have I, but not one
  Doth risk his life for England's sake!'

MATILDA BETHAM-EDWARDS

Westminster Gazette, 11 December 1914. *War Poems* (1917).

(26) Many Sisters to Many Brothers

When we fought campaigns (in the long Christmas rains)
  With soldiers spread in troops on the floor,
I shot as straight as you, my losses were as few,
  My victories as many, or more.
And when in naval battle, amid cannon's rattle,
  Fleet met fleet in the bath,
My cruisers were as trim, my battleships as grim,
  My submarines cut as swift a path.

Or, when it rained too long, and the strength of the strong
  Surged up and broke a way with blows,
I was as fit and keen, my fists hit as clean,
  Your black eye matched my bleeding nose.
Was there a scrap or ploy in which you, the boy,
  Could better me? You could not climb higher,
Ride straighter, run as quick (and to smoke made you sick)
  ... But I sit here, and you're under fire.

Oh, it's you that have the luck, out there in blood and muck:
    You were born beneath a kindly star;
All we dreamt, I and you, you can really go and do,
    And I can't, the way things are.
In a trench you are sitting, while I am knitting
    A hopeless sock that never gets done.
Well, here's luck, my dear; – and you've got it, no fear;
    But for me ... a war is poor fun.

ROSE MACAULAY

In the anthology *Poems of To-Day* (May 1915), but perhaps first published in a 1914 periodical.

(27) A Jingle on the Times

'I am a painter
    Of Earth's pied hue;
What can my pencil
    Do for you?' –
' – You can do nothing,
    Nothing, nothing,
Nations want nothing
    That you can do.'

'I am a sculptor,
    A worker who
Preserves dear features
    The tombs enmew.' –
' – Sculpture, sculpture!
    More than sculpture
For dear remembrance
    Have we to do.'

'I am a poet,
   And set in view
Life and its secrets
   Old and new.' –
' – Poets we read not,
   Heed not, feed not,
Men now need not
   What they do.'

'I'm a musician,
   And balm I strew
On the passions people
   Are prone unto.' –
' – Music? Passions
   Calmed by music?
Nothing but passions
   Today will do!'

'I am an actor;
   The world's strange crew
In long procession
   My masques review.' –
' – O it's not acting,
   Acting, acting
And glassing nature
   That's now to do!'

'I am an architect;
   Once I drew
Glorious buildings,
   And built them too.' –
' – That was in peace-time,
   Peace-time, peace-time,
Nought but demolishing
   Now will do.'

'I am a preacher:
I would ensue
Whatsoever things are
Lovely, true.' –
' – Preachers are wordy,
Wordy, wordy;
Prodding's the preaching
We've now to do.'

'How shall we ply, then,
Our old mysteries?' –
' – Silly ones! Must we
Show to you
What is the only
Good, artistic,
Cultured, Christian
Thing to do?

'To manners, amenities,
Bid we adieu, –
To the old lumber
Of Right and True!
Fighting, smiting,
Running through;
That's now the civilized
Thing to do.'

THOMAS HARDY

Written December 1914. Hardy was privately much more sceptical about the war than his public verses might suggest. He left this poem unpublished, although his wife had it printed in a pamphlet in 1917.

(28) On Receiving News of the War

Snow is a strange white word.
No ice or frost
Have asked of bud or bird
For Winter's cost.

Yet ice and frost and snow
From earth to sky
This Summer land doth know,
No man knows why.

In all men's hearts it is.
Some spirit old
Hath turned with malign kiss
Our lives to mould.

Red fangs have torn His face.
God's blood is shed.
He mourns from His lone place
His children dead.

O! ancient crimson curse!
Corrode, consume.
Give back this universe
Its pristine bloom.

ISAAC ROSENBERG

Poems (1922). Written in South Africa, where Rosenberg had gone to stay with his
sister to convalesce, 1914. Distance and lack of patriotic convictions contribute to his
detachment from war fever in England: lacking early enthusiasm, he would not be
disillusioned later.

(29) 1914

War broke: and now the Winter of the world
With perishing great darkness closes in.
The foul tornado, centred at Berlin,
Is over all the width of Europe whirled,
Rending the sails of progress. Rent or furled
Are all Art's ensigns. Verse wails. Now begin
Famines of thought and feeling. Love's wine's thin.
The grain of human Autumn rots, down-hurled.

For after Spring had bloomed in early Greece,
And Summer blazed her glory out with Rome,
An Autumn softly fell, a harvest home,
A slow grand age, and rich with all increase.
But now, for us, wild Winter, and the need
Of sowings for new Spring, and blood for seed.

WILFRED OWEN

Poems (1931). One draft is dated 1914. Owen was in the south of France when war broke, so he was unaffected by the early excitement. He sees the crisis as an aesthetic disaster, ruinous for art, poetry and love.

Winter of the world: 'This is the winter of the world; – and here / We die' (Shelley, *Revolt of Islam* IX.25).

rich with all increase: 'autumn, big with rich increase' (Shakespeare, Sonnet 97).

(30) 'All the hills and vales along'

All the hills and vales along
Earth is bursting into song,
And the singers are the chaps
Who are going to die perhaps.
  O sing, marching men,
  Till the valleys ring again.
  Give your gladness to earth's keeping,
  So be glad, when you are sleeping.

Cast away regret and rue,
Think what you are marching to.
Little live, great pass.
Jesus Christ and Barabbas
Were found the same day.
This died, that went his way.
  So sing with joyful breath.
  For why, you are going to death.
  Teeming earth will surely store
  All the gladness that you pour.

Earth that never doubts nor fears,
Earth that knows of death, not tears,
Earth that bore with joyful ease
Hemlock for Socrates,
Earth that blossomed and was glad
'Neath the cross that Christ had,
Shall rejoice and blossom too
When the bullet reaches you.
  Wherefore, men marching
  On the road to death, sing!
  Pour gladness on earth's head,
  So be merry, so be dead.

From the hills and valleys earth
Shouts back the sound of mirth,
Tramp of feet and lilt of song
Ringing all the road along.
All the music of their going,
Ringing swinging glad song-throwing,
Earth will echo still, when foot
Lies numb and voice mute.
   On, marching men, on
   To the gates of death with song.
   Sow your gladness for earth's reaping,
   So you may be glad, though sleeping.
   Strew your gladness on earth's bed,
   So be merry, so be dead.

CHARLES HAMILTON SORLEY

Marlborough and Other Poems (1916). Possibly begun as early as August 1914. 'The earth even more than Christ is the ultimate ideal of what man should strive to be' (Sorley, November 1914).

(31) To Germany

You are blind like us. Your hurt no man designed,
And no man claimed the conquest of your land.
But gropers both through fields of thought confined
We stumble and we do not understand.
You only saw your future bigly planned,
And we, the tapering paths of our own mind,
And in each other's dearest ways we stand,
And hiss and hate. And the blind fight the blind.

When it is peace, then we may view again
With new-won eyes each other's truer form
And wonder. Grown more loving-kind and warm
We'll grasp firm hands and laugh at the old pain,
When it is peace. But until peace, the storm
The darkness and the thunder and the rain.

CHARLES HAMILTON SORLEY

Marlborough and Other Poems (1916). Undated. Sorley spent the first half of 1914 as a student in Germany, returning home when war broke.

(32) 1914

I Peace

Now, God be thanked Who has matched us with His hour,
    And caught our youth, and wakened us from sleeping,
With hand made sure, clear eye, and sharpened power,
    To turn, as swimmers into cleanness leaping,
Glad from a world grown old and cold and weary,
    Leave the sick hearts that honour could not move,
And half-men, and their dirty songs and dreary,
    And all the little emptiness of love!

Oh! we, who have known shame, we have found release there,
    Where there's no ill, no grief, but sleep has mending,
        Naught broken save this body, lost but breath;
Nothing to shake the laughing heart's long peace there
    But only agony, and that has ending;
        And the worst friend and enemy is but Death.

II Safety

Dear! of all happy in the hour, most blest
　He who has found our hid security,
Assured in the dark tides of the world that rest,
　And heard our word, 'Who is so safe as we?'
We have found safety with all things undying,
　The winds, and morning, tears of men and mirth,
The deep night, and birds singing, and clouds flying,
　And sleep, and freedom, and the autumnal earth.
We have built a house that is not for Time's throwing.
　We have gained a peace unshaken by pain for ever.
War knows no power. Safe shall be my going,
　Secretly armed against all death's endeavour;
Safe though all safety's lost; safe where men fall;
And if these poor limbs die, safest of all.

III The Dead

Blow out, you bugles, over the rich Dead!
　There's none of these so lonely and poor of old,
　But, dying, has made us rarer gifts than gold.
These laid the world away; poured out the red
Sweet wine of youth; gave up the years to be
　Of work and joy, and that unhoped serene,
　That men call age; and those who would have been,
Their sons, they gave, their immortality.

Blow, bugles, blow! They brought us, for our dearth,
　Holiness, lacked so long, and Love, and Pain.
Honour has come back, as a king, to earth,
　And paid his subjects with a royal wage;
And Nobleness walks in our ways again;
　And we have come into our heritage.

IV The Dead

These hearts were woven of human joys and cares,
  Washed marvellously with sorrow, swift to mirth.
The years had given them kindness. Dawn was theirs,
  And sunset, and the colours of the earth.
These had seen movement, and heard music; known
  Slumber and waking; loved; gone proudly friended;
Felt the quick stir of wonder; sat alone;
  Touched flowers and furs and cheeks. All this is ended.

There are waters blown by changing winds to laughter
And lit by the rich skies, all day. And after,
  Frost, with a gesture, stays the waves that dance
And wandering loveliness. He leaves a white
  Unbroken glory, a gathered radiance,
A width, a shining peace, under the night.

V The Soldier

If I should die, think only this of me:
  That there's some corner of a foreign field
That is for ever England. There shall be
  In that rich earth a richer dust concealed;
A dust whom England bore, shaped, made aware,
  Gave once, her flowers to love, her ways to roam,
A body of England's, breathing English air,
  Washed by the rivers, blest by suns of home.

And think, this heart, all evil shed away,
  A pulse in the eternal mind, no less
    Gives somewhere back the thoughts by England given;
Her sights and sounds; dreams happy as her day;
  And laughter, learnt of friends; and gentleness,
    In hearts at peace, under an English heaven.

RUPERT BROOKE

1914

Written after Brooke's brief experience of the front at Antwerp in early October 1914: perhaps the first poems by a volunteer who had been in action. First published in *New Numbers* ('December 1914', but actually late February 1915); reprinted in *1914 and Other Poems* (May 1915), only a few weeks after Brooke's death. 'The Soldier' (originally 'The Recruit') came to public attention when the Dean of St Paul's quoted it in his Easter sermon. 'The thoughts to which [Brooke] gives expression ... will be shared by many thousands of young men moving resolutely into this, the hardest, the cruellest, and the least-rewarded of all the wars that men have fought' (Winston Churchill, obituary, *The Times*, 26 April).

1915

Nineteen-fiteen brought a growing sense of realism – military, political and economic. British casualties on the Western Front escalated from 11,500 at Neuve Chapelle in March to 62,000 at Loos in October, and during the summer the daily casualty rate in the Ypres Salient averaged 300 even when there was no significant military action. The Germans first used poison gas in April, during the Second Battle of Ypres; the Allies were soon to develop their own versions. Poetry from the home front became sterner and more anxious, and poets increasingly made use of religious imagery, finding comfort in thinking of soldiers as modern Christs, who would redeem themselves and the world.

The Liberal government fell in May, to be replaced by a National Coalition, still under Asquith. With the press clamouring for more effective armaments production, the dynamic Lloyd George was appointed Minister of Munitions. Public confidence, supported by propaganda and most newspapers, remained largely unshaken: the nation, its empire and its values would triumph in the end. Hopes that the United States might join the Allies grew in May when a German submarine sank the liner *Lusitania* with the loss of over a hundred American lives.

From Kitchener's army of volunteers, eventually to surpass two million, emerged voices of soldier-poets, all able to draw on personal military experience, their verse expressing not the simple enthusiasm of 1914 but a considered sense of dedication and contemplation. When Brooke died – conveniently for pro-war opinion on St George's Day – his *1914* sonnets rapidly became the most celebrated war poems of all, expressing what many people wanted to see as the highest ideals of British patriotism and selflessness. Some poets in uniform echoed his language and his theme of willing sacrifice, but as the year went on others began to find his certainty increasingly at odds with what they knew of the front line.

On the Western Front, the stalemate that had developed in late 1914 became ever more difficult to break as the trenches grew deeper, more complex and, especially on the German side, more professional. While Germany concentrated its efforts on its Eastern Front, Britain hoped to take advantage of superior naval strength by launching strikes from the south, avoiding what was becoming a war of attrition in France and Flanders. The results were disastrous: the Mesopotamia expedition and the landings at Gallipoli both failed, and a beach-head at Salonika made no headway. The focus returned to the Western Front, where the casualties at Loos included Sorley and Rudyard Kipling's only son. Hopes remained strong, nevertheless: with the New Armies steadily gaining in size and experience, many people at home and in uniform looked forward to 1916 with resolute optimism.

(33) On Being Asked for a War Poem

I think it better that in times like these
A poet's mouth be silent, for in truth
We have no gift to set a statesman right;
He has had enough of meddling who can please
A young girl in the indolence of her youth,
Or an old man upon a winter's night.

W. B. YEATS

Written 6 February 1915. *The Book of the Homeless* (1916), where the poem is entitled 'A Reason for Keeping Silent'. Revised for *The Wild Swans at Coole* (1917). The first version was more colloquial: 'I think it better that at times like these / We poets keep our mouths shut'. Yeats wrote to Henry James on 20 August 1915: 'I shall keep the neighbourhood of the seven sleepers of Ephesus, hoping to catch their comfortable snores till the bloody frivolity is over'.

(34) The Beau Ideal

Since Rose a classic taste possessed,
   It naturally follows
Her girlish fancy was obsessed
   By Belvedere Apollos.
And when she dreamed about a mate,
   If any hoped to suit, he
Must in his person illustrate
   A type of manly beauty.

He must be physically fit,
   A graceful, stalwart figure,
Of iron and elastic knit
   And full of verve and vigour.
Enough! I've made the bias plain
   That warped her heart and thrilled it.
It was a maggot of her brain,
   And Germany has killed it.

Today, the sound in wind and limb
   Don't flutter Rose one tittle.
Her maiden ardour cleaves to him
   Who's proved that he is brittle,
Whose healing cicatrices show
   The colours of a prism,
Whose back is bent into a bow
   By Flanders rheumatism.

The lad who troth with Rose would plight,
   Nor apprehend rejection
Must be in shabby khaki dight
   To compass her affection.
Who buys her an engagement ring
   And finds her kind and kissing,
Must have one member in a sling
   Or, preferably, missing.

JESSIE POPE

Daily Mail, 3 February 1915. *More War Poems* (1915). Early drafts of Owen's 'Dulce et Decorum Est' (*182*) are addressed to 'A certain Poetess' and 'To Jessie Pope, etc'.

(35) Epitaph: Neuve Chapelle

Tell them at home, there's nothing here to hide:
We took our orders, asked no questions, died.

H. W. GARROD

Worms and Epitaphs (1919). Simonides again: cf. (*23 note*). Neuve Chapelle: a three-day British offensive, March 1915.

(36) The Marionettes

Let the foul Scene proceed:
　　There's laughter in the wings;
'Tis sawdust that they bleed,
　　But a box Death brings.

How rare a skill is theirs
　　These extreme pangs to show,
How real a frenzy wears
　　Each feigner of woe!

Gigantic dins uprise!
　　Even the gods must feel
A smarting of the eyes
　　As these fumes upsweal.

Strange, such a Piece is free,
　　While we Spectators sit,
Aghast at its agony,
　　Yet absorbed in it!

Dark is the outer air,
　　Coldly the night draughts blow,
Mutely we stare, and stare
　　At the frenzied Show.

Yet heaven hath its quiet shroud
　　Of deep, immutable blue −
We cry 'An end!' We are bowed
　　By the dread, ''Tis true!'

While the Shape who hoofs applause
  Behind our deafened ear,
Hoots – angel-wise – 'the Cause!'
  And affrights even fear.

WALTER DE LA MARE

Westminster Gazette, 10 March 1915. *Motley and Other Poems* (1918). Another thoughtful response from one of the older Georgians. The *Gazette*, which supported the war, presumably approved of the last stanza.

(37) The Owl

Downhill I came, hungry, and yet not starved;
Cold, yet had heat within me that was proof
Against the North wind; tired, yet so that rest
Had seemed the sweetest thing under a roof.

Then at the inn I had food, fire, and rest,
Knowing how hungry, cold, and tired was I.
All of the night was quite barred out except
An owl's cry, a most melancholy cry

Shaken out long and clear upon the hill,
No merry note, nor cause of merriment,
But one telling me plain what I escaped
And others could not, that night, as in I went.

And salted was my food, and my repose,
Salted and sobered, too, by the bird's voice
Speaking for all who lay under the stars,
Soldiers and poor, unable to rejoice.

EDWARD THOMAS

Written in Hampshire, February 1915. *Poems* (1917). Thomas is uneasy at still being a civilian (he joined up in July).

(38) In Memoriam

The flowers left thick at nightfall in the wood
This Eastertide call into mind the men,
Now far from home, who, with their sweethearts, should
Have gathered them and will do never again.

EDWARD THOMAS

Written April 1915. *Poems* (1917).

(39) The Question

I wonder if the old cow died or not.
Gey bad she was the night I left, and sick.
Dick reckoned she would mend. He knows a lot –
At least he fancies so himself, does Dick.

Dick knows a lot. But maybe I did wrong
To leave the cow to him, and come away.
Over and over like a silly song
These words keep bumming in my head all day –

And all I think of, as I face the foe
And take my lucky chance of being shot,
Is this – that if I'm hit, I'll never know
Till Doomsday if the old cow died or not.

W. W. GIBSON

(40) Mad

Neck-deep in mud,
He mowed and raved –
He who had braved
The field of blood –
And as a lad
Just out of school
Yelled – *April Fool!*
And laughed like mad.

W. W. GIBSON

(41) Raining

The night I left my father said –
'You'll go and do some stupid thing:
You've no more sense in that fat head
Than Silly Billy Witterling.

'Not sense to come in when it rains –
Not sense enough for that you've got.
You'll get a bullet through your brains,
Before you know, as like as not.'

And now I'm lying in the trench
And shells and bullets through the night
Are raining in a steady drench –
I'm thinking the old man was right.

W. W. GIBSON

1915

(42) Victory

I watched it oozing quietly
Out of the gaping gash.
The lads thrust on to victory
With lunge and curse and crash.

Half-dazed, that uproar seemed to me
Like some old battle-sound
Heard long ago, as quietly
His blood soaked in the ground.

The lads thrust on to victory
With lunge and crash and shout.
I lay and watched, as quietly
His life was running out.

W. W. GIBSON

Four of ten poems by Gibson published under the title 'Battle', *Nation*, 24 April 1915 (the day he heard of Brooke's death). All included in *Battle* (September 1915). Cf. (*15*), (*16*). Like de la Mare (*36*), Gibson was appalled by the conflict. Most of his *Battle* poems are ironic and very short, intended to 'get at' civilian consciences. No soldier wrote like this so early in the war.

(43) Fragment

I strayed about the deck, an hour, tonight
Under a cloudy moonless sky; and peeped
In at the windows, watched my friends at table,
Or playing cards, or standing in the doorway,
Or coming out into the darkness. Still
No one could see me.

> I would have thought of them
> – Heedless, within a week of battle – in pity,
> Pride in their strength and in the weight and firmness
> And link'd beauty of bodies, and pity that
> This gay machine of splendour 'ld soon be broken,
> Thought little of, pashed, scattered ...
>
> Only, always,
> I could but see them – against the lamplight – pass
> Like coloured shadows, thinner than filmy glass,
> Slight bubbles, fainter than the wave's faint light,
> That broke to phosphorus out in the night,
> Perishing things and strange ghosts – soon to die
> To other ghosts – this one, or that, or I.

RUPERT BROOKE

Written April 1915 on the troopship to Gallipoli. *Collected Poems* (1918). Haunting, melancholy, sceptical, much more typical of Brooke than his famous sonnets, the lines remained unpublished while he was being turned into a national icon. They give a hint of the kind of poetry he might have written had he lived.

(44) Into Battle

> The naked earth is warm with spring,
>   And with green grass and bursting trees
> Leans to the sun's gaze glorying,
>   And quivers in the sunny breeze;
> And life is colour and warmth and light,
>   And a striving evermore for these;
> And he is dead who will not fight;
>   And who dies fighting has increase.

The fighting man shall from the sun
  Take warmth, and life from the glowing earth;
Speed with the light-foot winds to run,
  And with the trees to newer birth;
And find, when fighting shall be done,
  Great rest, and fullness after dearth.

All the bright company of Heaven
  Hold him in their high comradeship,
The Dog-Star, and the Sisters Seven,
  Orion's Belt and sworded hip.

The woodland trees that stand together,
  They stand to him each one a friend;
They gently speak in the windy weather;
  They guide to valley and ridge's end.

The kestrel hovering by day,
  And the little owls that call by night,
Bid him be swift and keen as they,
  As keen of ear, as swift of sight.

The blackbird sings to him, 'Brother, brother,
  If this be the last song you shall sing,
Sing well, for you may not sing another;
  Brother, sing.'

In dreary, doubtful, waiting hours,
  Before the brazen frenzy starts,
The horses show him nobler powers;
  O patient eyes, courageous hearts!

And when the burning moment breaks,
  And all things else are out of mind,
And only joy of battle takes
  Him by the throat, and makes him blind,

Through joy and blindness he shall know
  Not caring much to know, that still
Nor lead nor steel shall reach him, so
  That it be not the Destined Will.

The thundering line of battle stands,
  And in the air death moans and sings;
But Day shall clasp him with strong hands,
  And Night shall fold him in soft wings.

JULIAN GRENFELL

Written 29 April 1915. *The Times*, 28 May, with the announcement of Grenfell's death. The timing of his death and his aristocratic connections helped to make him an idealized figure second only to Brooke, who had died a month earlier. 'Into Battle' has appeared in many anthologies from 1915 onwards: its content is unique among Great War poems.

(45) 'I saw a man this morning'

I saw a man this morning
  Who did not wish to die:
I ask, and cannot answer,
  If otherwise wish I.

Fair broke the day this morning
  Against the Dardanelles;
The breeze blew soft, the morn's cheeks
  Were cold as cold sea-shells.

But other shells are waiting
  Across the Aegean Sea,
Shrapnel and high explosive,
  Shells and hells for me.

O hell of ships and cities,
Hell of men like me,
Fatal second Helen,
Why must I follow thee?

Achilles came to Troyland
And I to Chersonese:
He turned from wrath to battle,
And I from three days' peace.

Was it so hard, Achilles,
So very hard to die?
Thou knowest and I know not –
So much the happier I.

I will go back this morning
From Imbros over the sea;
Stand in the trench, Achilles,
Flame-capped, and shout for me.

PATRICK SHAW-STEWART

Ronald Knox, *Patrick Shaw-Stewart* (1920). Apparently Shaw-Stewart's only complete surviving poem, found in his copy of Housman's *A Shropshire Lad*, a book that clearly influenced the poem.
  Chersonese: Gallipoli peninsula, opposite Troy.
  wrath: see opening lines of the *Iliad*.
  Imbros: Allied base. Achilles sailed from Skyros (where Brooke was buried) to Troy.
  Flame-capped: Achilles' helmet was made by Hephaestus, god of fire.

(46) 'I tracked a dead man down a trench'

I tracked a dead man down a trench,
I knew not he was dead.
They told me he had gone that way,
And there his foot-marks led.

The trench was long and close and curved,
　　It seemed without an end;
And as I threaded each new bay
　　I thought to see my friend.

I went there stooping to the ground.
　　For, should I raise my head,
Death watched to spring; and how should then
　　A dead man find the dead?

At last I saw his back. He crouched
　　As still as still could be,
And when I called his name aloud
　　He did not answer me.

The floorway of the trench was wet
　　Where he was crouching dead:
The water of the pool was brown,
　　And round him it was red.

I stole up softly where he stayed
　　With head hung down all slack,
And on his shoulders laid my hands
　　And drew him gently back.

And then, as I had guessed, I saw
　　His head, and how the crown –
I saw then why he crouched so still,
　　And why his head hung down.

W. S. S. LYON

'Written in trenches by "Glencorse Wood", 19–20 April 1915.' *Easter at Ypres,
1915* (1916).
　　the crown: the crown of thorns – the dead man is Christ, who has taken on himself
the role of a common soldier.

(47) In Flanders Fields

In Flanders fields the poppies blow
Between the crosses, row on row,
    That mark our place; and in the sky
    The larks, still bravely singing, fly
Scarce heard amid the guns below.

We are the Dead. Short days ago
We lived, felt dawn, saw sunset glow,
    Loved and were loved, and now we lie
        In Flanders fields.

Take up our quarrel with the foe:
To you from failing hands we throw
    The torch; be yours to hold it high.
    If ye break faith with us who die
We shall not sleep, though poppies grow
        In Flanders fields.

JOHN MCCRAE

Written April 1915 at a dressing station near the line during Second Ypres. *Punch*, 8 December 1915. *In Flanders Fields* (1919). A near-sonnet, composed as a metrical experiment with only two rhymes, both open vowels to suggest hope. Echoes Brooke's fourth sonnet (*32*), which had been quoted in *The Times Literary Supplement*, 11 March: McCrae gives voice to the dead, calling on the living to keep faith and continue fighting. This call struck a 1970s critic as 'vicious' and 'stupid' (Paul Fussell, *The Great War and Modern Memory*, 250), but when the poem was first published it caught the public mood, reaffirming Brooke's message and soon becoming one of the most famous poems of the war. It probably inspired the post-war use of blood-red Flanders poppies as symbols of remembrance.

(48) Absolution

The anguish of the earth absolves our eyes
Till beauty shines in all that we can see.
War is our scourge; yet war has made us wise,
And, fighting for our freedom, we are free.

Horror of wounds and anger at the foe,
And loss of things desired; all these must pass.
We are the happy legion, for we know
Time's but a golden wind that shakes the grass.

There was an hour when we were loth to part
From life we longed to share no less than others.
Now, having claimed this heritage of heart,
What need we more, my comrades and my brothers?

SIEGFRIED SASSOON

Sassoon's first war poem, written May 1915 while training in England. *Westminster Gazette*, 28 March 1916. *The Old Huntsman* (1917). He said it was 'manifestly influenced by Rupert Brooke's famous sonnet-sequence' (*Siegfried's Journey*, 17). Ivor Gurney thought it showed 'the fault of minor poets who make beautiful lines of [no] particular significance. / *Why* is time a *wind*, a *golden* wind ... ?' (letter, 23 August 1917).

(49) Trenches: St Eloi

Over the flat slope of St Eloi
A wide wall of sand bags.
Night,
In the silence desultory men
Pottering over small fires, cleaning their mess tins:
To and fro, from the lines,
Men walk as on Piccadilly,
Making paths in the dark,
Through scattered dead horses,
Over a dead Belgian's belly.

The Germans have rockets. The English have no rockets.
Behind the line, cannon, hidden, lying back miles.
Before the line, chaos:

My mind is a corridor. The minds about me are corridors.
Nothing suggests itself. There is nothing to do but keep on.

T. E. HULME

First published as 'Poem: Abbreviated from the Conversation of Mr T. E. H.' in Ezra
Pound's *Catholic Anthology* (1915). The free verse and spare, Imagist style owe something
to Pound, who wrote down Hulme's remarks while visiting him in hospital, May 1915
(Hulme had been wounded near St Eloi in April). 'I want to avoid the infantry again',
Hulme told Marsh in 1915. 'I have had my fill of the trenches, I think.'
  no rockets: Hulme's 1915–16 articles about the war in the *New Age* deplore the
inadequacy of British munitions.

(50) Lusitania

Chaos! that coincides with this militant purpose.
Chaos! the heart of this earnest malignancy.
Chaos! that helps, chaos that gives to shatter
Mind-wrought, mind-unimagining energies
For topless ill, of dynamite and iron.
Soulless logic, inventive enginery.
Now you have got the peace-faring Lusitania,
Germany's gift – all earth they would give thee, Chaos.

ISAAC ROSENBERG

Written summer 1915, while Rosenberg was still a civilian. *Collected Works* (1937). The
sinking in May of the *Lusitania*, a liner carrying British and American passengers (and,
as emerged long afterwards, some munitions) was seen as a prime example of German
barbarity, provoking riots in England and a strong protest from the US President.

(51) The Anvil

Burned from the ore's rejected dross,
The iron whitens in the heat.
With plangent strokes of pain and loss
The hammers on the iron beat.
Searched by the fire, through death and dole
We feel the iron in our soul.

O dreadful Forge! If torn and bruised
The heart, more urgent comes our cry
Not to be spared but to be used,
Brain, sinew, and spirit, before we die.
Beat out the iron, edge it keen,
And shape us to the end we mean!

LAURENCE BINYON

The Times, 21 May 1915. *The Anvil* (1916). The strain on civilians is beginning to show: imagery of war as a forge or crucible had not been typical of work by idealists such as Binyon.

(52) Gathering Song

A word for you of the Prussian boast,
    Or never a word, but under the drum
The limber tread of a tramping host
    Out of the English counties come –
There are men who could count you the Warwick spires,
    And fishermen turning from Severn and Ouse;
They gather from half a hundred shires,
    And never a man of them all to choose.

They are coming out of the northern dales,
    Out of the sound of Bow they come,
Lomond calls to the hills of Wales –
    Hear them tramping under the drum:
From Derry to Cork, from Thames to Dee,
    With Kentish Hob and Collier Tyne,
They come to travel the Dover sea,
    A thousand thousand men of the line.

They come from the bright Canadian snows,
   And Brisbane's one with proud Bengal;
Over the Vaal and the Orange goes
   To the cape of the south a single call;
Though the term shall be for a year or ten
   You still shall hear it under the drum,
The limber tread of the marching men:
   They come, you lords of the boast, they come.

JOHN DRINKWATER

Swords and Ploughshares (May 1915). The ready response of volunteers from Britain, Ireland and the 'Colonies', celebrated in many 1914–15 poems, seemed an impressive contrast to Germany's boasts about its conscripted army.

(53) The Dilemma

God heard the embattled nations sing and shout
'Gott strafe England!' and 'God save the King!'
God this, God that, and God the other thing –
'Good God!' said God, 'I've got my work cut out.'

J. C. SQUIRE

Herald, 5 June 1915. *The Survival of the Fittest* (May 1916, soon reprinted). Squire's satirical verse was well known in this period, but he seems to have had doubts later: he omitted all his 1915–16 satires from his 1918 collection and reprinted only two of them in 1926.

(54) The Telegraph Boy

Death bids his heralds go their way
On red-rimmed bicycles today.
Arrayed in blue, with streak of red,
A boy bears tidings of the dead:
He pedals merrily along,
Whistling the chorus of a song;
Passing the time of day with friends,
Until the journey almost ends.
Then slowing down, he scans each gate
For the doomed name upon the plate.
That done, he loudly knocks and rings,
Hands in the yellow missive; sings
His song. The maid says at the door
'No answer,' and he's off once more.

***

No answer through the empty years!
No answer but a mother's tears!

EDWARD SHILLITO

Nation, 12 June 1915. *The Omega and Other Poems* (1916).
yellow missive: telegram from the War Office – cf. (*195*).

(55) The Fields of Flanders

Last year the fields were all glad and gay
With silver daisies and silver may;
There were kingcups gold by the river's edge
And primrose stars under every hedge.

This year the fields are trampled and brown,
The hedges are broken and beaten down,
And where the primroses used to grow
Are little black crosses set in a row.

And the flower of hopes, and the flowers of dreams,
The noble, fruitful, beautiful schemes,
The tree of life with its fruit and bud,
Are trampled down in the mud and the blood.

The changing seasons will bring again
The magic of Spring to our wood and plain:
Though the Spring be so green as never was seen
The crosses will still be black in the green.

The God of battles shall judge the foe
Who trampled our country and laid her low ...
God! Hold our hands on the reckoning day,
Lest all we owe them we should repay.

EDITH NESBIT

Dated 1915. *Westminster Gazette*, 15 June 1915. *Many Voices* (1922).

(56) Two Julys

I was so vague in 1914; tossed
  Upon too many purposes, and worthless;
Moody; to this world or the other lost,
  Essential nowhere; without calm and mirthless.
And now I have gained for many ends,
  See my straight road stretch out so white, so slender,
That happy road, the road of all my friends,
  Made glad with peace, and holy with surrender.

Proud, proud we fling to the winds of Time our token,
   And in our need there wells in us the power,
Given England's swords to keep her honour clean.
   Which they shall be which pierce, and which be broken,
We know not, but we know that every hour
   We must shine brighter, take an edge more keen.

CHARLES MASEFIELD

Written in trenches near Sanctuary Wood, July 1915. In Galloway Kyle's anthology, *More Songs by the Fighting Men* (1917). *Poems* (1919). The language derives from Brooke.

(57) O Fortunati

O happy to have lived these epic days!
   To have seen unfold, as doth a dream unfold,
   These glorious chivalries, these deeds of gold,
The glory of whose splendour gilds death's ways,
As a rich sunset fills dark woods with fire
   And blinds the traveller's eyes. Our eyes are blind
   With flaming heroism, that leaves our mind
Dumbstruck with pride. We have had our heart's desire!
O happy! Generations have lived and died
   And only dreamed such things as we have seen and known!
Splendour of men, death laughed at, death defied,
   Round the great world, on the winds, their tale is blown;
Whatever pass, these ever shall abide:
   In memory's Valhalla, an imperishable throne.

REX FRESTON

Probably written mid-1915, in England. *The Quest for Truth* (1916). A. G. West reacted furiously to this poem and others like it (*126*).

(58) Big Words

'I've whined of coming death, but now, no more!
It's weak and most ungracious. For, say I,
Though still a boy if years are counted, why!
I've lived those years from roof to cellar-floor,
And feel, like greybeards touching their fourscore,
Ready, so soon as the need comes, to die:
  And I'm satisfied.
For winning confidence in those quiet days
Of peace, poised sickly on the precipice side
Of Lliwedd crag by Snowdon, and in war
Finding it firmlier with me than before;
Winning a faith in the wisdom of God's ways
That once I lost, finding it justified
Even in this chaos; winning love that stays
And warms the heart like wine at Eastertide;
  Having earlier tried
False loves in plenty; oh! my cup of praise
Brims over, and I know I'll feel small sorrow,
Confess no sins and make no weak delays
If death ends all and I must die tomorrow.'

But on the firestep, waiting to attack,
He cursed, prayed, sweated, wished the proud words back.

ROBERT GRAVES

Written July 1915 (Graves was just twenty), except for the last two lines, which were added after the Battle of Loos in October. *Over the Brazier* (May 1916).

(59) Back to Rest

A leaping wind from England,
　The skies without a stain,
Clean cut against the morning
　Slim poplars after rain,
The foolish noise of sparrows
　And starlings in a wood –
After the grime of battle
　We know that these are good.

Death whining down from Heaven,
　Death roaring from the ground,
Death stinking in the nostril,
　Death shrill in every sound,
Doubting we charged and conquered –
　Hopeless we struck and stood.
Now when the fight is ended
　We know that it was good.

We that have seen the strongest
　Cry like a beaten child,
The sanest eyes unholy,
　The cleanest hands defiled,
We that have known the heart blood
　Less than the lees of wine,
We that have seen men broken,
　We know man is divine.

W. N. HODGSON

'Composed while marching to Rest Camp after severe fighting at Loos.' *New Witness*,
2 March 1916. *Verse and Prose in Peace and War* (1916). Hodgson was awarded the
MC after Loos.

(60) The Moles

I've been in a trench for fifteen days,
  I'm choked for the want of air;
It's harvest-time where my mother stays,
  And I'm wishing that I was there.

I've ceased to count in the scheme of things,
  My courage has waned and set;
It's trysting-time where the mavis sings,
  And I'm wishing I could forget.

With straightened shoulders and hearts that sang
  'For Freedom and Liberty!'
That was the battle-cry that rang
  From the men–that-we-used-to-be.

We've learnt the law of shot and shell,
  We've learnt the law of steel;
But the Law of the Trench is a cultured Hell,
  For it stifles the power to feel.

Death we have ventured many times
  Nor flinched at the sacrifice,
But if this be the debt of our youthful crimes –
  Lord God we have paid the price!

We have used our youth and lost the strength
  That the spirit of youth controls;
We have become no more at length
  Than partially human moles.

We're growing inanimate: bit by bit
  We're getting inert – decayed;
The score of our sins was boldly writ
  But Mother of God – we've paid!

And this is our Fate: when the Gods are kind
  Our existence shall simply cease –
A sniper's bullet – a trench that's mined –
  Godspeed, and a quick release!

CYRIL MORTON HORNE

Written in France, late 1915. *Songs of the Shrapnel Shell* (1918). In its Kiplingesque way, this is one of the earliest poems by a soldier about the realities of trench life.
    mavis: poetic word for a song thrush.

(61) 'When you see millions of the mouthless dead'

When you see millions of the mouthless dead
Across your dreams in pale battalions go,
Say not soft things as other men have said,
That you'll remember. For you need not so.
Give them not praise. For, deaf, how should they know
It is not curses heaped on each gashed head?
Nor tears. Their blind eyes see not your tears flow.
Nor honour. It is easy to be dead.
Say only this, 'They are dead.' Then add thereto,
'Yet many a better one has died before.'
Then, scanning all the o'ercrowded mass, should you
Perceive one face that you loved heretofore,
It is a spook. None wears the face you knew.
Great death has made all his for evermore.

CHARLES HAMILTON SORLEY

Found in Sorley's kit after his death at Loos in October 1915. *Marlborough and Other Poems* (1916).
    other men: probably a reference to Brooke.
    many a better ... : 'Thus died Patroclus, a better man than thou', said by Achilles (*Iliad* XXI) and quoted approvingly by Sorley in a November 1914 letter.

(62) The Redeemer

Darkness: the rain sluiced down; the mire was deep;
It was past twelve on a midwinter night,
When peaceful folk in beds lay snug asleep;
There, with much work to do before the light,
We lugged our clay-sucked boots as best we might
Along the trench; sometimes a bullet sang,
And droning shells burst with a hollow bang;
We were soaked, chilled and wretched, every one;
Darkness; the distant wink of a huge gun.

I turned in the black ditch, loathing the storm;
A rocket fizzed and burned with blanching flare,
And lit the face of what had been a form
Floundering in mirk. He stood before me there;
I say that He was Christ; stiff in the glare,
And leaning forward from His burdening task,
Both arms supporting it; His eyes on mine
Stared from the woeful head that seemed a mask
Of mortal pain in Hell's unholy shine.

No thorny crown, only a woollen cap
He wore – an English soldier, white and strong,
Who loved his time like any simple chap,
Good days of work and sport and homely song;
Now he has learned that nights are very long,
And dawn a watching of the windowed sky.
But to the end, unjudging, he'll endure
Horror and pain, not uncontent to die
That Lancaster on Lune may stand secure.

He faced me, reeling in his weariness,
Shouldering his load of planks, so hard to bear.
I say that He was Christ, who wrought to bless
All groping things with freedom bright as air,
And with His mercy washed and made them fair.
Then the flame sank, and all grew black as pitch,
While we began to struggle along the ditch;
And someone flung his burden in the muck,
Mumbling: 'O Christ Almighty, now I'm stuck!'

SIEGFRIED SASSOON

Written in France, November 1915. *Cambridge Magazine*, 29 April 1916. *The Old Huntsman* (1917). Sassoon's first front-line poem, originally ending: 'But in my heart I knew that I had seen / The suffering spirit of a world washed clean'. He rewrote this in March 1916, thinking the original version 'more than a little too pompous'. For other examples of soldier-Christ imagery, see (*46*), (*71*), (*72*), (*188*), (*189*), (*234*), (*236*).
   woollen cap: Sassoon's men were not supplied with steel helmets until February 1916.

(63) Let Us Drink

'We shall drink to them that sleep' – Campbell

Yes, you will do it, silently of course;
For after many a toast and much applause,
One is in love with silence, being hoarse,
– Such more than sorrow is your quiet's cause.

Yes, I can see you at it, in a room
Well-lit and warm, high-roofed and soft to the tread,
Satiate and briefly mindful of the tomb
With its poor victim of Teutonic lead.

Some unknown notability will rise,
Ridiculously solemn, glass abrim,
And say, 'To our dear brethren in the skies,' –
Dim are all eyes, all glasses still more dim.

Your pledge of sorrow but a cup to cheer,
Your sole remark a witless platitude,
Such as, 'Although it does not yet appear,
To suffer is the sole beatitude.

'Life has, of course, good moments such as this
(A glass of sherry we should never spurn),
But where our brethren are, 'tis perfect bliss;
Still, we are glad *our* lot was, – to return.'

Yes, I can see you and can see the dead,
Keen-eyed at last for Truth, with gentle mirth
Intent. And, having heard, smiling, they said:
'Strange are our little comrades of the earth.'

ALEXANDER ROBERTSON

New Age, 2 December 1915, lacking two stanzas. This text, except the title, from the anthology, *Soldier Poets* (1916). An early example of a soldier-poet satirizing civilian insensitivity, a theme soon to be taken up by many others, often more strongly. Robertson was to be killed on the first day of the Somme, 1 July 1916.

Epigraph: an ironic misquotation of Thomas Campbell's line, 'Let us think of them that sleep' ('The Battle of the Baltic').

(64) Au Champ d'Honneur

Mud-stained and rain-sodden, a sport for flies and lice,
Out of this vilest life into vile death he goes;
His grave will soon be ready, where the grey rat knows
There is fresh meat slain for her; – our mortal bodies rise,
In those foul scampering bellies, quick – and yet, those eyes
That stare on life still out of death, and will not close,
Seeing in a flash the Crown of Honour, and the Rose
Of Glory wreathed about the Cross of Sacrifice,

Died radiant. May some English traveller today
Leaving his city cares behind him, journeying west
To the brief solace of a sporting holiday,
Quicken again with boyish ardour, as he sees,
For a moment, Windsor Castle towering on the crest
And Eton still enshrined among remembering trees.

CHARLES SCOTT MONCRIEFF

New Witness, 23 December 1915. In the 1917 anthology, *The Muse in Arms*, where the title is 'The Field of Honour'. The original French title alludes to ancient chivalric values: in 1918 Scott Moncrieff began translating the French medieval epic, *The Song of Roland*, dedicating it to his new friend Wilfred Owen.

(65) 'Without Shedding of Blood ...'

God gave us England from of old,
But we held light the gift He gave;
Our royal birthright we have sold,
And now the land we lost for gold
  Only our blood can save.

  Not till thousands have been slain
  Shall the green wood be green again;
  Not till men shall fall and bleed
  Can brown ale taste like ale indeed.
  Blood and blood must yet be shed
    To make the roses red.

For minds made vile, and blind with greed,
For sins that spread from sire to son;
For loss of honour, loss of creed,
There yet remains one cure indeed –
  And there remains but one.

Malvern men must die and kill
That wind may blow on Malvern Hill;
Devonshire blood must fall like dew
That Devon's bays may yet be blue;
London must spill out lives like wine
That London's lights may shine.

Lord, for the years of ease and vice,
For hearts unmanned and souls decayed,
Thou hast required a sacrifice –
A bitter and a bloody price –
And lo! the price is paid.

We have given all things that were ours,
So that our weeds might yet be flowers;
We have covered half the earth with gore
That our houses might be homes once more;
The sword Thou hast demanded, Lord:
And, now, behold the sword!

GEOFFREY HOWARD

New Witness, 23 December 1915. Often anthologized during the war, but deplored in 1920 by Douglas Goldring as typical of how young public school officers could not face the truth. As Bernard Bergonzi points out (*Heroes' Twilight*, 62), Devon's bays would be just as blue in German-occupied England.

Title: 'without shedding of blood there is no remission [of sins]', a misleading use of Hebrews 9:22.

sword . . . demanded: Matthew 10:34.

(66) Marching – As Seen from the Left File

My eyes catch ruddy necks
Sturdily pressed back, –
All a red brick moving glint.
Like flaming pendulums, hands
Swing across the khaki –
Mustard-coloured khaki –
To the automatic feet.

We husband the ancient glory
In these bared necks and hands.
Not broke is the forge of Mars;
But a subtler brain beats iron
To shoe the hoofs of death,
(Who paws dynamic air now).
Blind fingers loose an iron cloud
To rain immortal darkness
On strong eyes.

ISAAC ROSENBERG

Written in England, late December 1915. *Poetry*, Chicago, December 1916. *Moses* (1916). Rosenberg's first poem after enlisting. He sees the marching column with a painter's eye, admiring its heroic strength.

(67) Nineteen-Fifteen

On a ploughland hill against the sky,
Over the barley, over the rye,
Time, which is now a black pine tree,
Holds out his arms and mocks at me –

'In the year of your Lord nineteen-fifteen
The acres are ploughed and the acres are green,
And the calves and the lambs and the foals are born,
But man the angel is all forlorn.

'The cropping cattle, the swallow's wing,
The wagon team and the pasture spring,
Move in their seasons and are most wise,
But man, whose image is in the skies,

'Who is master of all, whose hand achieves
The church and the barn and the homestead eaves –
How are the works of his wisdom seen
In the year of your Lord nineteen-fifteen?'

JOHN DRINKWATER

Sphere, 4 September 1915. *Olton Pools* (1916). The unspoilt English landscape is a reproach to a society at war – a civilian, Georgian view: contrast (*44*), (*65*).

(68) Before Marching and After

(In Memoriam F. W. G.)

Orion swung southward aslant
Where the starved Egdon pine-trees had thinned,
The Pleiads aloft seemed to pant
With the heather that twitched in the wind;
But he looked on indifferent to sights such as these,
Unswayed by love, friendship, home joy or home sorrow,
And wondered to what he would march on the morrow.

The crazed household clock – with its whirr
Rang midnight within as he stood,
He heard the low sighing of her
Who had striven from his birth for his good;
But he still only asked the spring starlight, the breeze,
What great thing or small thing his history would borrow
From that Game with Death he would play on the morrow.

When the heath wore the robe of late summer,
And the fuchsia-bells, hot in the sun,
Hung red by the door, a quick comer
Brought tidings that marching was done
For him who had joined in that game overseas
Where Death stood to win, though his name was to borrow
A brightness therefrom not to fade on the morrow.

THOMAS HARDY

Written September 1915. *Fortnightly Review*, October 1915. *Selected Poems* (1916).
  F. W. G.: Hardy's second cousin, Frank George, a lawyer, killed at Gallipoli in August 1915. Hardy had considered making him his heir.

(69) Christ in Flanders

We had forgotten You, or very nearly –
You did not seem to touch us very nearly –
  Of course we thought about You now and then;
Especially in any time of trouble –
We knew that You were good in time of trouble –
  But we are very ordinary men.

And there were always other things to think of –
There's lots of things a man has got to think of –
  His work, his home, his pleasure, and his wife;
And so we only thought of You on Sunday –
Sometimes, perhaps, not even on a Sunday –
  Because there's always lots to fill one's life.

And, all the while, in street or lane or byway –
In country lane, in city street, or byway –
  You walked among us, and we did not see,
Your Feet were bleeding as You walked our pavements –
How did we miss Your Footprints on our pavements? –
  Can there be other folk as blind as we?

Now we remember; over here in Flanders –
(It isn't strange to think of You in Flanders) –
  This hideous warfare seems to make things clear.
We never thought about You much in England –
But now that we are far away from England –
  We have no doubts, we know that You are here.

You helped us pass the jest along the trenches –
Where, in cold blood, we waited in the trenches –
  You touched its ribaldry and made it fine.
You stood beside us in our pain and weakness –
We're glad to think You understand our weakness –
  Somehow it seems to help us not to whine.

We think about You kneeling in the Garden –
Ah! God! The agony of that dread Garden –
  We know You prayed for us upon the Cross.
If anything could make us glad to bear it –
'Twould be the knowledge that You willed to bear it –
  Pain – death – the uttermost of human loss.

Though we forgot You – You will not forget us –
We feel so sure that You will not forget us –
  But stay with us until this dream is past.
And so we ask for courage, strength, and pardon –
Especially, I think, we ask for pardon –
  And that You'll stand beside us to the last.

LUCY WHITMELL

Spectator, 11 September 1915. One of the war's most popular poems, unsurprisingly
perhaps, given its combination of reassurance and easily acknowledged guilt.

(70) To My Pupils, Gone Before Their Day

You seemed so young, to know
So little, those few months or years ago,
Who may by now have disentwined
The inmost secrets of the Eternal Mind.

Yours seemed an easy part,
To construe, learn some trivial lines by heart:
Yet to your hands has God assigned
The burden of the sorrows of mankind.

You passed the brief school year
In expectation of some long career,
Then yielded up all years to find
That long career that none can leave behind.

If you had lived, some day
You would have passed my room, and chanced to say,
'I wonder if it's worth the grind
Of all those blunders he has underlined.'

Perhaps! If at the end
You in your turn shall teach me how to mend
The many errors whose effect
Eternity awaits us to correct.

GUY KENDALL

Spectator, 2 October 1915. *The Call* (1918). Written while Kendall was teaching at Charterhouse.

(71) Christs All!

Our Boys who have gone to the Front.

Ye are all christs in this your self-surrender, –
True sons of God, in seeking not your own.
Yours now the hardships, – yours shall be the splendour
Of the Great Triumph and THE KING'S 'Well done!'

Yours these rough Calvaries of high endeavour, –
Flame of the trench, and foam of wintry seas.
Nor Pain, nor Death, nor aught that is can sever
You from the Love that bears you on His knees.

Yes, you are christs, if less at times your seeming, –
Christ walks the earth in many a simple guise.
We know you christs, when, in your souls' redeeming,
The Christ-light blazes in your steadfast eyes.

Here – or hereafter, you shall see it ended, –
This mighty work to which your souls are set.
If from beyond – then, with the vision splendid,
You shall smile back and never know regret.

Or soon, or late, for each – the Life Immortal!
And not for us to choose the How or When.
Or late, or soon, – what matter? – since the Portal
Leads but to glories passing mortal ken.

O Lads! Dear Lads! Our christs of God's anointing!
Press on in hope! Your faith and courage prove!
Pass – by these High Ways of the Lord's appointing!
You cannot pass beyond our boundless love.

JOHN OXENHAM

'*All's Well!*' *Some Helpful Verse for These Dark Days of War* (November 1915). The war's
best-selling poet. Among the many soldiers to be sent one of Oxenham's little
khaki-coloured paperbacks by their mothers was Wilfred Owen in June 1917. Owen
commented that Oxenham 'evidently holds the Moslem doctrine – preached by Horatio
Bottomley, but not by the Nazarene – of salvation by *death in war*' (*Collected Letters*, 468).

(72) Three Hills

There is a hill in England,
  Green fields and a school I know,
Where the balls fly fast in summer,
  And the whispering elm-trees grow,
    A little hill, a dear hill,
    And the playing fields below.

There is a hill in Flanders,
  Heaped with a thousand slain,
Where the shells fly night and noontide
  And the ghosts that died in vain,
    A little hill, a hard hill
    To the souls that died in pain.

There is a hill in Jewry,
Three crosses pierce the sky,
On the midmost He is dying
To save all those who die,
  A little hill, a kind hill
To souls in jeopardy.

EVERARD OWEN

Dated Harrow, December 1915. *The Times*, 27 December 1915. *Three Hills and Other Poems* (1916). Written by a clergyman-schoolmaster at Harrow School, which is on a hill.
  hill in Flanders: presumably Hill 70, scene of fierce fighting at Loos.

(73) In Hospital

Under the shadow of a hawthorn brake,
  Where bluebells draw the sky down to the wood,
Where, 'mid brown leaves, the primroses awake
  And hidden violets smell of solitude;
Beneath green leaves bright-fluttered by the wing
Of fleeting, beautiful, immortal Spring,
I should have said, 'I love you,' and your eyes
Have said, 'I, too ....'. The gods saw otherwise.

For this is winter, and the London streets
    Are full of soldiers from that far, fierce fray
Where life knows death, and where poor glory meets
    Full-face with shame, and weeps and turns away.
And in the broken, trampled foreign wood
Is horror, and the terrible scent of blood,
And love shines tremulous, like a drowning star,
Under the shadow of the wings of war.

EDITH NESBIT

Westminster Gazette, 11 December 1915. *Many Voices* (1922).

(74) A Soldier's Face in a Starting Train

Clamour and shout,
And the long, packed train quite slowly moving out.
Some cried farewell,
Some with their tears told all they had to tell.
A muff, a swinging cap, a body's grace,
A waving hand,
And, like some weeping heart, the gaiety of the band;
Then, through the crowd, the loneliness of your face,
Glimpsed for a moment only: lost and gone
As the train went moving on.

Almost it seemed
You looked out from the train as one who dreamed
And watched some phantom show's queer pageant flit,
And were lonely, outside, watching it.

Just what you left – maybe had not to leave –
Of hearts to hope and grieve,
Just what you lost, won, dreaded, hoped to win,
These made your secret which your face locked in;
Your only testament
To me – you heard the call, and went.

With the turbulence and din
Of battle hammering near you, clipping you in;
A man's life as lightly going
As a wind's blowing;
Your life as like to be cut off as not
In the sore stress;
For all, be it much or little, that you gave,
God give you comfort in your inmost thought,
Vision and knowledge of what you fight to save,
And in that vision break your loneliness.

AGNES GROZIER HERBERTSON

Windsor Magazine, Christmas 1915. *The Quiet Heart* (1919).

(75) War

Over the World
Rages war.
Earth, sea and sky
Wince at his roar.
He tramples down
At every tread,
A million men,
A million dead.

1915

We say that we
Must crush the Hun,
Or else the World
Will be undone.
But Huns are we
As much as they.
All men are Huns,
Who fight and slay.

And if we win,
And crush the Huns,
In twenty years
We must fight their sons,
Who will rise against
Our victory,
Their fathers', their own
Ignominy.

And if their Kaiser
We dethrone,
They will his son restore,
Or some other one.
If we win by war,
War is a force,
And others to war
Will have recourse.

And through the World
Will rage new war.
Earth, sea and sky
Will wince at his roar.
He will trample down
At every tread,
Millions of men,
Millions of dead.

JOSEPH LEFTWICH

Dated 1915. *Along the Years* (1937). A pacifist friend of Rosenberg makes an early prophecy of the Second World War.

All men are Huns: militarists in Britain were often referred to as 'Prussians' or 'Prussianists' by their opponents.

(76) In Time of 'The Breaking of Nations'

I

Only a man harrowing clods
   In a slow silent walk
With an old horse that stumbles and nods
   Half asleep as they stalk.

II

Only thin smoke without flame
   From the heaps of couch-grass;
Yet this will go onward the same
   Though Dynasties pass.

III

Yonder a maid and her wight
 Come whispering by:
War's annals will cloud into night
 Ere their story die.

THOMAS HARDY

Written 1915. *Saturday Review*, 29 January 1916. *Selected Poems* (1916). Despite his handful of propagandist war poems, Hardy is at his best when taking the long view (appropriately, the inspiration for this poem came to him during the 1870 Franco-Prussian war).

 Title: Jeremiah 51:20. Hardy had recorded that the last night of 1914 had been a 'sad vigil during which no bells were heard … in the first New Year of this unprecedented "breaking of nations"'.

(77) The Oxen

Christmas Eve, and twelve of the clock.
 'Now they are all on their knees,'
An elder said as we sat in a flock
 By the embers in hearthside ease.

We pictured the meek mild creatures where
 They dwelt in their strawy pen,
Nor did it occur to one of us there
 To doubt they were kneeling then.

So fair a fancy few would weave
 In these years! Yet, I feel,
If someone said on Christmas Eve,
 'Come; see the oxen kneel

THE WINTER OF THE WORLD

'In the lonely barton by yonder coomb
 Our childhood used to know,'
I should go with him in the gloom,
 Hoping it might be so.

THOMAS HARDY

The Times, 24 December 1915. *Selected Poems* (1916). Not usually thought of as a war poem, but its references to *these years* and modern religious uncertainty make it strongly relevant to its time.

1916

arly in 1916 the British and French agreed to a huge military push later in the year, by which time Kitchener's army would be fully trained for a decisive breakthrough. At home, though, recruitment had been falling, and the government was obliged to introduce conscription in January, first for single men aged eighteen to forty, and then, in May, for married men.

At the Battle of Jutland in late May, the German navy failed to break the Grand Fleet, but Jutland was no decisive victory in the great Nelson tradition. Despite political and military diversions in Ireland, the Middle East and elsewhere, the generals remained convinced that the war was going to be won or lost on the Western Front. When the French came under intense pressure at Verdun, the long-awaited, long-prepared British offensive was brought forward: on 1 July the Battle of the Somme began.

In retrospect the Somme has often been seen as a turning-point in British poetry about the war. Soldiers' verse about self-sacrifice was certainly more common before the Somme than after, and civilians wrote less glibly as the casualties increased, but plenty of poets continued to believe that victory would be achieved sooner or later. By the end of the year, questions were being raised about British strategy, but there were no mutinies, conscription was generally accepted, and conscientious objectors received little sympathy at home or in the ranks (only 16,000 out of a possible eight million refused to enlist).

All the same, a gulf was opening between civilian understanding of the war and what the soldiers themselves knew. Men on leave felt unable to tell their families much about the horrors of the trenches, which partly explains why civilians were so shocked and deeply moved by the film of the Somme battles that was shown in cinemas all over the country in August. Soldier-poets began to express isolation, doubt and resentment, detesting the heroic tone that persisted in newspaper verse. The more thoughtful civilians tried to find words for the home front's sympathy, admiration and gratitude, but it was almost impossible to imagine front-line horrors and all too easy to sound complacent.

The Somme casualties were enormous on both sides – over a million for Britain, France and Germany combined. Germany tentatively suggested peace negotiations, but the offer was rejected: the British government could not be seen to be giving way to 'defeatist' moves. In early December Asquith was replaced as Prime Minister by Lloyd George, who was seen as a more energetic leader, determined to achieve total victory.

(78) In the Pink

So Davies wrote: 'This leaves me in the pink.'
Then scrawled his name: 'Your loving sweetheart, Willie.'
With crosses for a hug. He'd had a drink
Of rum and tea; and, though the barn was chilly,
For once his blood ran warm; he had pay to spend.
Winter was passing; soon the year would mend.

But he couldn't sleep that night; stiff in the dark
He groaned and thought of Sundays at the farm,
And how he'd go as cheerful as a lark
In his best suit, to wander arm in arm
With brown-eyed Gwen, and whisper in her ear
The simple, silly things she liked to hear.

And then he thought: tomorrow night we trudge
Up to the trenches, and my boots are rotten.
Five miles of stodgy clay and freezing sludge,
And everything but wretchedness forgotten.
Tonight he's in the pink; but soon he'll die.
And still the war goes on − *he* don't know why.

SIEGFRIED SASSOON

Written 10 February 1916. *Nation*, 28 October 1916. *The Old Huntsman* (1917).
Sassoon described this as his first 'outspoken' war poem. The *Westminster Gazette* refused
to print it because 'they thought it might prejudice recruiting!!'. The subject is an
imaginary soldier 'who probably got killed on the Somme in July, after months and
months of a dog's life and no leave' (*The War Poems*, 22).

(79) The Night Patrol

Over the top! The wire's thin here, unbarbed
Plain rusty coils, not staked, and low enough:
Full of old tins, though – 'When you're through, all three,
Aim quarter left for fifty yards or so,
Then straight for that new piece of German wire;
See if it's thick, and listen for a while
For sounds of working; don't run any risks;
About an hour; now, over!'
                      And we placed
Our hands on the topmost sandbags, leapt, and stood
A second with curved backs, then crept to the wire,
Wormed ourselves tinkling through, glanced back, and dropped.
The sodden ground was splashed with shallow pools,
And tufts of crackling cornstalks, two years old,
No man had reaped, and patches of spring grass,
Half-seen, as rose and sank the flares, were strewn
With the wrecks of our attack: the bandoliers,
Packs, rifles, bayonets, belts, and haversacks,
Shell fragments, and the huge whole forms of shells
Shot fruitlessly – and everywhere the dead.
Only the dead were always present – present
As a vile sickly smell of rottenness;
The rustling stubble and the early grass,
The slimy pools – the dead men stank through all,
Pungent and sharp; as bodies loomed before,
And as we passed, they stank: then dulled away
To that vague fœtor, all encompassing,
Infecting earth and air. They lay, all clothed,
Each in some new and piteous attitude
That we well marked to guide us back: as he,
Outside our wire, that lay on his back and crossed
His legs Crusader-wise; I smiled at that,
And thought on Elia and his Temple Church.
From him, at quarter left, lay a small corpse,
Down in a hollow, huddled as in bed,
That one of us put his hand on unawares.

Next was a bunch of half a dozen men
All blown to bits, an archipelago
Of corrupt fragments, vexing to us three,
Who had no light to see by, save the flares.
On such a trail, so lit, for ninety yards
We crawled on belly and elbows, till we saw,
Instead of lumpish dead before our eyes,
The stakes and crosslines of the German wire.
We lay in shelter of the last dead man,
Ourselves as dead, and heard their shovels ring
Turning the earth, then talk and cough at times.
A sentry fired and a machine-gun spat;
They shot a flare above us; when it fell
And spluttered out in the pools of No Man's Land,
We turned and crawled past the remembered dead:
Past him and him, and them and him, until,
For he lay some way apart, we caught the scent
Of the Crusader and slid past his legs,
And through the wire and home, and got our rum.

ARTHUR GRAEME WEST

Written March 1916. *Diary of a Dead Officer* (1919). West describes the patrol and his
cool detachment in a letter of 12 February 1916: 'I had a rather exciting time ... with
two other men on a patrol in the "no man's land" between the lines. A dangerous
business, and most repulsive on account of the smells and appearance of the heaps of
dead men ... I found myself much as I had expected ... more interested than afraid,
but more careful for my own life than anxious to approve any new martial ardour.'
  Elia: Charles Lamb (1775–1834), a resident of the Temple, where the church has
effigies of cross-legged Crusader knights.

(80) 'If I should die, be not concerned to know'

If I should die, be not concerned to know
   The manner of my ending, if I fell
Leading a forlorn charge against the foe,
   Strangled by gas, or shattered by a shell.
Nor seek to see me in this death-in-life
   Mid shirks and curses, oaths and blood and sweat,
Cold in the darkness, on the edge of strife,
   Bored and afraid, irresolute, and wet.

But if you think of me, remember one
   Who loved good dinners, curious parody,
Swimming, and lying naked in the sun,
   Latin hexameters, and heraldry,
Athenian subtleties of δηζ and ποιζ,
   Beethoven, Botticelli, beer, and boys.

PHILIP BAINBRIGGE

Undated. First published in Nevil Shute, *Slide Rule* (1954). Many wartime poems echoed Brooke, sometimes ironically. Bainbrigge's verse, often remarkably candid about his interest in boys, was written for private circulation among friends, including Charles Scott Moncrieff and perhaps, in 1918, Owen.

   Athenian subtleties: the Greek particles 'de' and 'poi' mean something like 'indeed' and 'somewhere' but often indicate no more than a shrug or a raised eyebrow. Bainbrigge adds a Greek *z* to each, to give the rhyme for 'boys', the sort of linguistic witticism that he and Scott Moncrieff delighted in.

(81) *from* Denial

If I should die – chatter only this:
'A bullet flew by that did not miss!'
I did not give life up because of a friend;
That bullet came thro', and that was the end!

R. WATSON KERR

The first of five stanzas. *War Daubs* (1919).

(82) The Mother

Written after reading Rupert Brooke's sonnet, 'The Soldier'

If you should die, think only this of me
In that still quietness where is space for thought,
Where parting, loss and bloodshed shall not be,
And men may rest themselves and dream of nought:
That in some place a mystic mile away
One whom you loved has drained the bitter cup
Till there is nought to drink; has faced the day
Once more, and now, has raised the standard up.

And think, my son, with eyes grown clear and dry
She lives as though for ever in your sight,
Loving the things *you* loved, with heart aglow
For country, honour, truth, traditions high,
– Proud that you paid their price. (And if some night
Her heart should break – well, lad, you will not know.)

MAY HERSCHEL-CLARKE

TP's Weekly, 1 April 1916. *Behind the Firing Line* (1917). A patriotic response to Brooke.

(83) To Any Diplomatist

Heeding nought else, your subtle game you played,
Took tricks and lost them, reckoned up the score,
Balanced defeats with triumphs, less with more,
And plotted how the next point might be made:
How some sly move with countermoves to meet,
How by some crafty stratagem to gain
This empty point of honour, how obtain
That barren symbol of a foe's defeat.

Engrossed, you never cared to realise
The folly of the things for which you fought,
The hideous peril which your striving brought –
A witless struggle for a worthless prize!
God! Were you fiends or fools, who, in your game,
Heedless, have set the circling world aflame?

W. N. EWER

Dated February 1916. *Five Souls* (1917).

(84) To W. in the Trenches

You live with Death: yet over there
You breathe a somewhat cleaner air.

J. C. SQUIRE

The dedication in Squire's *The Survival of the Fittest* (May 1916).
W.: his close friend William Smith, killed in April 1917.

(85) The Trinity

Cry 'God for Harry! England and Saint George!' – Henry V

Customs die hard in this our native land;
And still in Northern France, I understand,
Our gallant boys, as through the fray they forge,
Cry 'God for Harmsworth! England and Lloyd George!'

J. C. SQUIRE

The Survival of the Fittest (1916). Alfred Harmsworth, Lord Northcliffe, owned *The Times* and founded the *Daily Mail*, which led the campaign for increased munitions production. Lloyd George was Minister of Munitions from May 1915 to June 1916.

(86) The Higher Life for Clergymen

'Conscription is a step towards the Higher Life.' – A Living Dean
*' ... he who made the earthquake and the storm, Perchance made
battles too.'* – A Dead Archbishop

Christ, when you hung upon that tree accurst,
Bleeding, and bruised, and agonized by thirst,
Mocked, tantalized, and spat on and defiled,
On a near rising ground there stood and smiled,
Serene behind those ravening Hebrew beasts,
Annas and Caiaphas, the two high priests.

They felt uplifted, doubtless; for their god
Was Moloch who was always pleased with blood.
Under all names this one red God they love,
And when the evidence appeared to prove
The divine origin of him who died,
They thought 'twas Moloch they had crucified!

Nor will they change; when the last worst war is done,
And all mankind lies rotting in the sun,
High on the highest pile of skulls will kneel,
Thanking his god for that he did reveal
This crowning proof of his great grace to man,
A radiant, pink, well-nourished Anglican.

J. C. SQUIRE

The Survival of the Fittest (1916). Most Anglican clergy strongly supported the war effort.
   Annas and Caiaphas: high priests at the time of Christ's trial.
   Moloch: the Canaanite war god, to whom fathers sacrificed their sons.

(87) The Last Rally

(Under England's supplementary Conscription Act, the last of the married men joined her colours on June 24, 1916)

In the midnight, in the rain,
That drenches every sooty roof and licks each windowpane,
The bugles blow for the last rally
Once again.

Through the horror of the night,
Where glimmers yet northwestward one ghostly strip of white,
Squelching with heavy boots through the untrodden ploughlands,
The troops set out. Eyes right!

These are the last who go because they must,
Who toiled for years at something levelled now in dust;
Men of thirty, married, settled, who had built up walls of comfort
That crumbled at a thrust.

Now they have naked steel,
And the heavy, sopping rain that the clammy skin can feel,
And the leaden weight of rifle and the pack that grinds the entrails,
Wrestling with a half-cooked meal.

And there are oaths and blows,
The mud that sticks and flows,
The bad and smoky billet, and the aching legs at morning,
And the frost that numbs the toes;

And the senseless, changeless grind,
And the pettifogging mass of orders muddling every mind,
And the dull-red smudge of mutiny half rising up and burning,
Till they choke and stagger blind.

But for them no bugle flares;
No bright flags leap, no gay horizon glares;
They are conscripts, middle-aged, rheumatic, cautious, weary,
With slowly thinning hairs;
Only for one tonight
A woman weeps and moans and tries to smite
Her head against a table, and another rocks a cradle,
And another laughs with flashing eyes, sitting bolt upright.

JOHN GOULD FLETCHER

Century Magazine, Christmas 1916. The irregular metres and line lengths reflect
Fletcher's Modernist inclinations and his dislike of wartime rhetoric; see notes to (*1*)
and (*5*).

(88) Youth's Consecration

Lovers of Life! Dreamers with lifted eyes!
O Liberty, at thy command we challenge Death!
The monuments that show our fathers' faith
Shall be the altars of our sacrifice.
Dauntless, we fling our lives into the van,
Laughing at Death because within Youth's breast
Flame lambent fires of Freedom. Man for man
We yield to thee our heritage, our best.
Life's highest product, Youth, exults in life;
We are Olympian Gods in consciousness;
Mortality to us is sweet; yet less
We value Ease when Honour sounds the strife.
Lovers of Life, we pledge thee Liberty
And go to death, calmly, triumphantly.

J. W. STREETS

Poetry Review, August 1916. *The Undying Splendour* (1916). Streets was killed on the first day of the Somme. He wanted his poems to show that 'we go to meet death grim-lipped, clear-eyed and resolute-hearted'. His work was published and highly praised by Galloway Kyle as typical of 'the soul of young England'.

(89) Before Action

By all the glories of the day
    And the cool evening's benison,
By that last sunset touch that lay
    Upon the hills when day was done,
By beauty lavishly outpoured,
    And blessings carelessly received,
By all the days that I have lived,
    Make me a soldier, Lord.

By all of all man's hopes and fears,
  And all the wonders poets sing,
The laughter of unclouded years,
  And every sad and lovely thing;
By the romantic ages stored
  With high endeavour that was his,
By all his mad catastrophes,
  Make me a man, O Lord.

I, that on my familiar hill
  Saw with uncomprehending eyes
A hundred of Thy sunsets spill
  Their fresh and sanguine sacrifice,
Ere the sun swings his noonday sword
  Must say goodbye to all of this: –
By all delights that I shall miss,
  Help me to die, O Lord.

WILLIAM NOEL HODGSON

New Witness, 29 June 1916. Verse and Prose in Peace and War (November 1916).
Always printed with the date 29 June, so commentators have liked to imagine
Hodgson writing the poem two days before his death on 1 July, but the date actually
refers to first publication, not composition.

(90) A Petition

All that a man might ask, thou hast given me, England,
  Birthright and happy childhood's long heart's-ease,
And love whose range is deep beyond all sounding
  And wider than all seas.

A heart to front the world and find God in it,
  Eyes blind enow, but not too blind to see
The lovely things behind the dross and darkness,
  And lovelier things to be.

And friends whose loyalty time nor death shall weaken,
    And quenchless hope and laughter's golden store;
All that a man might ask thou hast given me, England,
    Yet grant thou one thing more:

That now when envious foes would spoil thy splendour,
    Unversed in arms, a dreamer such as I
May in thy ranks be deemed not all unworthy,
    England, for thee to die.

R. E. VERNÈDE

Written in trenches before the Somme offensive, 1916. *The Times*, 5 May 1917, accompanying a report of Vernède's death. *War Poems* (1917).

(91) A Soldier

He laughed. His blue eyes searched the morning,
Found the unceasing song of the lark
In a brown twinkle of wings, far out.
Great clouds, like galleons, sailed the distance.
The young spring day had slipped the cloak of dark
And stood up straight and naked with a shout.

Through the green wheat, like laughing schoolboys,
Tumbled the yellow mustard flowers, uncheck'd.
The wet earth reeked and smoked in the sun ...
He thought of the waking farm in England.
The deep thatch of the roof – all shadow-fleck'd –
The clank of pails at the pump ... the day begun.

'After the war ...' he thought. His heart beat faster
With a new love for things familiar and plain.
The Spring leaned down and whispered to him low
Of a slim, brown-throated woman he had kissed ...
He saw, in sons that were himself again,
The only immortality that man may know.

And then a sound grew out of the morning,
And a shell came, moving a destined way,
Thin and swift and lustful, making its moan.
A moment his brave white body knew the Spring,
The next, it lay
In a red ruin of blood and guts and bone.

* * *

Oh! nothing was tortured there! Nothing could know
How death blasphemed all men and their high birth
With his obscenities. Already moved,
Within those shattered tissues, that dim force,
Which is the ancient alchemy of Earth,
Changing him to the very flowers he loved.

* * *

'Nothing was tortured there!' Oh, pretty thought!
When God Himself might well bow down His head
And hide His haunted eyes before the dead.

T. P. Cameron Wilson

Manuscript dated June 1916, sent to Harold Monro. *Magpies in Picardy* (1919). On
3 May Wilson wrote: '*War* is an obscenity. Thank God we are fighting this to stop
war ... All those picturesque phrases of war writers ... are dangerous because they show
nothing of the individual horror, nothing of the fine personalities smashed suddenly
into red beastliness' (*War Letters of Fallen Englishmen*, 299–300).

(92) Magpies in Picardy

The magpies in Picardy
Are more than I can tell.
They flicker down the dusty roads
And cast a magic spell
On the men who march through Picardy,
Through Picardy to hell.

(The blackbird flies with panic,
The swallow goes with light,
The finches move like ladies,
The owl floats by at night;
But the great and flashing magpie
He flies as artists might.)

A magpie in Picardy
Told me secret things –
Of the music in white feathers,
And the sunlight that sings
And dances in deep shadows –
He told me with his wings.

(The hawk is cruel and rigid,
He watches from a height;
The rook is slow and sombre,
The robin loves to fight;
But the great and flashing magpie
He flies as lovers might.)

He told me that in Picardy,
An age ago or more,
While all his fathers still were eggs,
These dusty highways bore
Brown, singing soldiers marching out
Through Picardy to war.

He said that still through chaos
Works on the ancient plan,
And two things have altered not
Since first the world began –
The beauty of the wild green earth
And the bravery of man.

(For the sparrow flies unthinking
And quarrels in his flight;
The heron trails his legs behind,
The lark goes out of sight;
But the great and flashing magpie
He flies as poets might.)

T. P. CAMERON WILSON

Westminster Gazette, 16 August 1916. *Magpies in Picardy* (1919). 'There was a man once loved green fields like you, / He drew his knowledge from the wild birds' songs' (Marjorie Wilson, 'To Tony – Aged 3', *Spectator*, 26 October 1918). Marjorie was T. P. C. Wilson's sister, Tony his nephew.

(93) Song of the Dark Ages

We digged our trenches on the down
  Beside old barrows, and the wet
White chalk we shovelled from below;
It lay like drifts of thawing snow
  On parados and parapet:

Until a pick neither struck flint
  Nor split the yielding chalky soil,
But only calcined human bone:
Poor relic of that Age of Stone
  Whose ossuary was our spoil.

Home we marched singing in the rain,
　And all the while, beneath our song,
I mused how many springs should wane
And still our trenches scar the plain:
　The monument of an old wrong.

But then, I thought, the fair green sod
　Will wholly cover that white stain,
And soften, as it clothes the face
Of those old barrows, every trace
　Of violence to the patient plain.

And careless people, passing by
　Will speak of both in casual tone:
Saying: 'You see the toil they made:
The age of iron, pick and spade,
　Here jostles with the Age of Stone.'

Yet either from that happier race
　Will merit but a passing glance;
And they will leave us both alone:
Poor savages who wrought in stone –
　Poor savages who fought in France.

FRANCIS BRETT YOUNG

Dated 17 June 1916. *New Statesman*, 7 October 1916. *Five Degrees South* (1917).
A Hardyesque poem set near Hardy country: Young was in training on Salisbury plain
until March 1916. Gurney read and admired his poems, quoting the last lines of this
one in a letter of 31 October 1917.
　parados, parapet: upper sections of the back and front walls of a trench.

(94) To England – A Note

I watched the boys of England where they went
Through mud and water to do appointed things.
See one a stake, and one wire-netting brings,
And one comes slowly under a burden bent
Of ammunition. Though the strength be spent
They 'carry on' under the shadowing wings
Of Death the ever-present. And hark, one sings
Although no joy from the grey skies be lent.

Are these the heroes – these? – have kept from you
The power of primal savagery so long?
Shall break the devil's legions? These they are
Who do in silence what they might boast to do;
In the height of battle tell the world in song
How they do hate and fear the face of War.

IVOR GURNEY

Copied into a letter from the Front at the end of June. *Severn and Somme* (1917). After
the war Gurney's style became less conventional and more idiosyncratic, but his view
of the war scarcely changed.

 song: he said in a June letter that his comrades had sung, 'O my, I don't want to die,
I want to go home' while under fire.

(95) 'This is no case of petty right or wrong'

This is no case of petty right or wrong
That politicians or philosophers
Can judge. I hate not Germans, nor grow hot
With love of Englishmen, to please newspapers.
Beside my hate for one fat patriot
My hatred of the Kaiser is love true: –
A kind of god he is, banging a gong.

But I have not to choose between the two,
Or between justice and injustice. Dinned
With war and argument I read no more
Than in the storm smoking along the wind
Athwart the wood. Two witches' cauldrons roar.
From one the weather shall rise clear and gay;
Out of the other an England beautiful
And like her mother that died yesterday.
Little I know or care if, being dull,
I shall miss something that historians
Can rake out of the ashes when perchance
The phoenix broods serene above their ken.
But with the best and meanest Englishmen
I am one in crying, God save England, lest
We lose what never slaves and cattle blessed.
The ages made her that made us from dust:
She is all we know and live by, and we trust
She is good and must endure, loving her so:
And as we love ourselves we hate her foe.

EDWARD THOMAS

Written December 1915. *Poems* (1917). Thomas had enlisted as a private in July and become a map instructor.

(96) February Afternoon

Men heard this roar of parleying starlings, saw,
A thousand years ago even as now,
Black rooks with white gulls following the plough
So that the first are last until a caw
Commands that last are first again, – a law
Which was of old when one, like me, dreamed how
A thousand years might dust lie on his brow
Yet thus would birds do between hedge and shaw.

Time swims before me, making as a day
A thousand years, while the broad ploughland oak
Roars mill-like and men strike and bear the stroke
Of war as ever, audacious or resigned,
And God still sits aloft in the array
That we have wrought him, stone-deaf and stone-blind.

EDWARD THOMAS

Written February 1916. *Last Poems* (1918). Thomas was considering applying for a commission and active service, although he was almost over age and could have remained in England. His poems explore man's relationship with time, change and the natural world in a voice of tense resignation.

(97) As the Team's Head Brass

As the team's head brass flashed out on the turn
The lovers disappeared into the wood.
I sat among the boughs of the fallen elm
That strewed the angle of the fallow, and
Watched the plough narrowing a yellow square
Of charlock. Every time the horses turned
Instead of treading me down, the ploughman leaned
Upon the handles to say or ask a word,
About the weather, next about the war.
Scraping the share he faced towards the wood,
And screwed along the furrow till the brass flashed
Once more.
        The blizzard felled the elm whose crest
I sat in, by a woodpecker's round hole,
The ploughman said, 'When will they take it away?'
'When the war's over.' So the talk began –
One minute and an interval of ten,
A minute more and the same interval.
'Have you been out?' 'No.' 'And don't want to, perhaps?'
'If I could only come back again, I should.

I could spare an arm. I shouldn't want to lose
A leg. If I should lose my head, why, so,
I should want nothing more ... Have many gone
From here?' 'Yes.' 'Many lost?' 'Yes, a good few.
Only two teams work on the farm this year.
One of my mates is dead. The second day
In France they killed him. It was back in March,
The very night of the blizzard, too. Now if
He had stayed here we should have moved the tree.'
'And I should not have sat here. Everything
Would have been different. For it would have been
Another world.' 'Ay, and a better, though
If we could see all all might seem good.' Then
The lovers came out of the wood again:
The horses started and for the last time
I watched the clods crumble and topple over
After the ploughshare and the stumbling team.

EDWARD THOMAS

Written in camp at Romford, late May 1916. *Poems* (1917). By now Thomas has made up his mind to apply for service overseas.

    blizzard: a severe blizzard had hit the area on 28 March, bringing down many trees (*Romford Times*, 5 April).

(98) 'No one cares less than I'

'No one cares less than I,
Nobody knows but God,
Whether I am destined to lie
Under a foreign clod,'
Were the words I made to the bugle call in the morning.

But laughing, storming, scorning,
Only the bugles know
What the bugles say in the morning,
And they do not care, when they blow
The call that I heard and made words to early this morning.

EDWARD THOMAS

Written May 1916. *Last Poems* (1918). Inspired by Reveille, the morning bugle call, at
Romford. For a discussion of Thomas's bugle poems, see Andrew Motion, *The Poetry of
Edward Thomas*, 121–5.

(99) Lights Out

I have come to the borders of sleep,
The unfathomable deep
Forest where all must lose
Their way, however straight,
Or winding, soon or late;
They cannot choose.

Many a road and track
That, since the dawn's first crack,
Up to the forest brink,
Deceived the travellers,
Suddenly now blurs,
And in they sink.

Here love ends –
Despair, ambition ends;
All pleasure and all trouble,
Although most sweet or bitter,
Here ends in sleep that is sweeter
Than tasks most noble.

There is not any book
Or face of dearest look
That I would not turn from now
To go into the unknown
I must enter, and leave, alone,
I know not how.

The tall forest towers;
Its cloudy foliage lowers
Ahead, shelf above shelf;
Its silence I hear and obey
That I may lose my way
And myself.

EDWARD THOMAS

Written November 1916. *Poems* (1917). Like Owen's 'Futility' (*206*), a poem about the war but reaching far beyond it. Lights Out is the evening bugle call. Thomas, now an officer, is waiting to be sent abroad.

(100) Goliath and David

For D. C. T., killed at Fricourt, March 1916

Once an earlier David took
Smooth pebbles from the brook:
Out between the lines he went
To that one-sided tournament,
A shepherd boy who stood out fine
And young to fight a Philistine
Clad all in brazen mail. He swears
That he's killed lions, he's killed bears,
And those that scorn the God of Zion
Shall perish so like bear or lion.
But ... the historian of that fight
Had not the heart to tell it right.

Striding within javelin range
Goliath marvels at this strange
Goodly-faced boy so proud of strength.
David's clear eye measures the length;
With hand thrust back, he cramps one knee,
Poises a moment thoughtfully,
And hurls with a long vengeful swing.
The pebble, humming from the sling
Like a wild bee, flies a sure line
For the forehead of the Philistine;
Then ... but there comes a brazen clink,
And quicker than a man can think
Goliath's shield parries each cast.
Clang! clang! and clang! was David's last.

Scorn blazes in the Giant's eye,
Towering unhurt six cubits high.
Says foolish David, 'Damn your shield!
And damn my sling! But I'll not yield.'
He takes his staff of Mamre oak,
A knotted shepherd-staff that's broke
The skull of many a wolf and fox
Come filching lambs from Jesse's flocks.
Loud laughs Goliath, and that laugh
Can scatter chariots like blown chaff
To rout: but David, calm and brave,
Holds his ground, for God will save.
Steel crosses wood, a flash, and oh!
Shame for Beauty's overthrow!
(God's eyes are dim, His ears are shut.)

One cruel backhand sabre cut –
'I'm hit! I'm killed!' young David cries,
Throws blindly forward, chokes ... and dies.
And look, spike-helmeted, grey, grim,
Goliath straddles over him.

ROBERT GRAVES

Goliath and David (late 1916). *D. C. T.*: David Thomas, killed 18 March 1916 – a young officer loved platonically by Graves and Sassoon, and the subject of poems by both of them; 'Dick Tiltwood' in Sassoon's *Memoirs of an Infantry Officer*. In the biblical story David kills Goliath (I Samuel 17).

   spike-helmeted, grey: the giant is in German uniform.

(101) A Dead Boche

To you who'd read my songs of War
  And only hear of blood and fame,
I'll say (you've heard it said before)
  'War's Hell!' and if you doubt the same,
Today I found in Mametz Wood
A certain cure for lust of blood:

Where, propped against a shattered trunk,
  In a great mess of things unclean,
Sat a dead Boche; he scowled and stunk
  With clothes and face a sodden green,
Big-bellied, spectacled, crop-haired,
Dribbling black blood from nose and beard.

ROBERT GRAVES

Written July 1916 at the front. *Goliath and David* (late 1916). Graves describes the incident in *Goodbye to All That*.

  you who'd read: you who might wish to read.

  War's Hell!: echoes the famous comment by the American General Sherman in 1880 that war is 'all hell'.

(102) The Legion

'Is that the Three-and-Twentieth, Strabo mine,
Marching below, and we still gulping wine?'
From the sad magic of his fragrant cup
The red-faced old centurion started up,
Cursed, battered on the table. 'No,' he said,
'Not that! The Three-and-Twentieth Legion's dead,
Dead in the first year of this damned campaign –
The Legion's dead, dead, and won't rise again.
Pity? Rome pities her brave lads that die,
But we need pity also, you and I,
Whom Gallic spear and Belgian arrow miss,
Who live to see the Legion come to this,
Unsoldierlike, slovenly, bent on loot,
Grumblers, diseased, unskilled to thrust or shoot.
O brown cheek, muscled shoulder, sturdy thigh!
Where are they now? God! Watch it struggle by,
The sullen pack of ragged ugly swine.
Is that the Legion, Gracchus? Quick, the wine!'
'Strabo,' said Gracchus, 'you are strange tonight.
The Legion is the Legion; it's all right.
If these new men are slovenly, in your thinking,
God damn it! You'll not better them by drinking.
They all try, Strabo; trust their hearts and hands.
The Legion is the Legion while Rome stands,
And these same men before the autumn's fall
Shall bang old Vercingetorix out of Gaul.'

ROBERT GRAVES

Written late 1916. *Fairies and Fusiliers* (1917). Graves was immensely proud of his
regiment, the Royal Welch Fusiliers or '23rd', and its battle-hardened soldiers (he
himself had been listed as 'Died of Wounds' in July after a severe lung wound). Julius
Caesar's legions in Gaul (France) defeated barbarians under Vercingetorix. Graves
believes the fight must go on, and that the new recruits, often despised by veterans,
will prove worthy of the regiment. Owen told Sassoon in November 1917 that
'The Legion' was 'glorious' (*Collected Letters*, 511).

(103) August 1914

What in our lives is burnt
In the fire of this?
The heart's dear granary?
The much we shall miss?

Three lives hath one life –
Iron, honey, gold.
The gold, the honey gone –
Left is the hard and cold.

Iron are our lives
Molten right through our youth.
A burnt space through ripe fields,
A fair mouth's broken tooth.

ISAAC ROSENBERG

Written in France, summer 1916. *Collected Works* (1937).

(104) Returning, We Hear the Larks

Sombre the night is.
And though we have our lives, we know
What sinister threat lurks there.

Dragging these anguished limbs, we only know
This poison-blasted track opens on our camp –
On a little safe sleep.

But hark! joy – joy – strange joy.
Lo! heights of night ringing with unseen larks.
Music showering our upturned list'ning faces.

Death could drop from the dark
As easily as song –
But song only dropped,
Like a blind man's dreams on the sand
By dangerous tides,
Like a girl's dark hair for she dreams no ruin lies there,
Or her kisses where a serpent hides.

ISAAC ROSENBERG

Written summer 1916. *Poems* (1922). Rosenberg was working with the Royal Engineers, taking materials to the front line at night and returning at dawn.

(105) Break of Day in the Trenches

The darkness crumbles away.
It is the same old Druid Time as ever.
Only a live thing leaps my hand,
A queer sardonic rat,
As I pull the parapet's poppy
To stick behind my ear.
Droll rat, they would shoot you if they knew
Your cosmopolitan sympathies.
Now you have touched this English hand
You will do the same to a German
Soon, no doubt, if it be your pleasure
To cross the sleeping green between.
It seems you inwardly grin as you pass
Strong eyes, fine limbs, haughty athletes,
Less chanced than you for life,
Bonds to the whims of murder,
Sprawled in the bowels of the earth,
The torn fields of France.
What do you see in our eyes
At the shrieking iron and flame
Hurled through still heavens?

What quaver – what heart aghast?
Poppies whose roots are in man's veins
Drop, and are ever dropping,
But mine in my ear is safe –
Just a little white with the dust.

ISAAC ROSENBERG

Written in trenches, waiting for the Somme offensive, June 1916. *Poetry*, Chicago,
December 1916. *Poems* (1922). Fussell, 250–3, discusses the poem's images and literary
echoes, judging it to be 'the greatest poem of the war'.
  seems you inwardly grin: Rosenberg changes this in a late draft to 'seems,
odd thing, you grin'.

(106) Before Action

Over the down the road goes winding,
  A ribbon of white in the corn –
The green, young corn. O, the joy of binding
  The sheaves some harvest morn!

But we are called to another reaping,
  A harvest that will not wait.
The sheaves will be green. O, the world of weeping
  Of those without the gate!

For the road we go they may not travel,
  Nor share our harvesting;
But watch and weep. O, to unravel
  The riddle of this thing!

Yet over the down the white road leading
   Calls; and who lags behind?
Stout are our hearts; but O, the bleeding
   Of hearts we may not bind!

J. E. STEWART

Dated Somme, July 1916. *Poetry Review*, March 1917. A poem by an officer, pitying civilians yet recognizing that the coming slaughter will be a premature harvest.

(107) The Game

A company of the East Surrey Regiment is reported to have dribbled footballs, the gift of their captain who fell in the fight, for a mile and a quarter into the enemy trenches

On through the hail of slaughter
   Where gallant comrades fall,
Where blood is poured like water,
   They drive the trickling ball.
The fear of death before them
   Is but an empty name;
True to the land that bore them
   The Surreys play the game!

On without check or falter,
   They press towards the goal;
Who falls on freedom's altar
   The Lord shall rest his soul.
But still they charge, the living,
   Into that hell of flame;
Ungrudging in the giving,
   Our soldiers play the game!

And now at last is ended
   The task so well begun.
Though savagely defended
   The lines of death are won.
In this, their hour of glory,
   A deathless place they claim
In England's splendid story,
   The men who played the game!

C. E. C. H. BURTON ('TOUCHSTONE')

Daily Mail, 12 July 1916. Captain W. P. Nevill's sporting exploit on the first day of the Somme became a famous example of the British amateur spirit.

(108) The Nurse

Here in the long white ward I stand,
   Pausing a little breathless space,
Touching a restless fevered hand,
   Murmuring comfort's commonplace –

Long enough pause to feel the cold
   Fingers of fear about my heart;
Just for a moment, uncontrolled,
   All the pent tears of pity start.

While here I strive, as best I may,
   Strangers' long hours of pain to ease,
Dumbly I question – *Far away*
   Lies my beloved even as these?

G. M. MITCHELL

Punch, 30 August 1916. The public had been fed with optimistic reports during the opening days of the Somme battle, but by the end of August the huge losses were becoming obvious.

(109) To a Clerk, Now at the Wars

Here at your desk I sit and work,
As once you used to do;
I wonder if you'll ever guess
How much I envy you.

You'll win a world I'll never know,
Who ride the barriers down;
And my life's bounded by a desk,
And the grey streets of a town.

MAY WEDDERBURN CANNAN

War Worker, August 1916. *In War Time* (1917). One of the great socio-economic changes of the war was that women took men's places in clerical occupations.
    win a world: Cannan's fiancé had written to her proudly in July about his experiences on the Somme – 'But it was different', she commented, 'if you weren't there' (*Grey Ghosts and Voices*, 109).

(110) Love, 1916

One said to me, 'Seek Love, for he is Joy
Called by another name'.
A Second said, 'Seek Love, for he is Power
Which is called Fame'.
Last said a Third, 'Seek Love, his name is Peace'.
I called him thrice,
And answer came, 'Love now
Is christened Sacrifice'.

MAY WEDDERBURN CANNAN

Dated August 1916. *In War Time* (1917).

(111) Hardness of Heart

In the first watch no death but made us mourn;
Now tearless eyes run down the daily roll,
Whose names are written in the book of death;
For sealed are now the springs of tears, as when
The tropic sun makes dry the torrent's course
After the rains. They are too many now
For mortal eyes to weep, and none can see
But God alone the Thing itself and live.
We look to seaward, and behold a cry!
To skyward, and they fall as stricken birds
On autumn fields; and earth cries out its toll,
From the Great River to the world's end – toll
Of dead, and maimed and lost; we dare not stay;
Tears are not endless and we have no more.

EDWARD SHILLITO

The Omega (1916).

(112) The Dancers

(During a Great Battle, 1916)

The floors are slippery with blood:
The world gyrates too. God is good
That while His wind blows out the light
For those who hourly die for us –
We still can dance, each night.

The music has grown numb with death –
But we will suck their dying breath,
The whispered name they breathed to chance,
To swell our music, make it loud
That we may dance, – may dance.

124

We are the dull blind carrion-fly
That dance and batten. Though God die
Mad from the horror of the light –
The light is mad, too, flecked with blood, –
We dance, we dance, each night.

EDITH SITWELL

Clowns' Houses (1918).

(113) Nostra Culpa

We knew, this thing at least we knew, – the worth
Of life: this was our secret learned at birth.
We knew that Force the world has deified,
How weak it is. We spoke not, so men died.
Upon a world down-trampled, blood-defiled,
Fearing that men should praise us less, we smiled.

We knew the sword accursed, yet with the strong
Proclaimed the sword triumphant. Yea, this wrong
Unto our children, unto those unborn
We did, blaspheming God. We feared the scorn
Of men; men worshipped pride; so were they led,
We followed. Dare we now lament our dead?

Shadows and echoes, harlots! We betrayed
Our sons; because men laughed we were afraid.
That silent wisdom which was ours we kept
Deep-buried; thousands perished; still we slept.
Children were slaughtered, women raped, the weak
Downtrodden. Very quiet was our sleep.

Ours was the vision, but the vision lay
Too far, too strange; we chose an easier way.
The light, the unknown light, dazzled our eyes. –
Oh! sisters in our choice were we not wise?
When all men hated, could we pity or plead
For love with those who taught the Devil's creed?

Reap we with pride the harvest! It was sown
By our own toil. Rejoice! It is our own.
This is the flesh we might have saved – our hands,
Our hands prepared these blood-drenched, dreadful lands,
What shall we plead? That we were deaf and blind?
We mothers and we murderers of mankind.

MARGARET SACKVILLE

The Pageant of War (1916).
   Title: 'our fault'.
   proclaimed the sword triumphant: men and women across the political spectrum
supported the war ('Every sword that is drawn against Germany now is a sword drawn
for peace', H. G. Wells, 1914), but Sackville was staunchly pacifist throughout.

(114) My Boy Jack

'Have you news of my boy Jack?'
    Not this tide.
'When d'you think that he'll come back?'
    Not with this wind blowing, and this tide.

'Has any one else had word of him?'
    Not this tide.
For what is sunk will hardly swim,
    Not with this wind blowing, and this tide.

1916

'Oh, dear, what comfort can I find?'
  None this tide,
  Nor any tide,
Except he did not shame his kind –
  Not even with that wind blowing, and that tide.

Then hold your head up all the more,
  This tide,
  And every tide;
Because he was the son you bore,
  And gave to that wind blowing and that tide!

RUDYARD KIPLING

Daily Telegraph, 18 October 1916. *Sea Warfare* (1916). Published almost a year to the day that Kipling's son John was reported missing at Loos. The loss did not turn Kipling against the war as is sometimes claimed – in fact, it strengthened his insistence on the need for victory.

(115) The Question

1916

Brethren, how shall it fare with me
  When the war is laid aside,
If it be proven that I am he
  For whom a world has died?

If it be proven that all my good,
  And the greater good I will make,
Were purchased me by a multitude
  Who suffered for my sake?

That I was delivered by mere mankind
  Vowed to one sacrifice,
And not, as I hold them, battle-blind,
  But dying with open eyes?

That they did not ask me to draw the sword
  When they stood to endure their lot –
That they only looked to me for a word,
  And I answered I knew them not?

If it be found, when the battle clears,
  Their death has set me free,
Then how shall I live with myself through the years
  Which they have bought for me?

Brethren, how must it fare with me,
  Or how am I justified,
If it be proven that I am he
  For whom mankind has died;
If it be proven that I am he
  Who being questioned denied?

RUDYARD KIPLING

Published as a pamphlet, 1916. *The Years Between* (1919). Aimed at the USA, a country
Kipling regarded as one of the great bastions of natural justice. He repeatedly criticized
American neutrality in 1914–17.

  I knew them not: underlying the poem and its title is the story of Peter's denial of
Christ (Matthew 26:69–75). Harry Ricketts (*Kipling*, 331) suggests that Kipling's
poetry after John's death contains more allusions to the New Testament than to the
Old, particularly to sacrifice and betrayal.

(116) To the Vanguard

Oh little mighty Force that stood for England!
That, with your bodies for a living shield,
Guarded her slow awaking, that defied
The sudden challenge of tremendous odds
And fought the rushing legions to a stand –
Then stark in grim endurance held the line.
O little Force that in your agony
Stood fast while England girt her armour on,
Held high our honour in your wounded hands,
Carried our honour safe with bleeding feet –
We have no glory great enough for you,
The very soul of Britain keeps your day!
Procession? – Marches forth a Race in Arms;
And, for the thunder of the crowd's applause,
Crash upon crash the voice of monstrous guns,
Fed by the sweat, served by the life of England,
Shouting your battle-cry across the world.

Oh, little mighty Force, your way is ours,
This land inviolate your monument.

BEATRIX BRICE

The Times, 2 November 1916. Also published as a 1916 Christmas card. To the Vanguard, and Other Songs of the Seven Divisions (?1917). Sung at a great Choral Commemoration of the First Seven Divisions (the original BEF) at the Albert Hall, December 1917, an event apparently instigated by Brice herself.

Her poem contains many of the motifs of patriotic civilian verse: the heroic Spartans at Thermopylae; the British amateur approach to war (slow awaking); archaic chivalry (girt her armour on) and classical warfare (legions); soldiers as Christs (wounded hands ... bleeding feet) and biblical echoes ('present your bodies a living sacrifice', Romans 12:1) – and the contribution of women as munitions workers.

(117) Advent, 1916

I dreamt last night Christ came to earth again
To bless His own. My soul from place to place
On her dream-quest sped, seeking for His face
Through temple and town and lovely land, in vain.
Then came I to a place where death and pain
Had made of God's sweet world a waste forlorn,
With shattered trees and meadows gashed and torn,
Where the grim trenches scarred the shell-seared plain.

And through that Golgotha of blood and clay,
Where watchers cursed the sick dawn, heavy-eyed,
There (in my dream) Christ passed upon His way,
Where His cross marks their nameless graves who died
Slain for the world's salvation, where all day
For others' sake strong men are crucified.

EVA DOBELL

A Bunch of Cotswold Grasses (1919).

(118) Spreading Manure

There are forty steaming heaps in the one tree field,
  Lying in four rows of ten,
They must be all spread out ere the earth will yield
  As it should (And it won't, even then).

Drive the great fork in, fling it out wide;
  Jerk it with a shoulder throw,
The stuff must lie even, two feet on each side.
  Not in patches, but level ... so!

1916

When the heap is thrown you must go all round
   And flatten it out with the spade,
It must lie quite close and trim till the ground
   Is like bread spread with marmalade.

The north-east wind stabs and cuts our breaths,
   The soaked clay numbs our feet,
We are palsied like people gripped by death
   In the beating of the frozen sleet.

I think no soldier is so cold as we,
   Sitting in the frozen mud.
I wish I was out there, for it might be
   A shell would burst to heat my blood.

I wish I was out there, for I should creep
   In my dug-out and hide my head,
I should feel no cold when they lay me deep
   To sleep in a six-foot bed.

I wish I was out there, and off the open land:
   A deep trench I could just endure.
But things being other, I needs must stand
   Frozen, and spread wet manure.

ROSE MACAULAY

One of five poems under the title 'On the Land 1916', *Three Days* (1919). Many
women volunteered to replace men as land workers; like soldiers in the trenches, they
suffered in the exceptionally harsh winter of 1916–17.

(119) A War Film

I saw,
With a catch of the breath and the heart's uplifting,
Sorrow and pride,
   The 'week's great draw' –
The Mons Retreat;
The 'Old Contemptibles' who fought, and died,
The horror and the anguish and the glory.

As in a dream,
Still hearing machine-guns rattle and shells scream,
I came out into the street.

When the day was done,
My little son
Wondered at bath-time why I kissed him so,
Naked upon my knee.
How could he know
The sudden terror that assaulted me? ...
The body I had borne
Nine moons beneath my heart,
A part of me ...
If, someday,
It should be taken away
To War. Tortured. Torn.
Slain.
Rotting in No Man's Land, out in the rain –
My little son ...
Yet all those men had mothers, every one.

How should he know
Why I kissed and kissed and kissed him, crooning his name?
He thought that I was daft.
He thought it was a game,
And laughed, and laughed.

TERESA HOOLEY

Perhaps written 1914–15 (the film is of 1914 scenes). *Songs of All Seasons* (1927).
War films were censored, never showing British corpses, but they were the nearest
people at home could get to experiencing the front line and they were a *great draw*,
filling the cinemas.

(120) The War Films

O living pictures of the dead,
  O songs without a sound,
O fellowship whose phantom tread
  Hallows a phantom ground –
How in a gleam have these revealed
  The faith we had not found.

We have sought God in a cloudy Heaven,
  We have passed by God on earth:
His seven sins and his sorrows seven,
  His wayworn mood and mirth,
Like a ragged cloak have hid from us
  The secret of his birth.

Brother of men, when now I see
  The lads go forth in line,
Thou knowest my heart is hungry in me
  As for thy bread and wine:
Thou knowest my heart is bowed in me
  To take their death for mine.

HENRY NEWBOLT

The Times, 14 October 1916. *St George's Day* (1918). The official Somme film, made to strengthen morale at home, was first shown in London on 10 August 1916. One or two front-line scenes were necessarily faked, but much was genuine, and many soldiers as well as civilians were deeply impressed. Newbolt was moved by the long columns of marching men: 'the effect was to make me love them passionately and to make me feel that the world would be well lost to die with them' (*Later Life and Letters*, 230–1).

(121) Somme Film 1916

There is no cause, sweet wanderers in the dark,
  For you to cry aloud from cypress trees
To a forgetful world; since you are seen
Of all twice nightly at the cinema,
While the munition makers clap their hands.

C. H. B. KITCHIN

Curtains (1919).
  munition makers: the film included many scenes of big guns, shells and ammunition dumps to encourage munition workers at home.

(122) Home Service

'At least it wasn't your fault' I hear them console
When they come back, the few that will come back.
I feel those handshakes now. 'Well, on the whole
You didn't miss much. I wish I had your knack
Of stopping out. You still can call your soul
Your own, at any rate. What a priceless slack
You've had, old chap. It must have been top-hole.
How's poetry? I bet you've written a stack.'

What shall I say? That it's been damnable?
That all the time my soul was never my own?
That we've slaved hard at endless make-believe?
It isn't only actual war that's hell,
I'll say. It's spending youth and hope alone
Among pretences that have ceased to deceive.

GEOFFREY FABER

Dated September 1916. *The Buried Stream* (1941). Faber's preface, dated October 1916, sums up the contradictions of war: 'an appalling perversion of human energy ... a searching ordeal ... a revelation of the human spirit. It is vile – and it is glorious.' He thought this poem was too 'colloquial' (yet later he was to publish the work of T. S. Eliot).

(123) Officers' Mess (1916)

I

I search the room with all my mind,
Peering among those eyes;
For I am feverish to find
A brain with which my brain may talk,
Not that I think myself too wise,
But that I'm lonely, and I walk
Round the large place and wonder – No:
There's nobody, I fear,
Lonely as I, and here.

How they hate me. I'm a fool.
I can't play Bridge; I'm bad at Pool;
I cannot drone a comic song;
I can't talk Shop; I can't use Slang;
My jokes are bad, my stories long:
My voice will falter, break or hang,
Not blurt the sour sarcastic word,
And so my swearing sounds absurd.

II

But came the talk: I found
Three or four others for an argument.
I forced their pace. They shifted their dull ground,
And went
Sprawling about the passages of Thought.
We tugged each other's words until they tore.
They asked me my philosophy: I brought
Bits of it forth and laid them on the floor.
They laughed, and so I kicked the bits about,
Then put them in my pocket one by one,
I, sorry I had brought them out,
They, grateful for the fun.

And when these words had thus been sent
Jerking about, like beetles round a wall,
Then one by one to dismal sleep we went:
There was no happiness at all
In that short hopeless argument
Through yawns and on the way to bed
Among men waiting to be dead.

HAROLD MONRO

Probably written in 1916. *Poetry*, Chicago, February 1921. *Collected Poems* (1933). Monro volunteered in early June 1916, three weeks before he was due to be conscripted – cf. (*87*). He became an officer almost immediately but never served abroad. For him, as for Gibson, Faber and others, home service was inglorious and humiliating.

(124) To My Daughter Betty, the Gift of God

In wiser days, my darling rosebud, blown
To beauty proud as was your mother's prime,
In that desired, delayed, incredible time,
You'll ask why I abandoned you, my own.
And the dear heart that was your baby throne,
To dice with death. And oh! they'll give you rhyme
And reason: some will call the thing sublime,
And some decry it in a knowing tone,
So here, while the mad guns curse overhead,

And tired men sigh with mud for couch and floor,
Know that we fools, now with the foolish dead,
Died not for flag, not King, nor Emperor,
But for a dream, born in a herdsman's shed,
And for the secret Scripture of the poor.

T. M. KETTLE

Written in 'the field, before Guillemont, Somme, September 4, 1916'. Kettle was
killed four days later. *Poems and Parodies* (1916).
   not for flag … King … Emperor. Kettle was an Irish nationalist.
   shed: the stable where Christ was born.

(125) Who Made the Law?

Who made the Law that men should die in meadows?
Who spake the word that blood should splash in lanes?
Who gave it forth that gardens should be bone-yards?
Who spread the hills with flesh, and blood, and brains?
          Who made the Law?

Who made the Law that Death should stalk the village?
Who spake the word to kill among the sheaves,
Who gave it forth that death should lurk in hedgerows,
Who flung the dead among the fallen leaves?
          Who made the law?

Those who return shall find that peace endures,
Find old things old, and know the things they knew,
Walk in the garden, slumber by the fireside,
Share the peace of dawn, and dream amid the dew –
          Those who return.

Those who return shall till the ancient pastures,
Clean-hearted men shall guide the plough-horse reins,
Some shall grow apples and flowers in the valleys,
Some shall go courting in summer down the lanes –
       THOSE WHO RETURN.

But who made the Law? The Trees shall whisper to him:
'See, see the blood – the splashes on our bark!'
Walking the meadows, he shall hear bones crackle,
And fleshless mouths shall gibber in silent lanes at dark.
       Who made the Law?

Who made the Law? At noon upon the hillside
His ears shall hear a moan, his cheeks shall feel a breath,
And all along the valleys, past gardens, croft, and homesteads,
He who made the Law,
HE who made the Law,
HE who made the Law shall walk alone with Death.
       WHO made the Law?

                        LESLIE COULSON

Dated October 1916. Found in Coulson's kit after his death in action on the 8th.
From an Outpost (1917). On 30 June, just before taking part in the first day of the
Somme, he had written: 'If I should fall, do not grieve for me. I shall be one with the
wind and the sun and the flowers'. His attitude changed between then and October.
In another late poem, 'Judgement', he promises that after death his soul will summon
God to 'tell me *why*'.

(126) 'God! How I hate you, you young cheerful men'

On a University Undergraduate moved to verse by the war.

God! How I hate you, you young cheerful men,
Whose pious poetry blossoms on your graves
As soon as you are in them, nurtured up
By the salt of your corruption, and the tears
Of mothers, local vicars, college deans,
And flanked by prefaces and photographs
From all your minor poet friends – the fools –
Who paint their sentimental elegies
Where sure, no angel treads; and, living, share
The dead's brief immortality.

                                Oh Christ!
To think that one could spread the ductile wax
Of his fluid youth to Oxford's glowing fires
And take her seal so ill! Hark how one chants –
'Oh happy to have lived these epic days' –
'These epic days'! And *he'd* been to France,
And seen the trenches, glimpsed the huddled dead
In the periscope, hung in the rusting wire:
Choked by their sickly foetor, day and night
Blown down his throat: stumbled through ruined hearths,
Proved all that muddy brown monotony,
Where blood's the only coloured thing. Perhaps
Had seen a man killed, a sentry shot at night,
Hunched as he fell, his feet on the firing-step,
His neck against the back slope of the trench,
And the rest doubled up between, his head
Smashed like an egg-shell, and the warm grey brain
Spattered all bloody on the parados:
Had flashed a torch on his face, and known his friend,
Shot, breathing hardly, in ten minutes – gone!
Yet still God's in His heaven, all is right
In the best possible of worlds. The woe,
Even His scaled eyes *must* see, is partial, only
A seeming woe, we cannot understand.

God loves us, God looks down on this our strife
And smiles in pity, blows a pipe at times
And calls some warriors home. We do not die,
God would not let us, He is too 'intense',
Too 'passionate', a whole day sorrows He
Because a grass-blade dies. How rare life is!
On earth, the love and fellowship of men,
Men sternly banded: banded for what end?
Banded to maim and kill their fellow men –
For even Huns are men. In heaven above
A genial umpire, a good judge of sport,
Won't let us hurt each other! Let's rejoice
God keeps us faithful, pens us still in fold.
Ah, what a faith is ours (almost, it seems,
Large as a mustard-seed) – we trust and trust,
Nothing can shake us! Ah, how good God is
To suffer us be born just now, when youth
That else would rust, can slake his blade in gore,
Where very God Himself does seem to walk
The bloody fields of Flanders He so loves!

ARTHUR GRAEME WEST

A shorter version, 'War Poets', in the *New Age*, 6 October 1916. *Diary of a Dead Officer*
(1919). West quotes from two poems by his contemporary at Oxford, Rex Freston,
'O Fortunati' (*57*) and 'To the Atheists' ('God will never let me die / He is too
passionate and intense for that'; 'God, Who sorrows all a summer's day / Because a
blade of grass has died'). Freston's book, published after his death, is typical of the
memorial volumes described in West's opening lines.
   no angel treads: 'fools rush in where angels fear to tread' (Pope, *Essay on Criticism*).
   he'd been to France: actually, Freston seems to have written almost all his poems while
still in England.
   all is right: echoes Voltaire's satire ('all is for the best in the best of possible
worlds', *Candide*).
   mustard seed: Matthew 17:20.

(127) A Soldier's Testament

If I come to die
  In this inhuman strife,
I grudge it not, if I
  By laying down my life
Do aught at all to bring
  A day of charity,
When pride of lord or king
  Un-powerful shall be
To spend the nations' store,
  To spill the peoples' blood;
Whereafter evermore
  Humanity's full flood
Untroubled on shall roll
  In a rich tide of peace,
And the world's wondrous soul
  Uncrucified increase.

But if my life be given
  Merely that lords and kings
May say, 'We well have striven!
  See! Where our banner flings
Its folds upon the breeze
  (Thanks, noble sirs, to you!).
See how the lands and seas
  Have changed their pristine hue ...'
If after I am dead
  On goes the same old game,
With monarchs seeing red
  And ministers aflame,
And nations drowning deep
  In quarrels not their own,
And peoples called to reap
  The woes they have not sown; ...

If all we who are slain
  Have died, despite our hope,
Only to twist again
  The old kaleidoscope –
Why then, by God! we're sold!
  Cheated and wronged! betrayed!
Our youth and lives and gold
  Wasted – the homes we'd made
Shattered – in folly blind,
  By treachery and spite,
By cowardice of mind
  And little men and light! ...

If there be none to build
  Out of this ruined world
The temple we have willed
  With our flag there unfurled,
If rainbow none there shine
  Across these skies of woe,
If seed of yours and mine
  Through this same hell must go,
Then may my soul and those
  Of all who died in vain
(Be they of friends or foes)
  Rise and come back again
From peace that knows no end,
  From faith that knows not doubt,
To haunt and sear and rend
  The men that sent us out.

ELIOT CRAWSHAY-WILLIAMS

Written 28 November 1916 in Egypt. *Nation*, 3 February 1917, under the pseudonym 'Eques'. *The Gutter and the Stars* (1918). A commanding officer who had recently killed men in battle starts to doubt the political aims of the war.

(128) Grotesque

These are the damned circles Dante trod,
Terrible in hopelessness,
But even skulls have their humour,
An eyeless and sardonic mockery:
And we,
Sitting with streaming eyes in the acrid smoke,
That murks our foul, damp billet,
Chant bitterly, with raucous voices
As a choir of frogs
In hideous irony, our patriotic songs.

FREDERIC MANNING

Eidola (1917). Manning is said to have written most of his war poems in the second half of 1916, while he was serving on the Somme. They show the influence of his Modernist friends, Pound and Aldington.

circles: the seven circles of Hell in Dante's *Inferno*.

(129) Relieved

We are weary and silent,
There is only the rhythm of marching feet;
Tho' we move tranced, we keep it
As clockwork toys.

But each man is alone in this multitude;
We know not the world in which we move,
Seeing not the dawn, earth pale and shadowy,
Level lands of tenuous grays and greens;
For our eyeballs have been seared with fire.

Only we have our secret thoughts,
Our sense floats out from us, delicately apprehensive,
To the very fringes of our being,
Where light drowns.

FREDERIC MANNING

Eidola (1917). 'Eidola' means 'visions' in Greek.

(130) Autarcheia

I am alone: even ranked with multitudes:
And they alone, each man.
                    So are we free.
For some few friends of me, some earth of mine,
Some shrines, some dreams I dream, some hopes that emerge
From the rude stone of life vaguely, and tend
Toward form in me: the progeny of dreams
I father; even this England which is mine
Whereof no man has seen the loveliness
As with mine eyes: and even too, my God
Whom none have known as I: for these I fight,
For mine own self, that thus in giving self
Prodigally, as a mere breath in the air,

I may possess myself, and spend me so
Mingling with earth, and dreams, and God: and being
In them the master of all these in me,
Perfected thus.

     Fight for your own dreams, you.

           FREDERIC MANNING

Eidola (1917).

 Title (originally in Greek lettering): translated by Manning after the war as 'self-mastery' – 'the condition of any free activity of the mind, of all right choice'. In battle 'one undergoes a kind of katharsis (as Aristotle described the function of tragedy) ... it is precisely at such moments that a man becomes most intensely himself' (quoted, J. Marwil, 'Frederic Manning', *St Louis Literary Supplement*, June–July 1977, 12–14). A similar insight informs Manning's war novel, *The Middle Parts of Fortune* (1929).

(131) German Prisoners

When first I saw you in the curious street,
Like some platoon of soldier ghosts in grey,
My mad impulse was all to smite and slay,
To spit upon you – tread you 'neath my feet.
But when I saw how each sad soul did greet
My gaze with no sign of defiant frown,
How from tired eyes looked spirits broken down,
How each face showed the pale flag of defeat,
And doubt, despair, and disillusionment,
And how were grievous wounds on many a head,
And on your garb red-faced was other red;
And how you stooped as men whose strength was spent,
I knew that we had suffered each as other,
And could have grasped your hand and cried, 'My brother!'

           JOSEPH LEE

Spectator, 4 November 1916. *Work-a-Day Warriors* (1917).

(132) Before the Assault

If thro' this roar o' the guns one prayer may reach Thee,
  Lord of all Life, whose mercies never sleep,
Not in our time, not now, Lord, we beseech thee
  To grant us peace. The sword has bit too deep.

We may not rest. We hear the wail of mothers
  Mourning the sons who fill some nameless grave:
Past us, in dreams, the ghosts march of our brothers
  Who were most valiant ... whom we could not save.

We may not rest. What though our eyes be holden,
  In sleep we see dear eyes yet wet with tears,
And locks that once were, oh, so fair and golden,
  Grown grey in hours more pitiless than years.

We see all fair things fouled – homes love's hands builded
  Shattered to dust beside their withered vines,
Shattered the towers that once Thy sunsets gilded,
  And Christ struck yet again within His shrines.

Over them hangs the dust of death, beside them
  The dead lie countless – and the foe laughs still;
We may not rest, while those cruel mouths deride them,
  We, who were proud, yet could not work Thy will.

We have failed – we have been more weak than these betrayers –
  In strength or in faith we have failed; our pride was vain.
How can we rest, who have not slain the slayers?
  What peace for us, who have seen Thy children slain?

Hark, the roar grows ... the thunders reawaken –
  We ask one thing, Lord, only one thing now:
Hearts high as theirs, who went to death unshaken,
  Courage like theirs to make and keep their vow.

To stay not till these hosts whom mercies harden,
  Who know no glory save of sword and fire,
Find in our fire the splendour of Thy pardon,
  Meet from our steel the mercy they desire ...

Then to our children there shall be no handing
  Of fates so vain – of passions so abhorr'd ...
But Peace ... the Peace which passeth understanding ...
  Not in our time ... but in their time, O Lord.

R. E. VERNÈDE

Observer, 17 December 1916. *War Poems* (1917). Unlike Coulson (*125*), whose thinking changed during the Somme, Vernède began this poem in about February 1916, fought on the Somme all summer and finished the poem in England in November (*Letters to His Wife*, viii). His belief in the rightness of the cause had not faltered. In December he chose to return to the trenches, where he was killed in April 1917.

    Peace ... understanding: Philippians 4:7.

(133) *from* Sed Miles

[...]
It's often said
You're a long time dead,
And the grey worms eat,
Through the nails of your feet,
Through the white of your thighs,
To the whites of your eyes;
You feel pretty cheap
As a drab little heap
Of powder and smell;
For a Fritz gas shell
Leaves more behind
In the way of rind.

1916

But when West you go,
It's nice to know
You've done your bit
In spite of it;
And Blighty's name
And Blighty's fame
Will find in your
Demise, manure,
To sprout and spread
Till English red
Is the favourite hue
For Bartholomew,

[...]
When West you go,
It's nice to know
You've done your bit
In spite of it.

A. E. TOMLINSON

From a 54-line poem, dated December 1916. *Candour* (1922).
    Title: an ironic allusion to Newbolt's 'Clifton Chapel': 'Qui ante diem periit: / Sed miles, sed pro patria' ('Who died before his day, but as a soldier and for his country').
    Bartholomew: map publishers (British territories were shown in red).

(134) Resolve

Let me not think of blood tonight –
So doing
It will be harder still to fight:
Peace's wooing
Sucks blood making me white
And tremulous –
Thus, thus
I will harden yet my heart
Gaze into horror's face
Unafraid, without a trace
Of tenderness!

R. WATSON KERR

War Daubs (1919).

(135) Welcome Death

When you've been dead beat, and had to go on
While others died; when your turn to be gone
Is overdue; when you're pushed ahead
('Go on till you die' is all they said),
Then die – and you're glad to be dead!

R. C. G. DARTFORD

In the anthology *Soldier Poets Second Series* (1917). Dartford had been badly wounded at Loos; he wrote his few war poems in 1916 on the Somme, where he saw his CO killed in front of him.

(136) After the 'Offensive'

This is the end of it, this the cold silence
Succeeding the violence
That rioted here.
This is the end of it – grim and austere.

This is the end of it – where the tide spread,
Runnels of blood
Debris of dead.
This is the end of it: ebb follows flood.

Waves of strong men
That will surge not again,
Scattered and riven
You lie, and you rot;
What have you not given?
And what – have you got?

THEO VAN BEEK

Undated. *English Review*, April 1919. Van Beek, an artillery officer, fought on the Somme. This poem may have been among those that he read at the Aeolian Hall in London during the war, wearing uniform and risking disciplinary action (he was reprimanded).

(137) The Refugees

Past the marching men, where the great road runs,
    Out of burning Ypres, three pale women came.
One was a widow (listen to the guns!) –
    She wheeled a heaped-up barrow. One walked lame
And dragged two tired children at her side,

Frightened and coughing with the dust. The third
Nestled a dead child on her breast, and tried
    To suckle him. They never spoke a word ...
So they came down along the great Ypres road.
    A soldier stayed his mirth to watch them pass,
Turned, and in silence helped them with their load,
    And led them to a field and gave them bread ...
I saw them hide their faces in the grass
    And cry, as women cried when Christ was dead.

WILLIAM G. SHAKESPEARE

Spectator, 5 December 1916. *Ypres and Other Poems* (1916).

(138) *from* Otherworld

[...]
My friend said to me as I marched by his side in the night
Through the mud of Waterloo Road,
'This is the finest draft that has ever left England,
Picked men, all non-commissioned officers, held back for months.'
And the head of the column, out of sight away in the darkness,
Roared out a marching chorus,
Taken up and humorously turned by the men in the rear.
Windows opened, and women's voices cheered on the soldiers,
Who answered with jests and offered to kiss them
(And the kiss was taken, but not in a way they knew).
Through the mud, through the mud they went.
And at the bends of the road the lamp of the column-leader
Burned the blackness with red for a moment.

1916

Four-deep they went, strong young men,
Jesting and singing and laughing,
With broad backs bearing their packs,
And broad chests breathing great breaths of the cold, damp air, –
Life at its cleanest,
Moving swiftly through the half-dead evil
And the filth of the sleeping city.
And when they arrived at London Bridge,
And stood in the gas-lit, frowsy station,
The sweat was on their face, and the hall was filled
With the smell of healthy men.
What was my friend doing there,
The singer of beautiful things, the beautiful singer?
What was any man of that company –
Clerk, shopkeeper, labourer, poet –
Doing each with the other,
Clothed and loaded alike and marching together,
With the thought of each man's heart and brain written off,
And their common manhood
Trained to move in one direction and to fit one shape?
What is war? ...What are nations?
My friend has gone from me; I could not have even him
And yet in those men
There was so much kindliness, so much humour,
And so little desire to kill.
[...]

F. S. FLINT

Otherworld: Cadences (1920). In December 1916 Flint accompanied his friend Richard Aldington when the latter's unit marched from Waterloo to London Bridge station, one more draft of men destined for France. As a committed Modernist, like Aldington, Flint writes in 'unrhymed cadence' and unornamented language.

1917

There had been an exchange of diplomatic 'peace notes' between Germany and America in December 1916, but on 1 February 1917 Germany resumed attacks on neutral shipping, and that brought the USA into the war as an 'Associate Power' of the Allies. President Woodrow Wilson expressed his country's aims in liberal, even idealistic, terms and the overthrow of the Russian Tsar in March added to hopes that this might be a war for democracy.

Yet there was no real chance of peace in 1917. After a bitter winter that caused much suffering in the trenches, the Germans retreated to their new, seemingly impregnable Hindenburg Line. A major French offensive along the River Aisne in April, supported by the British at Arras, proved disastrous, despite Canadian success at Vimy Ridge. Germany's resumption of submarine attacks was intended to starve Britain out of the war, and for a time it came near to succeeding, causing severe food shortages and inflation. The mood on the home front was less than optimistic, but the government still refused to consider peace moves and seemed reluctant to define its war aims. The grimness of most 1917 verse reflected the realities of a war of attrition. Soldiers kept going, although some poets among them felt they were fighting to save each other and their own self-respect, rather than for any larger cause.

In June Siegfried Sassoon wrote his famous protest, accusing the government of prolonging the war unnecessarily, having secretly changed its aims from liberation to conquest. He met Wilfred Owen in August, and during the next few months the two poets wrote many of their angriest poems against the war – but such poems were not at all typical of 1917. Other poets in the army, with views very different from those of Sassoon and Owen, wrote verse that was much nearer the attitudes of most soldiers.

German attempts to impose a blockade failed after Britain introduced a convoy system, while the Allied blockade of German ports became increasingly effective. American troops began arriving in France, though they needed more training. At the end of July, on the same day that Sassoon's protest appeared in *The Times*, the Third Battle of Ypres, later known as Passchendaele, began. It lasted until December: intensive shelling and heavy rain destroyed the area's canals and drainage systems, and the campaign became a byword for useless attrition. Peace talk broke out again. On 29 November the *Daily Telegraph* published a letter from the respected former Foreign Secretary Lord Lansdowne, who argued that continuing the war would 'spell ruin for the civilised world'; he was ferociously attacked as a 'defeatist' in the popular press. Meanwhile, the Communists triumphed in Russia and decided to cease fighting, eventually leaving Germany free to concentrate its forces in the west.

(139) January Full Moon, Ypres

Vantaged snow on the gray pilasters
Gleams to the sight so wan and ghostly;
The wolfish shadows in the eerie places
   Sprawl in the mist-light.

Sharp-fanged searches the frost, and shackles
The sleeping water in broken cellars,
And calm and fierce the witch-moon watches,
   Curious of evil.

Flares from the horseshoe of trenches beckon,
Momently soaring and sinking, and often
Peer through the naked fire-swept windows
   Mocking the fallen.

Quiet, uneasily quiet – the guns hushed,
Scarcely a rifle-shot cracks through the salient,
Only the Cloth Hall sentry's challenge
   To someone crunching through the frozen snows.

EDMUND BLUNDEN

Written January 1917. *Poems 1914–30* (1930).

(140) Les Halles d'Ypres

A tangle of iron rods and spluttered beams,
   On brickwork past the skill of a mason to mend:
A wall with a bright blue poster – odd as dreams
   Is the city's latter end.

A shapeless obelisk looms Saint Martin's spire,
   Now a lean aiming-mark for the German guns;
And the Cloth Hall crouches beside, disfigured with fire,
   The glory of Flanders once.

Only the foursquare tower still bears the trace
   Of beauty that was, and strong embattled age,
And gilded ceremonies and pride of place –
   Before this senseless rage.

And still you may see (below the noon serene,
   The mysterious, changeless vault of sharp blue light),
The pigeons come to the tower, and flaunt and preen,
   And flicker in playful flight.

EDMUND BLUNDEN

Written January 1917. *Poems 1914–30* (1930). This and the preceding poem are among the very few that survive from the verse Blunden wrote at the front.

(141) On the Somme

Who heard the thunder of the great guns firing?
   Who watched the line where the great shells roared?
Who drove the foeman back, and followed his retiring,
   When we threw him out of Pommiers to the glory of the Lord?

Englishmen and Scotsmen, in the grey fog of morning
   Watched the dim, black clouds that reeked, and strove to break the gloom;
And Irishmen that stood with them, impatient for the warning,
   When the thundering around them would cease and give them room –

Room to move forward as the grey mist lifted,
   Quietly and swiftly – the white steel bare;
Happy, swift, and quiet, as the fog still drifted;
   They moved along the tortured slope and met the foeman there.

Stalwart men and wonderful, brave beyond believing –
  Little time to mourn for friends that dropped without a word!
(Wait until the work is done, and then give way to grieving) –
  So they hummed the latest ragtime to the glory of the Lord.

All across the No Man's Land and through the ruined wiring,
  Each officer that led them, with a walking-cane for sword,
Cared not a button though the foeman went on firing
  While they dribbled over footballs to the glory of the Lord.

And when they brought their captives back, hungry and downhearted,
  They called them 'Fritz' and slapped their backs, and, all with one
    accord,
They shared with them what food they'd left from when the long day
    started,
  And gave them smokes and bully to the glory of the Lord.

CLAUDE PENROSE

Dated 26 March 1917 in *Poems* (1919). If Burton's civilian verses about the first day of the Somme (*107*) seem absurd today, this later doggerel about the same event is less easy to dismiss. Penrose, who won the MC and was twice wounded during the battle, was an officer with a record of courage and leadership.
  bully: tinned beef.

(142) 'Glad that I killed yer'

Hear my voice; hearken unto my speech: for I have slain a man – Genesis 4:23

    Glad that I killed yer –
      It was you or me:
        Our bayonets locked,
     And then I pulled mine free;
       My heart beat like to burst;
      But Gawd, I got in first –
    Glad that I killed yer!

Glad that I killed yer,
   Though you are so young:
     How still you lie
   With both your arms outflung:
     There's red blood on your hair –
     Well, what the Hell I care? –
Glad that I killed yer!

Glad that I killed yer –
   You're my enemy;
     I had to hate –
   And you – you hated me;
     You mightn't be to blame –
     I killed yer just the same –
Glad that I killed yer!

Glad that I killed yer –
   That's the game o' war;
     But for my luck
   I'd lie just like you are;
     Your blood is on my hand –
     Surely you understand
I *had* to kill yer?

Glad that I killed yer –
   Yet I can't forget
     The look you gave me
   When we turned – and met –
     Why do you follow me with staring eye?
     Was it so difficult a thing to die –
Gawd! when *I* killed yer?

Glad that I killed yer –
  Yet I'm sorry, too,
    For those will wait
  So long at home for you:
    I have a mother living down at Bow –
    Thank Gawd for this that yours will never know
'Twas I that killed yer!

Glad that I killed yer –
  It was you or me:
    It does seem strange,
  But it had got to be.
    My heart beat like to burst,
    But Gawd, I got in first –
Glad that I killed yer!

JOSEPH LEE

Work-a-Day Warriors (1917). Relatively few poems by soldiers deal openly with killing the enemy – and most of those that do focus on remorse and guilt.

(143) Servitude

If it were not for England, who would bear
This heavy servitude one moment more?
To keep a brothel, sweep and wash the floor
Of filthiest hovels were noble to compare
With this brass-cleaning life. Now here, now there
Harried in foolishness, scanned curiously o'er
By fools made brazen by conceit, and store
Of antique witticisms thin and bare.

Only the love of comrades sweetens all,
Whose laughing spirit will not be outdone.
As night-watching men wait for the sun
To hearten them, so wait I on such boys
As neither brass nor Hell-fire may appal,
Nor guns, nor sergeant-major's bluster and noise.

IVOR GURNEY

Written February 1917. *Severn and Somme* (November 1917). The third of five 'Sonnets 1917', described by Gurney as 'a sort of counterblast' against Brooke's '1914' sonnets (*32*), 'the protest of the physical against the exalted spiritual, of the cumulative weight of small facts against the one large. Of informed opinion against uninformed ... Old ladies won't like them, but soldiers may.' As always, Gurney writes from the point of view of the private soldier.

Hell-fire: originally 'Bosches' but, like many other soldiers, Gurney had no strong feelings against Germans.

(144) The Other Side

There are not any, save the men that died,
Whose minds have probed into the heart of war.

Sometimes we stumble on a secret door
And listening guess what lies the other side.
Sometimes a moment's sudden pain
Flings back the veil that hangs between
Guessing and knowing; then lets it fall again
Before we understand what we have seen.

In and out everywhere,
Distorted in a twisted glass,
Fragmentary visions pass.
We try to fit them one with another,
Like a child putting a puzzle together,
When half the pieces are not there.

1917

Out of a dim obscurity
Certain things stand plain and clear,
Certain things we are forced to see,
Certain things we are forced to hear.

* * *

A subaltern dying between the lines,
  Wondering why.
A father with nothing left of life
  But the will to die.

A young girl born for laughter and spring,
Left to her shame and her loneliness.
What is one woman more or less
To men who've forgotten everything?

A thin line swinging forward to kill,
  And a man driven mad by the din.

Music-hall songs about 'Kaiser Bill'
  And 'the march through the streets of Berlin'.

Grey-beards prattling round a fire
Of the good the war has done.

Three men rotting upon the wire;
And each of them had a son.

A soldier who once was fresh and clean
Lost to himself in whoring and drink,
Blind to what will be and what has been,
Only aware that he must not think.

In the pulpit a parson preaching lies,
Babbling of honour and sacrifice.

***

Fragments flutter in and out.
Christ! what is it all about?

ALEC WAUGH

Dated Hampstead, March 1917. *Resentment* (1918). Modelled on the poem 'Strange Meetings' by his friend Monro. Waugh was still a teenager and had not yet been in action, but his scepticism is typical of 1917; it can be seen again in his 1917 novel, *The Loom of Youth*.

(145) Trench Idyll

We sat together in the trench,
He on a lump of frozen earth
Blown in the night before,
I on an unexploded shell;
And smoked and talked, like exiles,
Of how pleasant London was,
Its women, restaurants, night clubs, theatres,
How at that very hour
The taxi-cabs were taking folk to dine ...
Then we sat silent for a while
As a machine-gun swept the parapet.

He said:
'I've been here on and off two years
And seen only one man killed.'

'That's odd.'

'The bullet hit him in the throat;
He fell in a heap on the fire-step,
And called out "My God! *Dead*" '

'Good Lord, how terrible!'

'Well, as to that, the nastiest job I've had
Was last year on this very front
Taking the discs at night from men
Who'd hung for six months on the wire
Just over there.
The worst of all was
They fell to pieces at a touch.
Thank God we couldn't see their faces;
They had gas helmets on ... '

I shivered;
'It's rather cold here, sir, suppose we move?'

RICHARD ALDINGTON

Undated. *Images of War* (1919). A 'hard', 'dry' modern poem, written in 'unrhymed cadence' – cf. (*138*) – free, as Pound and Monro would have wished, from 'emotional slither' and sentimental ornament.

(146) Concert

These antique prostitutions –
I deplore my own vague cynicism,
Undressing with indifferent eyes each girl,
Seeing them naked on that paltry stage
Stared at by half a thousand lustful eyes.

These antique prostitutions –
Am I dead? Withered? Grown old?
That not the least flush of desire
Tinges my unmoved flesh,
And that instead of women's living bodies
I see dead men – you understand? – dead men
With sullen, dark red gashes
Luminous in a foul trench?

These antique prostitutions.

RICHARD ALDINGTON

Undated. *Art and Letters* (winter 1918–19). *Images of War* (1919). Many poems by soldiers express passionate love of comrades, 'passing the love of women': cf. (*164*), (*178*), (*188*), (*202*) and the anthology *Lads: Love Poetry of the Trenches* (1989), ed. Martin Taylor.

(147) Comrades in Arms

Not ours the zeal that passes with the years,
  The will too faint to battle with desire;
In the dim twilight-time of doubts and fears
  Our lips were singing and our eyes afire.

We have become a glory and a name,
  We who were weak, by this one faith made strong
That somewhere past the powder and the flame
  God is the arbiter of right and wrong.

And if beyond the day's long labour Death
  Stand in our path and shroud us in his pall,
Bartering honour for this wasted breath,
  Ah then! it were the greatest good of all,

Thus, with the last shot fired, the last fight over,
 The golden sunset fading in the sky,
To feel the night around us like a lover,
 And turn our face and smile to her, and die.

P. H. B. LYON

Lyon remembered writing this in 1917. *Songs of Youth and War* (1918). Another poem by
a serving, decorated officer: conventional attitudes still persist.
 glory and a name: 'I have become a name', Tennyson, 'Ulysses'.

(148) Two Fusiliers

And have we done with War at last?
Well, we've been lucky devils both,
And there's no need of pledge or oath
To bind our lovely friendship fast,
By firmer stuff
Close bound enough.

By wire and wood and stake we're bound,
By Fricourt and by Festubert,
By whipping rain, by the sun's glare,
By all the misery and loud sound,
By a Spring day,
By Picard clay.

Show me the two so closely bound
As we, by the wet bond of blood,
By friendship, blossoming from mud,
By Death: we faced him, and we found
Beauty in Death,
In dead men breath.

ROBERT GRAVES

Written 1917, probably in April or May. *Fairies and Fusiliers* (November 1917). The
two Royal Welch Fusiliers are Graves himself, sent home as permanently unfit after his
second, brief period at the front in early 1917, and Sassoon, invalided home wounded
in April. Graves's imagery is echoed in Owen's 'Apologia' (*183*).

(149) The Dead Soldiers

'God only Acts and Is in existing beings or Men'

I

Spectrum Trench. Autumn. Nineteen-Sixteen.
And Zenith. (The Border Regiment will remember.)
A little north of where Lesboeufs had been.
(The Australians took it over in December.)
Just as the scythe had caught them, there they lay,
A sheaf for Death, ungarnered and untied:
A crescent moon of men who showed the way
When first the Tanks crept out, till they too died:
Guardsmen I think, but one could hardly tell,
It was a forward slope, beyond the crest,
Muddier than any place in Dante's hell,
Where sniping gave us very little rest.
At night one stumbled over them and swore;
Each day the rain hid them a little more.

II

Fantastic forms, in postured attitudes,
Twisted and bent, or lying deathly prone;
Their individual hopes my thought eludes,
But each man had a hope to call his own.
Much else? – God knows. But not for me the thought,
'Your mothers made your bodies: God your souls,
And, for because you dutifully fought,
God will go mad and make of half-lives, wholes.'
No. God in every one of you was slain;
For killing men is always killing God,
Though Life destroyed shall come to life again
And loveliness rise from the sodden sod.
But if of life we do destroy the best,
God wanders wide, and weeps in his unrest.

MAX PLOWMAN

Dated April 1917. *A Lap Full of Seed* (1917). Plowman was badly concussed at Lesboeufs, January 1917. A year later he wrote to the authorities resigning from the army (see biographical note), again using the words *killing men is always killing God*.

(150) The Supreme Sacrifice

O valiant Hearts, who to your glory came
Through dust of conflict and through battle-flame;
Tranquil you lie, your knightly virtue proved,
Your memory hallowed in the Land you loved.

Proudly you gathered, rank on rank to war,
As who had heard God's message from afar;
All you had hoped for, all you had, you gave
To save Mankind – yourselves you scorned to save.

Splendid you passed, the great surrender made,
Into the light that nevermore shall fade;
Deep your contentment in that blest abode,
Who wait the last clear trumpet-call of God.

Long years ago, as earth lay dark and still,
Rose a loud cry upon a lonely hill,
While in the frailty of our human clay
Christ, our Redeemer, passed the self-same way.

Still stands His Cross from that dread hour to this
Like some bright star above the dark abyss;
Still, through the veil, the Victor's pitying eyes
Look down to bless our lesser Calvaries.

These were His servants; in His steps they trod
Following through death the martyr'd Son of God:
Victor He rose; victorious too shall rise
They who have drunk His cup of Sacrifice.

O risen Lord, O Shepherd of our Dead,
Whose Cross has bought them and Whose Staff has led –
In glorious hope their proud and sorrowing Land
Commits her Children to Thy gracious hand.

J. S. ARKWRIGHT

Written winter 1916–17. *Hereford Times*, 21 July 1917. *The Supreme Sacrifice
and Other Poems in Time of War* (1919). A popular hymn, in the metre and rhyme
scheme of 'Abide with Me', by a civilian with no experience of the battlefield. Often
anthologized, set to music by several composers, regularly sung at Remembrance Day
services – until the 1950s, when it began to be condemned as sentimental, even
unchristian, for its implied faith in salvation by death in war.
   yourselves … save: Luke 23:35.

(151) A Call to National Service

Up and be doing, all who have a hand
To lift, a back to bend. It must not be
In times like these that vaguely linger we
To air our vaunts and hopes; and leave our land

Untended as a wild of weeds and sand.
– Say, then, 'I come!' And go, O women and men
Of palace, ploughshare, easel, counter, pen;
That scareless, scathless, England still may stand.

Would years but let me stir as once I stirred
At many a dawn to take the forward track,
And with a stride plunged on to enterprise,
I now would speed like yester wind that whirred
Through yielding pines; and serve with never a slack,
So loud for promptness all around outcries!

THOMAS HARDY

Written in a hurry at the request of the National Service department, March 1917.
The Times, 12 March 1917. *Moments of Vision* (1917). 'I cannot do patriotic poems very
well – seeing the other side too much' (Hardy to John Galsworthy, 15 August 1918).
Germany had resumed unrestricted submarine warfare, aiming to starve Britain
into surrender; part of the government's response was a huge campaign to expand
food production.

(152) I Looked Up from My Writing

I looked up from my writing,
    And gave a start to see,
As if rapt in my inditing,
    The moon's full gaze on me.

THE WINTER OF THE WORLD

Her meditative misty head
　Was spectral in its air,
And I involuntarily said,
　'What are you doing there?'

'Oh, I've been scanning pond and hole
　And waterway hereabout
For the body of one with a sunken soul
　Who has put his life-light out.

'Did you hear his frenzied tattle?
　It was sorrow for his son
Who is slain in brutish battle,
　Though he has injured none.

'And now I am curious to look
　Into the blinkered mind
Of one who wants to write a book
　In a world of such a kind.'

Her temper overwrought me,
　And I edged to shun her view,
For I felt assured she thought me
　One who should drown him too.

THOMAS HARDY

Moments of Vision (1917). The book may be *Moments of Vision* itself, his largest single collection of poems.

(153) Recruited – Poplar

March 1917

THEY SAY – THEY SAY

(And that's the bugles going all the day
Past Coopers' Arms and round by Stepney way
Till you'll be mad for hearing of them play)

THEY SAY – THEY SAY

You were the finest stuff men ever had
To make into a soldier. And they say
They put the needed strength and spirit in you,
Straightened your shoulders, made you clean and true,
And fit for England's service – I can say
They clothed you warm, and fed and worked you fair
The first time in your life, on Derby Day;
Maybe that did a little – Anyway
They made a man of you this year, the sort
That England's rich and proud to own, they say

– THEY SAY – THEY SAY –

And so they went and killed you. That's their way.

MARGARET POSTGATE

Poems (1918).

(154) 'A Fight to a Finish'

'Fight the year out!' the Warlords said:
What said the dying among the dead?

'To the last man!' cried the profiteers:
What said the poor in the starveling years?

'War is good!' yelled the Jingo-kind:
What said the wounded, the maimed and blind?

'Fight on!' the Armament-kings besought:
Nobody asked what the women thought.

'On!' echoed Hate where the fiends kept tryst:
Asked the Church, even, what said Christ?

S. GERTRUDE FORD

'A Fight to a Finish' and Other Songs of Peace (1917). Ford sometimes published with
Galloway Kyle, but her collection of pacifist poems would not have been to his taste:
like a number of other pacifist books, it was published by C. W. Daniel.
   Title: a notorious phrase from a September 1916 speech by Lloyd George ('The
fight must be to a finish – to a knock-out'). Cf. (*176*).

(155) To the United States of America

Brothers in blood! They who this wrong began
To wreck our commonwealth, will rue the day
When first they challenged freemen to the fray,
And with the Briton dared the American.
   Now are we pledged to win the Rights of man;
Labour and justice now shall have their way,
And in a League of Peace – God grant we may –
Transform the earth, not patch up the old plan.

Sure is our hope since he, who led your nation,
Spake for mankind; and ye arose in awe
Of that high call to work the world's salvation;
   Clearing your minds of all estranging blindness
In the vision of Beauty, and the Spirit's law,
Freedom and Honour and sweet Loving-kindness.

ROBERT BRIDGES

Written 30 April 1917. Published next day in *The Times*. *October and Other Poems* (1920).
German attacks on neutral shipping brought the USA into the war in April. The
Poet Laureate's language is still that of 1914.

   he, who led: President Woodrow Wilson, whose hopes for international co-operation
and what would now be called 'human rights' were an inspiration to many people
in Britain.

(156) Mesopotamia

1917

They shall not return to us, the resolute, the young,
   The eager and whole-hearted whom we gave:
But the men who left them thriftily to die in their own dung,
   Shall they come with years and honour to the grave?

They shall not return to us, the strong men coldly slain
   In sight of help denied from day to day:
But the men who edged their agonies and chid them in their pain,
   Are they too strong and wise to put away?

Our dead shall not return to us while Day and Night divide –
   Never while the bars of sunset hold:
But the idle-minded overlings who quibbled while they died,
   Shall they thrust for high employments as of old?

Shall we only threaten and be angry for an hour?
　When the storm is ended shall we find
How softly but how swiftly they have sidled back to power
　By the favour and contrivance of their kind?

Even while they soothe us, while they promise large amends,
　Even while they make a show of fear,
Do they call upon their debtors, and take council with their friends,
　To confirm and re-establish each career?

Their lives cannot repay us — their death could not undo —
　The shame that they have laid upon our race.
But the slothfulness that wasted and the arrogance that slew,
　Shall we leave it unabated in its place?

RUDYARD KIPLING

Morning Post, 11 July 1917. *The Years Between* (1919). The Mesopotamia campaign had ended in humiliating surrender at Kut, April 1916. Captives were held in appalling conditions, many dying of dysentery and other diseases. Parliament demanded a government inquiry: Kipling, as ever on the side of the ordinary soldier and critical of administrative incompetence, comments on its findings (he had retained his independence by refusing a knighthood from Lloyd George's government).

(157) The Children

These were our children who died for our lands: they were dear in our
　　sight.
　We have only the memory left of their home-treasured sayings and
　　laughter.
　The price of our loss shall be paid to our hands, not another's
　　hereafter.
Neither the Alien nor Priest shall decide on it. That is our right.

　　But who shall return us the children?

At the hour the Barbarian chose to disclose his pretences,
  And raged against Man, they engaged, on the breasts that they bared
      for us,
  The first felon-stroke of the sword he had long-time prepared for us –
Their bodies were all our defence while we wrought our defences.

They bought us anew with their blood, forbearing to blame us,
Those hours which we had not made good when the judgment
  o'ercame us.
They believed us and perished for it. Our statecraft, our learning
Delivered them bound to the Pit and alive to the burning
Whither they mirthfully hastened as jostling for honour –
Not since her birth has our Earth seen such worth loosed upon her.

Nor was their agony brief, or once only imposed on them.
  The wounded, the war-spent, the sick received no exemption:
  Being cured they returned and endured and achieved our
      redemption,
Hopeless themselves of relief, till Death, marvelling, closed on them.

That flesh we had nursed from the first in all cleanness was given
To corruption unveiled and assailed by the malice of Heaven –
By the heart-shaking jests of Decay where it lolled on the wires –
To be blanched or gay-painted by fumes – to be cindered by fires –
To be senselessly tossed and retossed in stale mutilation
    From crater to crater. For this we shall take expiation.

    But who shall return us our children?

RUDYARD KIPLING

A Diversity of Creatures (1917). Beneath Kipling's forceful public voice lies grief at the loss of his son. He was one of the very few civilian poets willing to describe battlefield horrors – the last stanza reflects his agonizing knowledge of what may have happened to his son's body, which was never found in Kipling's lifetime.

(158) Epitaph on an Army of Mercenaries

These, in the day when heaven was falling,
The hour when earth's foundations fled,
Followed their mercenary calling
And took their wages and are dead.

Their shoulders held the sky suspended;
They stood, and earth's foundations stay;
What God abandoned, these defended,
And saved the sum of things for pay.

A. E. HOUSMAN

Written, according to Housman himself, in September 1917. *The Times*, 31 October 1917, under a leader on 'The Anniversary of Ypres'. *Last Poems* (1922). While the Third Battle of Ypres (Passchendaele) was grinding on into the mud, the nation celebrated a more uplifting example of British courage, the third anniversary of Gheluvelt (*23*) and 'First Ypres'. Several newspapers carried commemorative verses; others did so on 15 December, the day of the Choral Commemoration (*116 note*).

The original BEF of 1914 consisted entirely of *mercenaries*, professional Regular soldiers; like Hercules, who for a time did Atlas's job of carrying the sky, they performed an essential task on behalf of others. Kipling thought the epitaph 'the finest lines of poetry written during the war' (A. Lycett, *Kipling*, 582).

(159) Dead Man's Dump

The plunging limbers over the shattered track
Racketed with their rusty freight,
Stuck out like many crowns of thorns,
And the rusty stakes like sceptres old
To stay the flood of brutish men
Upon our brothers dear.

The wheels lurched over sprawled dead
But pained them not, though their bones crunched,
Their shut mouths made no moan,
They lie there huddled, friend and foeman,
Man born of man, and born of woman,
And shells go crying over them
From night till night and now.

Earth has waited for them
All the time of their growth
Fretting for their decay:
Now she has them at last!
In the strength of their strength
Suspended – stopped and held.

What fierce imaginings their dark souls lit
Earth! have they gone into you?
Somewhere they must have gone,
And flung on your hard back
Is their souls' sack,
Emptied of God-ancestralled essences.
Who hurled them out? Who hurled?

None saw their spirits' shadow shake the grass,
Or stood aside for the half used life to pass
Out of those doomed nostrils and the doomed mouth,
When the swift iron burning bee
Drained the wild honey of their youth.

What of us, who flung on the shrieking pyre,
Walk, our usual thoughts untouched,
Our lucky limbs as on ichor fed,
Immortal seeming ever?
Perhaps when the flames beat loud on us,
A fear may choke in our veins
And the startled blood may stop.

The air is loud with death,
The dark air spurts with fire
The explosions ceaseless are.
Timelessly now, some minutes past,
These dead strode time with vigorous life,
Till the shrapnel called 'an end!'
But not to all. In bleeding pangs
Some borne on stretchers dreamed of home,
Dear things, war-blotted from their hearts.

A man's brains splattered on
A stretcher-bearer's face;
His shook shoulders slipped their load,
But when they bent to look again
The drowning soul was sunk too deep
For human tenderness.

They left this dead with the older dead,
Stretched at the cross roads.

Burnt black by strange decay
Their sinister faces lie
The lid over each eye,
The grass and coloured clay
More motion have than they,
Joined to the great sunk silences.

Here is one not long dead;
His dark hearing caught our far wheels,
And the choked soul stretched weak hands
To reach the living word the far wheels said,
The blood-dazed intelligence beating for light,
Crying through the suspense of the far torturing wheels
Swift for the end to break,
Or the wheels to break,
Cried as the tide of the world broke over his sight.

Will they come? Will they ever come?
Even as the mixed hoofs of the mules,
The quivering-bellied mules,
And the rushing wheels all mixed
With his tortured upturned sight,
So we crashed round the bend,
We heard his weak scream,
We heard his very last sound,
And our wheels grazed his dead face.

ISAAC ROSENBERG

Completed by May 1917. *Poems* (1922). Unlike many soldier-poets, Rosenberg really did write poems in the trenches: manuscripts of this and other poems are torn and muddy. He worked with impressive courage: 'I will not leave a corner of my consciousness covered up, but saturate myself with the strange and extraordinary conditions of this life, and it will all refine itself into poetry later' (August 1916).

limbers: wheeled, detachable sections of gun carriages, used for carrying barbed wire and other materials to the front.

crowns ... sceptres ... brutish: conventional wartime imagery, portraying Tommies as Christs and kings, and the enemy as brutish (but see Jon Silkin, *Out of Battle*, 281–2, for a different reading of these lines).

souls' sack: the body.

ichor: in Greek myth, fluid in the veins of the gods.

(160) Soldier: Twentieth Century

I love you, great new Titan!
Am I not you?
Napoleon and Caesar
Out of you grew.

Out of unthinkable torture,
Eyes kissed by death,
Won back to the world again,
Lost and won in a breath,

Cruel men are made immortal,
Out of your pain born.
They have stolen the sun's power
With their feet on your shoulders worn.

Let them shrink from your girth,
That has outgrown the pallid days,
When you slept like Circe's swine,
Or a word in the brain's ways.

ISAAC ROSENBERG

Written late 1917. *Poems* (1922). The Titans were giants who, in Greek myth, fought against Zeus in the first of all wars. The enchantress Circe turned Odysseus's sailors into swine.

(161) Daughters of War

Space beats the ruddy freedom of their limbs –
Their naked dances with man's spirit naked
By the root side of the tree of life
(The underside of things
And shut from earth's profoundest eyes).

I saw in prophetic gleams
These mighty daughters in their dances
Beckon each soul aghast from its crimson corpse
To mix in their glittering dances.
I heard the mighty daughters' giant sighs
In sleepless passion for the sons of valour,
And envy of the days of flesh
Barring their love with mortal boughs across, –

The mortal boughs – the mortal tree of life,
The old bark burnt with iron wars
They blow to a live flame
To char the young green days
And reach the occult soul; – they have no softer lure –
No softer lure than the savage ways of death.
We were satisfied of our Lords the moon and the sun
To take our wage of sleep and bread and warmth –
These maidens came – these strong ever-living Amazons,
And in an easy might their wrists
Of night's sway and noon's sway the sceptres brake,
Clouding the wild – the soft lustres of our eyes.

Clouding the wild lustres, the clinging tender lights;
Driving the darkness into the flame of day,
With the Amazonian wind of them
Over our corroding faces
That must be broken – broken for evermore
So the soul can leap out
Into their huge embraces.
Though there are human faces
Best sculptures of Deity,
And sinews lusted after
By the Archangels tall,
Even these must leap to the love-heat of these maidens
From the flame of terrene days,
Leaving grey ashes to the wind – to the wind.

One (whose great lifted face,
Where wisdom's strength and beauty's strength
And the thewed strength of large beasts
Moved and merged, gloomed and lit)
Was speaking, surely, as the earth-men's earth fell away;
Whose new hearing drunk the sound
Where pictures lutes and mountains mixed
With the loosed spirit of a thought,
Essenced to language, thus –

'My sisters force their males
From the doomed earth, from the doomed glee
And hankering of hearts.
Frail hands gleam up through the human quagmire, and
lips of ash
Seem to wail, as in sad faded paintings
Far sunken and strange.
My sisters have their males
Clean of the dust of old days
That clings about those white hands
And yearns in those voices sad.
But these shall not see them,
Or think of them in any days or years,
They are my sisters' lovers in other days and years.'

ISAAC ROSENBERG

Begun c. October 1916, completed after June 1917. *Poems* (1922). Rosenberg saw this as his most important poem, although he knew it was obscure. 'The end is an attempt to imagine the severance of all human relationship and the fading away of human love'; 'I have ... striven to get that sense of inexorableness the human (or unhuman) side of this war has. It even penetrates behind human life for the "Amazon" who speaks ... is imagined to be without her lover yet, while all her sisters have theirs, the released spirits of the slain earth men.'

(162) After the Battle

So they are satisfied with our Brigade,
   And it remains to parcel out the bays!
And we shall have the usual Thanks Parade,
   The beaming General, and the soapy praise.

You will come up in your capacious car
　To find your heroes sulking in the rain,
To tell us how magnificent we are,
　And how you hope we'll do the same again.

And we, who knew your old abusive tongue,
　Who heard you hector us a week before,
We who have bled to boost you up a rung –
　A KCB perhaps, perhaps a Corps –

We who must mourn those spaces in the Mess
　And somehow fill those hollows in the heart,
We do not want your Sermon on Success,
　Your greasy benisons on Being Smart.

We only want to take our wounds away
　To some warm village where the tumult ends,
And drowsing in the sunshine many a day,
　Forget our aches, forget that we had friends.

Weary we are of blood and noise and pain;
　This was a week we shall not soon forget;
And if, indeed, we have to fight again,
　We little wish to think about it yet.

We have done well; we like to hear it said.
　Say it, and then, for God's sake, say no more.
Fight, if you must, fresh battles far ahead,
　But keep them dark behind your chateau door!

A. P. HERBERT

New Statesman, 30 June 1917. *The Bomber Gipsy* (1918).

(163) Beaucourt Revisited

I wandered up to Beaucourt; I took the river track,
And saw the lines we lived in before the Boche went back;
But Peace was now in Pottage, the front was far ahead,
The front had journeyed Eastward, and only left the dead.

And I thought, How long we lay there, and watched across the wire,
While the guns roared round the valley, and set the skies afire!
But now there are homes in Hamel and tents in the Vale of Hell,
And a camp at Suicide Corner, where half a regiment fell.

The new troops follow after, and tread the land we won,
To them 'tis so much hillside re-wrested from the Hun;
We only walk with reverence this sullen mile of mud;
The shell-holes hold our history, and half of them our blood.

Here, at the head of Peche Street, 'twas death to show your face;
To me it seemed like magic to linger in the place;
For me how many spirits hung round the Kentish Caves,
But the new men see no spirits – they only see the graves.

I found the half-dug ditches we fashioned for the fight,
We lost a score of men there – young James was killed that night;
I saw the star shells staring, I heard the bullets hail,
But the new troops pass unheeding – they never heard the tale.

I crossed the blood-red ribbon, that once was No-Man's Land,
I saw a misty daybreak and a creeping minute-hand;
And here the lads went over, and there was Harmsworth shot,
And here was William lying – but the new men know them not.

And I said, 'There is still the river, and still the stiff, stark trees,
To treasure here our story, but there are only these';
But under the white wood crosses the dead men answered low,
'The new men know not Beaucourt, but we are here – we know.'

A. P. HERBERT

The Mudhook: Journal of the 63rd Division, September 1917. The Bomber Gipsy (1918).
The Royal Naval Division captured Beaucourt in November 1916 at heavy cost: out of
400 men, fewer than twenty answered the roll-call that night. Casualties included
Herbert's close friends James Cook and William Ker, and Vere Harmsworth, son of Lord
Rothermere.
   The language (fight, tale, treasure) and ballad metre are heroic, but, as so often in the
war's poetry, the heroism lies in sacrifice, not killing, to be understood and celebrated –
as in the previous poem – only by men who have taken part.

(164) In Memoriam

*Private D. Sutherland killed in action in the German
trench, May 16 1916, and the others who died*

So you were David's father
And he was your only son,
And the new-cut peats are rotting
And the work is left undone,
Because of an old man weeping,
Just an old man in pain,
For David, his son David,
That will not come again.

Oh, the letters he wrote you,
And I can see them still,
Not a word of the fighting
But just the sheep on the hill
And how you should get the crops in
Ere the year got stormier,
And the Bosches have got his body,
And I was his officer.

You were only David's father.
But I had fifty sons
When we went up in the evening
Under the arch of the guns,
And we came back at twilight –
O God! I heard them call
To me for help and pity
That could not help at all.

Oh, never will I forget you,
My men that trusted me,
More my sons than your fathers',
For they could only see
The little helpless babies
And the young men in their pride.
They could not see you dying,
And hold you while you died.

Happy and young and gallant,
They saw their first-born go,
But not the strong limbs broken
And the beautiful men brought low,
The piteous writhing bodies,
The screamed, 'Don't leave me, Sir,'
For they were only your fathers
But I was your officer.

E. A. MACKINTOSH

A Highland Regiment (1917). An officer's first duty was to care for his men, a duty
ultimately based on love as many wartime documents testify (see, for example, Donald
Hankey, *A Student in Arms*, 1916, a much admired book reprinted a dozen times in its
first year).

Young officer-poets who wrote about their men often used the language of love
poetry – cf. (*146 note*). Mackintosh had carried the badly wounded Sutherland out of
a German trench, pursued by the enemy, but the man had died before he could be got
to safety.

(165) To Sylvia

Two months ago the skies were blue,
The fields were fresh and green,
And green the willow tree stood up,
With the lazy stream between.

Two months ago we sat and watched
The river drifting by –
And now – you're back at your work again
And here in a ditch I lie.

God knows – my dear – I did not want
To rise and leave you so,
But the dead men's hands were beckoning
And I knew that I must go.

The dead men's eyes were watching, lass,
Their lips were asking too,
We faced it out and paid the price –
Are we betrayed by you?

The days are long between, dear lass,
Before we meet again,
Long days of mud and work for me,
For you long care and pain.

But you'll forgive me yet, my dear,
Because of what you know,
I can look my dead friends in the face
As I couldn't two months ago.

E. A. MACKINTOSH

Dated 20 October 1917. The dedicatory poem in *War, the Liberator* (1918). Mackintosh became engaged to Sylvia Marsh in 1917 while teaching cadets in Cambridge. He returned to the trenches in October and was killed a month later.

(166) Death

Because I have made light of death
And mocked at wounds and pain,
The doom is laid on me to die –
Like the humble men in days gone by –
That angered me to hear them cry
For pity to me in vain.

I shall not go out suddenly
As many a man has done.
But I shall lie as those men lay –
Longing for death the whole long day –
Praying as I heard those men pray,
And none shall heed me, none.

The fierce waves will go surging on
Before they tend to me.
Oh, God of battles I pray you send
No word of pity – no help, no friend,
That if my spirit break at the end
None may be there to see.

E. A. MACKINTOSH

War, the Liberator (1918).

(167) War, the Liberator

(To the Authoress of 'Non-Combatants')

Surely War is vile to you, you who can but know of it,
Broken men and broken hearts, and boys too young to die,
You that never knew its joy, never felt the glow of it,
Valour and the pride of men, soaring to the sky.

Death's a fearful thing to you, terrible in suddenness,
Lips that will not laugh again, tongues that will not sing,
You that have not ever seen their sudden life of happiness,
The moment they looked down on death, a cowed and beaten thing.

Say what life would theirs have been, that it should make you weep for them,
A small grey world imprisoning the wings of their desire?
Happier than they could tell who knew not life would keep for them
Fragments of the high Romance, the old Heroic fire.
All they dreamed of childishly, bravery and fame for them,
Charges at the cannon's mouth, enemies they slew,
Bright across the waking world their romances came for them,
Is not life a little price when our dreams come true?

All the terrors of the night, doubts and thoughts tormenting us,
Boy-minds painting quiveringly the awful face of fear,
These are gone for ever now, truth is come contenting us,
Night with all its tricks is gone and our eyes are clear.
Now in all the time to come, memory will cover us,
Trenches that we did not lose, charges that we made,
Since a voice, when first we heard shells go shrilling over us,
Said within us, 'This is Death – and I am not afraid!'

Since we felt our spirits tower, smiling and contemptuous,
O'er the little frightened things, running to and fro,
Looked on Death and saw a slave blustering and presumptuous,
Daring vainly still to bring Man his master low.
Though we knew that at the last, he would have his lust of us,
Carelessly we braved his might, felt and knew not why
Something stronger than ourselves, moving in the dust of us,
Something in the Soul of Man still too great to die.

E. A. MACKINTOSH

War, the Liberator (1918). Said to be Mackintosh's last poem, probably written in October
1917. A remarkable statement, confidently expressed in strong rhythms and rhymes.
   '*Non-combatants*': a poem by Evelyn Underhill (*Theophanies*, 1916) about the
uncomplaining bravery of women who allow their men to face the terrors of war.
By contrast, also in October, Owen was writing 'Dulce et Decorum Est' (*182*),
attacking another woman poet for celebrating the glory of war.

(168) To His Love

He's gone, and all our plans
   Are useless indeed.
We'll walk no more on Cotswold
   Where the sheep feed
   Quietly and take no heed.

His body that was so quick
   Is not as you
Knew it, on Severn river
   Under the blue
   Driving our small boat through.

You would not know him now ...
   But still he died
Nobly, so cover him over
   With violets of pride
   Purple from Severn side.

Cover him, cover him soon!
   And with thick-set
Masses of memoried flowers –
   Hide that red wet
   Thing I must somehow forget.

IVOR GURNEY

Completed late 1917 at a camp in Northumberland. *War's Embers* (1919). Said to refer to Gurney's friend F. W. Harvey, although Gurney had long known that Harvey had been captured, not killed.

(169) *from* Rhapsode

Why should we sing to you of little things –
You who lack all imagination?
[...]

You hope that we shall tell you that they found
    their happiness in fighting,
Or that they died with a song on their lips,
Or that we shall use the old familiar phrases
With which your paid servants please you in
    the Press:
But we are poets,
And shall tell the truth.

OSBERT SITWELL

Dated September 1917. *Nation*, 27 October 1917. *Argonaut and Juggernaut* (1919).
Extract from an 87-line poem. Like his friend Sassoon, Sitwell was one of the few
soldier-poets to voice political opposition to the war in 1917.

(170) The Modern Abraham

To Siegfried Sassoon

His purple fingers clutch a large cigar –
    Plump, mottled fingers, with a ring or two.
He rests back in his fat armchair. The war
    Has made this change in him. As he looks through
His cheque-book with a tragic look he sighs:
    'Disabled Soldiers' Fund' he reads afresh,
And through his meat-red face peer angry eyes –
    The spirit piercing through its mound of flesh.

They should not ask me to subscribe again!
   Consider me and all that I have done –
I've fought for Britain with my might and main;
   I make explosives – and I gave a son.
My factory, converted for the fight
   (I do not like to boast of what I've spent),
Now manufactures gas and dynamite,
   Which only pays me seventy per cent.
And if I had ten other sons to send
   I'd make them serve my country to the end,
So all the neighbours should flock round and say:
   'Oh! look what Mr Abraham has done.
He loves his country in the elder way;
   Poor gentleman, he's lost another son!'

OSBERT SITWELL

Dated 1917. *Nation*, 2 February 1918. *Argonaut and Juggernaut* (1919). Dedicated to
Sassoon, whose satires were the model for Sitwell's. Both poets had painful memories
of their own fathers. Owen, who would certainly have known this poem, wrote his
own version in 1918, 'The Parable of the Old Man and the Young'. For the original
story, see Genesis 22:1–14.

(171) The Diners

'It isn't good enough,' you said;
   'They send us out to face the flame
For these whose rotten souls are dead,
   These beasts who've sold themselves to shame.

'And must we fall, as others fell,
   And add our quota to the dust,
To royalise this house of hell,
   To keep ajar the doors of lust?'

You said, 'The powder on that face,
   Those sensual lips, that painted hair,
We fight to save them from disgrace,
   To keep such sacred honour fair.

'Her honour spotless must abide,
   Tho' God should hide his face from earth:
That flabby-finger'd man beside –
   I guess he knows her honour's worth!

'I guess the reptile understands
   What women are, when lights are dim
And men wear diamonds on their hands –
   And so she's sold herself to him!'

You ceased. I look'd around the hall,
   Above the music and the din
I thought I heard dead voices call
   While haunting, tortured eyes looked in.

ALFRED NORMAN

Dated Hull, September 1917. *Ditchling Beacon* (1918). Norman, an airman, was killed
in 1918.

(172) *from* The Other Side

Being a letter from Major Average of the Royal Field Artillery in Flanders,
acknowledging a presentation copy of a book of war-verse, written by a former
subaltern of his battery – now in England

[...]
Lord, if I'd half *your* brains, I'd write a book:
None of your sentimental platitudes,
But something real, vital; that should strip
The glamour from this outrage we call war,
Showing it naked, hideous, stupid, vile –
One vast abomination. So that they
Who, coming after, till the ransomed fields
Where our lean corpses rotted in the ooze,
Reading my written words, should understand
This stark stupendous horror, visualize
The unutterable foulness of it all...
I'd show them, not your glamorous 'glorious game',
Which men play 'jesting' 'for their honour's sake' –
(A kind of Military Tournament,
With just a hint of danger – bound in cloth!) –
But War, – as war is now, and always was:
A dirty, loathsome, servile murder-job: –
Men, lousy, sleepless, ulcerous, afraid,
Toiling their hearts out in the pulling slime
That wrenches gumboot down from bleeding heel
And cakes in itching armpits, navel, ears:
Men stunned to brainlessness, and gibbering:
Men driving men to death and worse than death:
Men maimed and blinded: men against machines –
Flesh versus iron, concrete, flame and wire:
Men choking out their souls in poison-gas:
Men squelched into the slime by trampling feet:
Men, disembowelled by guns five miles away,
Cursing, with their last breath, the living God
Because he made them, in His image, men ...

So – were your talent mine – I'd write of war
For those who, coming after, know it not.

And if posterity should ask of me
What high, what base emotions keyed weak flesh
To face such torments, I would answer: 'You!
Not for themselves, O daughters, grandsons, sons,
Your tortured forebears wrought this miracle;
Not for themselves, *accomplished utterly*
This loathliest task of murderous servitude;
But just because they realized that thus,
And only thus, by sacrifice, might they
Secure a world worth living in – *for you*.'...

Good-night, my soldier-poet. *Dormez bien!*

GILBERT FRANKAU

Extract from a 170-line poem dated 'The Barn, 31/10/17'. *The Judgement of Valhalla*
(March 1918). Realism, however harsh, does not necessarily indicate opposition to the
war. Like West (*126*), Frankau loathes *sentimental platitudes*, and like Sitwell (*169*) he
wants to *tell the truth*, but unlike them he believes fervently in the war.
  The Barn: at Kidmore End, near Reading, where Frankau was convalescing. By odd
coincidence, the local doctor, named Gandy, treated two poets who were at opposite
political extremes: Frankau in 1917 and Owen, who had cousins in the village, in 1912.

(173) The Deserter

'I'm sorry I done it, Major.'
We bandaged the livid face;
And led him out, ere the wan sun rose,
To die his death of disgrace.

The bolt-heads locked to the cartridge;
The rifles steadied to rest,
As cold stock nestled at colder cheek
And foresight lined on the breast.

'*Fire!*' called the Sergeant-Major.
The muzzles flamed as he spoke:
And the shameless soul of a nameless man
Went up in the cordite-smoke.

GILBERT FRANKAU

Dated 'The Barn, 6/12/17'. *The Judgement of Valhalla* (1918). Taken on its own, this poem has sometimes been read as ironic, even pitying. But it is the introduction to a longer, pitiless poem, 'The Judgement of Valhalla', in which the deserter's soul seeks admission to the hall of dead heroes and is contemptuously refused: 'they will not drink with a coward's soul, the stark red men who slew'.

(174) The Rear-Guard

Groping along the tunnel, step by step,
 He winked his prying torch with patching glare
From side to side, and sniffed the unwholesome air.

Tins, boxes, bottles, shapes too vague to know;
A mirror smashed, the mattress from a bed;
And he, exploring fifty feet below
The rosy gloom of battle overhead.

Tripping, he grabbed the wall; saw someone lie
Humped at his feet, half-hidden by a rug,
And stooped to give the sleeper's arm a tug.
'I'm looking for headquarters.' No reply.
'God blast your neck!' (For days he'd had no sleep.)
'Get up and guide me through this stinking place.'
Savage, he kicked a soft, unanswering heap,
And flashed his beam across the livid face
Terribly glaring up, whose eyes yet wore
Agony dying hard ten days before;
And fists of fingers clutched a blackening wound.

Alone he staggered on until he found
Dawn's ghost that filtered down a shafted stair
To the dazed, muttering creatures underground
Who hear the boom of shells in muffled sound.
At last, with sweat of horror in his hair,
He climbed through darkness to the twilight air,
Unloading hell behind him step by step.

SIEGFRIED SASSOON

Written in a London hospital, 22 April 1917, six days after Sassoon had been wounded
in the shoulder. *The Hydra: Journal of the Craiglockhart War Hospital*, 15 September 1917
(Owen, the current editor, must have chosen the poem: he had introduced himself to
Sassoon in August). *Counter-Attack* (1918). On 23 April Sassoon wrote that 'a curse is
on my head, / That shall not be unsaid' ('To the Warmongers'): he had come back
from France determined to tell the truth about 'horrors from the abyss'.

(175) Does It Matter?

Does it matter? – losing your legs? ...
For people will always be kind,
And you need not show that you mind
When the others come in after hunting
To gobble their muffins and eggs.

Does it matter? – losing your sight? ...
There's such splendid work for the blind;
And people will always be kind,
As you sit on the terrace remembering
And turning your face to the light.

Do they matter? – those dreams from the pit? …
You can drink and forget and be glad,
And people won't say that you're mad;
For they'll know that you've fought for your country
And no one will worry a bit.

SIEGFRIED SASSOON

This and the next eight poems were written at Craiglockhart, autumn 1917.
Cambridge Magazine, 6 October 1917. *Counter-Attack* (1918). Sassoon made his
public protest against the war in July 1917, encouraged by civilian pacifists. The
authorities announced he was shellshocked and sent him to Craiglockhart, where
he wrote many of his most savage anti-war poems.

(176) Fight to a Finish

The boys came back. Bands played and flags were flying,
    And Yellow-Pressmen thronged the sunlit street
To cheer the soldiers who'd refrained from dying,
    And hear the music of returning feet.
'Of all the thrills and ardours War has brought,
This moment is the finest.' (So they thought.)

Snapping their bayonets on to charge the mob,
    Grim Fusiliers broke ranks with glint of steel,
At last the boys had found a cushy job.

* * *

I heard the Yellow-Pressmen grunt and squeal;
And with my trusty bombers turned and went
To clear those Junkers out of Parliament.

SIEGFRIED SASSOON

Cambridge Magazine, 27 October 1917. *Counter-Attack* (1918).
  Title: see (*154*).
  Yellow-Pressmen: journalists working for jingoist newspapers (*John Bull, Daily Mail* and others).
  Junkers: Prussian gentry, regarded as archetypal militarists.

(177) Glory of Women

You love us when we're heroes, home on leave,
Or wounded in a mentionable place.
You worship decorations; you believe
That chivalry redeems the war's disgrace.
You make us shells. You listen with delight,
By tales of dirt and danger fondly thrilled.
You crown our distant ardours while we fight,
And mourn our laurelled memories when we're killed.
You can't believe that British troops 'retire'
When hell's last horror breaks them, and they run,
Trampling the terrible corpses – blind with blood.
    O German mother dreaming by the fire,
While you are knitting socks to send your son
His face is trodden deeper in the mud.

SIEGFRIED SASSOON

Cambridge Magazine, 8 December 1917. *Counter-Attack* (1918). Women's ignorance of front-line conditions was often satirized by soldier-poets.

(178) Banishment

I am banished from the patient men who fight.
They smote my heart to pity, built my pride.
Shoulder to aching shoulder, side by side,
They trudged away from life's broad wealds of light.
Their wrongs were mine; and ever in my sight
They went arrayed in honour. But they died, –
Not one by one: and mutinous I cried
To those who sent them out into the night.

The darkness tells how vainly I have striven
To free them from the pit where they must dwell
In outcast gloom convulsed and jagged and riven
By grappling guns. Love drove me to rebel.
Love drives me back to grope with them through hell;
And in their tortured eyes I stand forgiven.

SIEGFRIED SASSOON

Counter-Attack (1918). Sassoon's *mutinous* protest had been deplored by many of his
fellow-soldiers, and he felt more and more guilty at being safely out of the fighting.
In the end he thought his protest had been ill-advised, perhaps even mistaken. In
December 1917, driven by love, duty and shame, he returned to active service.

(179) Anthem for Doomed Youth

What passing-bells for these who die as cattle?
 Only the monstrous anger of the guns.
Only the stuttering rifles' rapid rattle
 Can patter out their hasty orisons.
No mockeries for them; no prayers nor bells,
 Nor any voice of mourning save the choirs, –
The shrill, demented choirs of wailing shells;
 And bugles calling for them from sad shires.

What candles may be held to speed them all?
  Not in the hands of boys, but in their eyes
  Shall shine the holy glimmers of goodbyes.
The pallor of girls' brows shall be their pall;
  Their flowers the tenderness of silent minds,
  And each slow dusk a drawing-down of blinds.

WILFRED OWEN

Written September 1917. *Poems* (1920). Sassoon suggested the words 'Anthem' and
'Doomed', and altered 'our guns' to 'the guns', making the phrase less anti-German.
But Owen had not yet fully absorbed his new friend's ideas. The consolatory last line
undermines the anger of the first (see Silkin, 210–11).
   Much of the imagery comes from patriotic war literature – for example, Brice
(*monstrous guns* [*116*]; Ian Hay, *The First Hundred Thousand*, a very popular 1915 novel,
in which a machine gun begins to '*patter* out a *stuttering* malediction'; Binyon, 'For the
Fallen', 1914 ('At the going down of the sun ... / We will remember them').
   silent minds: Sassoon altered Owen's 'silent' to 'patient' in the manuscript; Blunden's
1931 edition prefers 'silent', but other editors have reverted to 'patient'.

(180) The Next War

'War's a joke for me and you,
While we know such dreams are true.' – Sassoon

Out there, we've walked quite friendly up to Death;
  Sat down and eaten with him, cool and bland, –
  Pardoned his spilling mess-tins in our hand.
We've sniffed the green thick odour of his breath, –
Our eyes wept, but our courage didn't writhe.
  He's spat at us with bullets and he's coughed
  Shrapnel. We chorused when he sang aloft;
We whistled while he shaved us with his scythe.

Oh, Death was never enemy of ours!
  We laughed at him, we leagued with him, old chum.
No soldier's paid to kick against his powers.
  We laughed, knowing that better men would come,
And greater wars; when each proud fighter brags
He wars on Death – for Life; not men – for flags.

WILFRED OWEN

Published anonymously (by Owen as editor, text as above) in *The Hydra*, 29 September 1917. *Art and Letters*, spring 1920. *Poems* (1931).
  Epigraph: from Sassoon, 'A Letter Home' (addressed to Robert Graves).
we: Owen had probably been (unfairly) accused of cowardice in May and was now being treated for shellshock, but here, with new-found confidence, he associates himself with Sassoon and Graves, not only as poets but also as experienced, courageous soldiers.

(181) Inspection

'You! What d'you mean by this?' I rapped.
'You dare come on parade like this?'
'Please, sir, it's– ' ' 'Old yer mouth,' the sergeant snapped.
'I take 'is name, sir?' – 'Please, and then dismiss.'

Some days 'confined to camp' he got
For being 'dirty on parade'.
He told me, afterwards, the damned spot
Was blood, his own. 'Well, blood is dirt,' I said.

'Blood's dirt,' he laughed, looking away
Far off to where his wound had bled
And almost merged for ever into clay.
'The world is washing out its stains,' he said.
'It doesn't like our cheeks so red.
Young blood's its great objection.
But when we're duly white-washed, being dead,
The race will bear Field-Marshal God's inspection.'

WILFRED OWEN

Undated, but in Sassoon's style and almost certainly written at Craiglockhart.
Poems (1931).
   damned spot: *Macbeth*, V.i. Like many soldiers, Lady Macbeth has killed: the blood she
sees on her hand is a sign of guilt that cannot be washed away. But soldiers were also
often portrayed as sacrificial victims, their blood cleansing the world of its sins (*stains*).
   white-washed: kerbs and bollards in a camp had to be whitewashed before a general
inspection, much to the troops' exasperation.

(182) Dulce et Decorum Est

Bent double, like old beggars under sacks,
Knock-kneed, coughing like hags, we cursed through sludge,
Till on the haunting flares we turned our backs
And towards our distant rest began to trudge.
Men marched asleep. Many had lost their boots
But limped on, blood-shod. All went lame; all blind;
Drunk with fatigue; deaf even to the hoots
Of tired, outstripped Five-Nines that dropped behind.

Gas! GAS! Quick, boys! – An ecstasy of fumbling,
Fitting the clumsy helmets just in time;
But someone still was yelling out and stumbling,
And flound'ring like a man in fire or lime ...
Dim, through the misty panes and thick green light,
As under a green sea, I saw him drowning.

In all my dreams, before my helpless sight,
He plunges at me, guttering, choking, drowning.

If in some smothering dreams you too could pace
Behind the wagon that we flung him in,
And watch the white eyes writhing in his face,
His hanging face, like a devil's sick of sin;
If you could hear, at every jolt, the blood
Come gargling from the froth-corrupted lungs,
Obscene as cancer, bitter as the cud
Of vile, incurable sores on innocent tongues, –
My friend, you would not tell with such high zest
To children ardent for some desperate glory,
The old Lie: Dulce et decorum est
Pro patria mori.

WILFRED OWEN

Written October 1917. *Poems* (1920). Since the 1960s, perhaps the most famous poem of the war, but Owen has not yet reached his final, mature voice.

Title: Horace, *Odes* III.ii.13. 'It is sweet and meet to die for one's country' (Owen's translation).

Five-Nines: 5.9 calibre shells.

My friend: Jessie Pope – see (*34 note*).

(183) Apologia pro Poemate Meo

I, too, saw God through mud, –
    The mud that cracked on cheeks when wretches smiled.
    War brought more glory to their eyes than blood,
    And gave their laughs more glee than shakes a child.

Merry it was to laugh there –
    Where death becomes absurd and life absurder.
    For power was on us as we slashed bones bare
    Not to feel sickness or remorse of murder.

I, too, have dropped off fear –
    Behind the barrage, dead as my platoon,
    And sailed my spirit surging, light and clear
    Past the entanglement where hopes lay strewn;

And witnessed exultation –
    Faces that used to curse me, scowl for scowl,
    Shine and lift up with passion of oblation,
    Seraphic for an hour; though they were foul.

I have made fellowships –
    Untold of happy lovers in old song.
    For love is not the binding of fair lips
    With the soft silk of eyes that look and long,

By Joy, whose ribbon slips, –
    But wound with war's hard wire whose stakes are strong;
    Bound with the bandage of the arm that drips;
    Knit in the webbing of the rifle-thong.

I have perceived much beauty
    In the hoarse oaths that kept our courage straight;
    Heard music in the silentness of duty;
    Found peace where shell-storms spouted reddest spate.

Nevertheless, except you share
    With them in hell the sorrowful dark of hell,
    Whose world is but the trembling of a flare,
    And heaven but as the highway for a shell,

You shall not hear their mirth:
  You shall not come to think them well content
  By any jest of mine. These men are worth
  Your tears. You are not worth their merriment.

WILFRED OWEN

Poems (1920). Probably written in Scarborough, December 1917. One draft is dated November 1917, but the poem seems to be an answer to advice from Graves in December to 'cheer up and write more optimistically ... a poet should have a spirit above wars' (*I, too, have ... sailed my spirit* ...). Graves thought Owen needed to move away from Sassoon's influence: his advice is already beginning to take effect.

   Title: 'A defence of my poem' – probably the first version of 'A Terre' (*191*), which Graves had just seen.

(184) Unidentified

Look well at this man. Look!
Come up out of your graves, philosophers,
And you who founded churches, and all you
Who for ten thousand years have talked of God.
Come out of your uncomfortable tombs, astronomers,
Who raked the heavens with your mighty eyes,
And died, unanswered questions on your lips,
For you have something interesting to learn
By looking at this man.

Stand all about, you many-legioned ghosts;
Fill up the desert with your shadowy forms,
And in the vast resounding waste of death,
Watch him while he dies;
He will not notice you.
Observe his ugliness.
See how he stands there planted in the mud like some old battered
    image of a faith forgotten by its God.

Note his naked neck and jutting jaw under the iron hat that's jammed
    upon his head;
See how he rounds his shoulders, bends his back inside his clumsy coat;
And how he leans ahead, gripping with grimy fists
The muzzle of his gun that digs its butt-end down into the mud
    between the solid columns of his legs.

Look close, come close, pale ghosts!
Come back out of the dim unfinished past;
Crowd up across the edges of the earth,
Where the horizon, like a red hot wire, twists underneath tremendous
    smoking blows.
Come up, come up across the quaking ground that gapes in sudden
    holes beneath your feet;
Come fearlessly across the twisting field where bones of men stick
    through the tortured mud.
Ghosts have no need to fear.

Look close at this man. Look!
He waits for death;
He watches it approach;
His little bloodshot eyes can see it bearing down on every side;
He feels it coming underneath his feet, running, burrowing underneath
    the ground;
He hears it screaming in the frantic air.
Death that tears the shrieking sky in two,
That suddenly explodes out of the festering bowels of the earth –
Dreadful and horrid death.
He takes the impact of it on his back, his chest, his belly and his arms;
Spreads his legs upon its lurching form;
Plants his feet upon its face and breathes deep into his pumping lungs
    the gassy breath of death.
He does not move.
In all the running landscape there's a solitary thing that's motionless:
The figure of this man.

The sky long since has fallen from its dome.
Terror let loose like a gigantic wind has torn it from the ceiling of the
    world,
And it is flapping down in frantic shreds.
The earth ages ago leaped screaming up out of the fastness of its
    ancient laws.
There is no centre now to hold it down.
It rolls and writhes, a shifting tortured thing, a floating mass of matter
    set adrift.
And in between the fluttering tatters of the ruined sky,
And the convulsions of the maddened earth,
The man stands solid.
Something holds him there.

What holds him, timid ghosts?
What do you say, you shocked and shuddering ghosts,
Dragged from your sheltered vaults;
You who once died in quiet lamp-lit rooms;
Who were companioned to the end by friends;
And closed your eyes in languor on a world
That you had fashioned for your pleasant selves?
You scorned this man.
He was for you an ordinary man.
Some of you pitied him, prayed over his soul, worried him with stories
    of Heaven and Hell.
Promised him Heaven if he would be ashamed of being what he was,
And everlasting sorrow if he died as he had lived, an ordinary man.
You gave him Gods he could not know, and images of God; laws he
    could not keep, and punishment.
You were afraid of him.
Everything about him that was his very own
Made you afraid of him.
His love of women, food and drink, and fun,
His clumsy reach for life, his open grabbing fist,
His stupid open gaping heart and mouth.
He was a hungry man,
And you were afraid of him.
None of you trusted him;
No one of you was his friend.

Look at him now. Look well, look long.
Your hungry brute, your ordinary man;
Your fornicator, drunkard, anarchist;
Your ruthless rough seed-sowing male;
Your angry greedy egotist;
Your lost, bewildered, childish dunce;
'Come close and look into his haggard face.
It is too late to do him justice now, or even speak to him.
But look.
Look at the stillness of his face.
It's made of little fragile bones and flesh, tissued of quivering muscles
    fine as silk;
Exquisite nerves, soft membrane warm with blood,
That travels smoothly through the tender veins.
One blow, one minute more, and that man's face will be a mass of
    matter, horrid slime and little brittle splinters.
He knows.
He waits.
His face remains quite still.
And underneath the bullet-spattered helmet on his head
His steady eyes look out.
What is it that looks out?
What is deep mirrored in those bloodshot eyes?
Terror? No.
Despair? Perhaps.
What else?
Ah, poor ghosts – poor blind unseeing ghosts!
It is his self you see;
His self that does remember what he loved and what he wanted, and
    what he never had;
His self that can regret, that can reproach its own self now; his self that
    gave itself, let loose its hold of all but just itself.
Is that, then, nothing? Just his naked self, pinning down a shaking
    world,
A single rivet driven down to hold a universe together.

Go back, poor ghosts. Go back into your graves.
He has no use for you, this nameless man.
Scholars, philosophers, men of God, leave this man alone.
No lamp you lit will show his soul the way;
No name restore his lost identity.
The guns will chant his death march down the world;
The flare of cannon light his dying;
The mute and nameless men beneath his feet will welcome him beside
    them in the mud.
Take one last look and leave him standing there,
Unfriended, unrewarded, and unknown.

MARY BORDEN

English Review, December 1917. *The Forbidden Zone* (1929). Borden (an American heiress married to a British missionary and later to a senior British general) financed, directed and worked in a field hospital for French soldiers for much of the war. Her poem, in the style of Walt Whitman, describes a French *poilu*, recognizably akin to the soldiers in Henri Barbusse's *Le Feu* (1916), the grim anti-war novel that also influenced Owen and Sassoon in 1917. Yet, angry though the poem is, the 'unidentified' man can be seen as a prototype for that sanctified, post-war hero, the Unknown Warrior.

1918

The year began quietly on the Western Front. Britain and France were recovering from their 1917 campaigns; America was still training its troops and increasing their numbers; and Germany was negotiating final peace terms with Communist Russia. For some it was a period of reflection. In January President Wilson announced his 'Fourteen Points', laying down principles of national self-determination, collective security, open diplomacy, free trade and international justice. Lloyd George at last set out British war aims, taking care to echo some of the President's ideas. Some poets, including Owen at home and Read at the front, had time to think about their poetic aims.

But on 21 March a huge military crisis broke in France. Having dictated crippling peace terms to Russia and moved seventy divisions westwards, Germany launched the first of a series of massive attacks, forcing the Allies to retreat in chaos. Trench warfare abruptly ended as the Western Front became mobile again for the first time since 1914. In the next two months daily British casualty rates exceeded those of the Somme or Passchendaele. Among the dead was one of the war's most outstanding poets, Isaac Rosenberg. On 12 April Field Marshal Haig issued his famous order forbidding retreat: 'With our backs to the wall, and believing in the justice of our cause, each one of us must fight to the end.'

The mood at home was grave, and many poets responded to it,

some rallying to the cause in language like that of 1914, some reacting angrily to the surge of patriotic rhetoric, some struggling against despair. Even Sassoon accepted that there was no longer any chance for peace negotiations nor any use for further protest. Owen wrote some of his most profound poems, elegies for the present and warnings for the future.

By July the Germans had suffered over half a million casualties and their advance was faltering. The Allies, their command now unified under the French General Foch, launched successful counter-offensives, including a series of well-planned, flexible attacks by Haig in August. The German population was facing starvation as a result of the blockade, and their front-line troops, who were subsisting on very poor rations, began surrendering in large numbers. On 4 November the British crossed the Sambre canal, a success that finally persuaded Germany to seek an armistice. One of the casualties during the crossing was Owen, perhaps the last soldier-poet to be killed in the war. Turkey and Austria capitulated, and on 9 November the Kaiser abdicated. As the British armies reached Mons, scene of their first engagement in 1914, a German political delegation signed the armistice in the early hours of 11 November, and at eleven o'clock fighting on the Western Front came to an end. Celebrations erupted in the Allied capitals and church bells rang out, but in the victorious armies – and in the poetry of the survivors – the response was rather quieter.

(185) *from* **Footsloggers**

To C. F. G. M.

I

What is love of one's land? ...

I don't know very well.

It is something that sleeps
For a year – for a day –
For a month – something that keeps
Very hidden and quiet and still
And then takes
The quiet heart like a wave,
The quiet brain like a spell,
The quiet will
Like a tornado; and that shakes
The whole of the soul.
[...]

V

Well, of course

One loves one's men. One takes a mort of trouble
To get them spick and span upon parades:
You strafe them, slang them, mediate between
Their wives and loves, and you inspect their toenails
And wangle leaves for them from the Adjutant
Until your Company office is your home
And all your mind ...

This is the way it goes:

First your Platoon and then your Company,9
Then the Battalion, then Brigade, Division,
And the whole BEF in France ... and then
Our Land, with its burden of civilians,
Who take it out of us as little dogs
Worry Newfoundlands ...

So, in the Flanders mud,
We bear the State upon our rain-soaked backs,
Breathe life into the State from our rattling lungs,
Anoint the State with the rivulets of sweat
From our tin helmets.
[...]

IX

For me, going out to France
Is like the exhaustion of dawn
After a dance ...
You have rushed around to get your money,
To get your revolver, complete your equipment;
You have had your moments, sweeter – ah, sweeter than honey;
You have got your valise all ready for shipment:
You have gone to confession and wangled your blessing,
You have bought your air-pillow and sewn in your coat
A pocket to hold your first field-dressing,
And you've paid the leech who bled you, the vampire ...
And you've been to the Theatre and the Empire,
And you've bidden goodbye to the band and the goat ...
And, like a ship that floats free of her berth,
There's nothing that holds you now to the earth,
And you're near enough to a yawn ...
'Good luck' and 'Goodbye' it has been, and 'So long, old chap'
'Cheerio: you'll be back in a month' – 'You'll have driven the
    Huns off the map.'
And one little pressure of the hand
From the thing you love next to the love of the land,
Since you leave her, out of love of your land ...
But that little, long, gentle and eloquent pressure
Shall go with you under the whine of the shells,
Into the mire and the stress,
Into the seven hundred hells,
Until you come down on your stretcher
To the CCS ...
And back to Blighty again –
Or until you go under the sod.

X

But, in the 1:10 train,
Running between the green and the grain,
Something like the peace of God
Descended over the hum and the drone
Of the wheels and the wine and the buzz of the talk,
And one thought:
'In two days' time we enter the Unknown,
And this is what we die for!'
And thro' the square
Of glass
At my elbow, as limpid as air,
I watched our England pass ...
The great downs moving slowly,
Far away,
The farmsteads quiet and lowly,
Passing away;
The fields newly mown
With the swathes of hay.
And the wheat just beginning to brown,
Whirling away ...
And I thought:
'In two days' time we enter the Unknown,
But *this* is what we die for ... As we ought ...'
For it is for the sake of the wolds and the wealds
That we die,
And for the sake of the quiet fields,
And the path through the stackyard gate ...
[...]

FORD MADOX HUEFFER

Extracts from a 255-line poem, dated '24/12/17–1/1/18'. On *Heaven and Poems Written on Active Service* (1918). Established as an influential avant-garde writer before the war, Hueffer (later Ford) paradoxically uses free verse to make the conventional patriotic celebration of the English countryside; mocks the 'State', yet dedicates the poem to his friend C. F. G. Masterman, director of official propaganda, 1914–17; and views the traditional countryside from a train, an industrial symbol of change. The details of an officer's relationship with the troops, learned from experience on the Somme in 1916, were to be developed in his post-war tetralogy, *Parade's End*.
   CCS: Casualty Clearing Station.

(186) *from* The Glory of War

[...]
My sergeant–major's dead, killed as we entered the village;
You will not find his body tho' you look for it;
A shell burst on him, leaving his legs, strangely enough, untouched.
Happy man, he died for England;
Happy ones are they who die for England.
[...]

H. F. CONSTANTINE

Dated February 1918. *English Review*, September 1918. With this poem, the *Review* printed another by Major Constantine blaming the war unequivocally on the Kaiser and the Kaiser's God.

(187) The Scene of War

And perhaps some outer horror,
some hideousness to stamp beauty
a mark
on our hearts.   H. D.

I Villages Démolis

The villages are strewn
In red and yellow heaps of rubble:

Here and there
Interior walls
Lie upturned and interrogate the skies amazedly

Walls that once held
Within their cubic confines
A soul that now lies strewn
In red and yellow
Heaps of rubble.

II The Crucifix

His body is smashed
Through the belly and chest,
And the head hangs lopsided
From one nailed hand.
  Emblem of agony,
    We have smashed you!

III Fear

Fear is a wave
Beating through the air
And on taut nerves impinging
Till there it wins
Vibrating chords.
All goes well
So long as you tune the instrument
To simulate composure.

(So you will become
A gallant gentleman.)

But when the strings are broken ...
Then you will grovel on the earth
And your rabbit eyes
Will fill with the fragments of your shattered soul.

IV The Happy Warrior

His wild heart beats with painful sobs,
His strained hands clench an ice-cold rifle,
His aching jaws grip a hot parched tongue,
And his wide eyes search unconsciously.

He cannot shriek.

Bloody saliva
Dribbles down his shapeless jacket.

I saw him stab
And stab again
A well-killed Boche.

This is the happy warrior,
This is he ...

V Liedholz

When I captured Liedholz
I had a blackened face
Like a nigger's,
And my teeth like white mosaics shone.

We met in the night at half-past one,
Between the lines.
Liedholz shot at me
And I at him;
And in the ensuing tumult he surrendered to me.

Before we reached our wire
He told me he had a wife and three children.
In the dug-out we gave him a whiskey.
Going to the Brigade with my prisoner at dawn,
The early sun made the land delightful,
And larks rose singing from the plain.

In broken French we discussed
Beethoven, Nietzsche and the International.

He was a professor
Living at Spandau;
And not too intelligible.

But my black face and nigger's teeth
Amused him.

VI The Refugees

Mute figures with bowed heads
They travel along the road:
Old women, incredibly old,
And a hand-cart of chattels.

They do not weep:
Their eyes are too dark for tears.

Past them have hastened
Processions of retreating gunteams,
Baggage-wagons and swift horsemen.
Now they struggle along
With the rearguard of a broken army.

We will hold the enemy towards nightfall
And they will move
Mutely into the dark behind us,
Only the creaking cart
Disturbing their sorrowful serenity.

HERBERT READ

Naked Warriors (1919). Read wrote in his diary, 14 March 1918, that his book would be 'a protest against all the glory camouflage that is written about the war ... the truth should be told'. (A week later he was leading his men against the German offensive, displaying his usual calm bravery and skill.) The apparently random juxtaposition of the six poems is typically Modernist (cf. *The Waste Land*), as is the pursuit of what Read called 'some disinterested beauty'.

H.D.: Hilda Dolittle, the Imagist poet.

The Happy Warrior: Wordsworth, 'Character of the Happy Warrior' ('This is the happy Warrior; this is He / That every Man in arms should wish to be').

Liedholz: Read describes this incident in his diary, 1 August 1917, and a short story, 'The Raid'.

Nietzsche: German philosopher.

International: a socialist organization (Read was a Marxist in this period).

Refugees: fleeing the German advance.

(188) *from* **My Company**

[...]

II

My men go wearily
With their monstrous burdens.

They bear wooden planks
And iron sheeting
Through the area of death.

When a flare curves through the sky
They rest immobile.

Then on again,
Sweating and blaspheming –
'Oh, bloody Christ!'

My men, my modern Christs,
Your bloody agony confronts the world.

III

A man of mine
        lies on the wire.
It is death to fetch his soulless corpse.

A man of mine
        lies on the wire;
And he will rot
And first his lips
The worms will eat.

It is not thus I would have him kissed
But with the warm passionate lips
Of his comrade here.
[...]

HERBERT READ

Naked Warriors (1919). Two sections from 'My Company', originally a six-section poem but in Read's *Collected Poems* (1966) reduced to four sections and printed as part of 'The Scene of War'. Again, two of the pervasive themes of the war's poetry: soldiers as Christs, and intense comradeship.

(189) Solomon in All His Glory

Still I see them coming, coming
    In their ragged broken line,
Walking wounded in the sunlight,
    Clothed in majesty divine.

For the fairest of the lilies,
    That God's summer ever sees,
Ne'er was clothed in royal beauty
    Such as decks the least of these.

Tattered, torn, and bloody khaki,
    Gleams of white flesh in the sun,
Raiment worthy of their beauty
    And the great things they have done.

Purple robes and snowy linen
  Have for earthly kings sufficed,
But these bloody sweaty tatters
  Were the robes of Jesus Christ.

G. A. STUDDERT KENNEDY

Fifth Gloucester Gazette, January 1919 (an early version, entitled 'Walking Wounded'
and signed 'Woodbine Willie'). *The Unutterable Beauty* (1927).
  Title: 'even Solomon in all his glory was not arrayed like one of these'
(Matthew 6:29).

(190) Miners

There was a whispering in my hearth,
  A sigh of the coal,
Grown wistful of a former earth
  It might recall.

I listened for a tale of leaves
  And smothered ferns;
Frond-forests; and the low sly lives
  Before the fawns.

My fire might show steam-phantoms simmer
  From Time's old cauldron,
Before the birds made nests in summer,
  Or men had children.

But the coals were murmuring of their mine,
  And moans down there
Of boys that slept wry sleep, and men
  Writhing for air.

1918

I saw white bones in the cinder-shard,
   Bones without number.
For many hearts with coal are charred,
   And few remember.

I thought of all that worked dark pits
   Of war, and died
Digging the rock where Death reputes
   Peace lies indeed:

Comforted years will sit soft-chaired,
   In rooms of amber,
The years will stretch their hands, well-cheered
   By our life's ember;

The centuries will burn rich loads
   With which we groaned,
Whose warmth shall lull their dreaming lids,
   While songs are crooned;
But they will not dream of us poor lads
   Lost in the ground.

WILFRED OWEN

Written 13–14 January 1917, Scarborough. *Nation*, 26 January 1917 (text as above: Owen checked the proof). *Poems* (1931). One of only five poems published in Owen's lifetime. On 12 January a pit explosion at Halmerend, near Stoke-on-Trent, killed about 140 men and boys. 'Wrote a poem on the Colliery Disaster: but I get mixed up with the War at the end' (*Poems*, 1931, 125). As Graves hoped, Owen has moved away from 'Sassoonish' satire.

(191) À Terre

(Being the philosophy of many soldiers)

Sit on the bed. I'm blind, and three parts shell.
Be careful; can't shake hands now; never shall.
Both arms have mutinied against me, – brutes.
My fingers fidget like ten idle brats.

I tried to peg out soldierly, – no use!
One dies of war like any old disease.
This bandage feels like pennies on my eyes.
I have my medals? – Discs to make eyes close.
My glorious ribbons? – Ripped from my own back
In scarlet shreds. (That's for your poetry book.)

A short life and a merry one, my buck!
We used to say we'd hate to live dead-old, –
Yet now ... I'd willingly be puffy, bald,
And patriotic. Buffers catch from boys
At least the jokes hurled at them. I suppose
Little I'd ever teach a son, but hitting,
Shooting, war, hunting, all the arts of hurting.
Well, that's what I learnt, – that, and making money.

Your fifty years ahead seem none too many?
Tell me how long I've got? God! For one year
To help myself to nothing more than air!
One Spring! Is one too good to spare, too long?
Spring wind would work its own way to my lung,
And grow me legs as quick as lilac-shoots.

My servant's lamed, but listen how he shouts!
When I'm lugged out, he'll still be good for that.
Here in this mummy-case, you know, I've thought
How well I might have swept his floors for ever.
I'd ask no nights off when the bustle's over,
Enjoying so the dirt. Who's prejudiced
Against a grimed hand when his own's quite dust,
Less live than specks that in the sun-shafts turn,
Less warm than dust that mixes with arms' tan?
I'd love to be a sweep, now, black as Town,
Yes; or a muckman. Must I be his load?

O Life, Life, let me breathe, – a dug-out rat!
Not worse than ours the existences rats lead –
Nosing along at night down some safe rut,
They find a shell-proof home before they rot.
Dead men may envy living mites in cheese,
Or good germs even. Microbes have their joys,
And subdivide, and never come to death.
Certainly flowers have the easiest time on earth.
'I shall be one with nature, herb, and stone',
Shelley would tell me. Shelley would be stunned:
The dullest Tommy hugs that fancy now.
'Pushing up daisies' is their creed, you know.
To grain, then, go my fat, to buds my sap,
For all the usefulness there is in soap.
D'you think the Boche will ever stew man-soup?
Some day, no doubt, if ...

Friend, be very sure
I shall be better off with plants that share
More peaceably the meadow and the shower.
Soft rains will touch me, – as they could touch once,
And nothing but the sun shall make me ware.
Your guns may crash around me. I'll not hear;
Or, if I wince, I shall not know I wince.
Don't take my soul's poor comfort for your jest.
Soldiers may grow a soul when turned to fronds,
But here the thing's best left at home with friends.

My soul's a little grief, grappling your chest,
To climb your throat on sobs; easily chased
On other sighs and wiped by fresher winds.

Carry my crying spirit till it's weaned
To do without what blood remained these wounds.

WILFRED OWEN

First drafted, December 1917; rewritten, April 1918, Ripon. One of seven Owen
poems in Edith Sitwell's anthology, *Wheels, 1919. Poems* (1920). A Georgian monologue,
influenced by Masefield's notorious *The Everlasting Mercy* (1911) and Sassoon's *The
Daffodil Murderer* (1913).

pennies: coins used to be placed on a corpse's eyelids to keep them shut.

poetry book: cf. Owen's famous statement at Ripon, 'Above all I am not concerned
with Poetry'.

one with nature: Shelley, 'Adonais', XLII.

pushing up daisies: dead (a common expression among the troops).

man-soup: according to a 1917 propaganda story, Germany had a 'corpse factory'
where bodies were boiled down for fat.

(192) Through These Pale Cold Days

Through these pale cold days
What dark faces burn
Out of three thousand years,
And their wild eyes yearn,

While underneath their brows
Like waifs their spirits grope
For the pools of Hebron again –
For Lebanon's summer slope.

They leave these blond still days
In dust behind their tread
They see with living eyes
How long they have been dead.

ISAAC ROSENBERG

Rosenberg's last poem, written March 1918 in France. *Collected Works* (1937). Enclosed in his last letter (to Edward Marsh, 28 March), postmarked the day after his death. The letter mentions his hope of joining the Jewish Battalion: in the poem that hope becomes the yearning of the exiled Jews for their homeland thousands of years before and, more widely, the longing of all soldiers for home even though they know they may already be as dust. Rosenberg was killed on 1 April.

Hebron: one of ancient Israel's holy cities.
Lebanon: Mount Lebanon.

(193) À Outrance

21 March 1918

The foe has flung his gage,
  His hands clutch at the spoil,
Not ours his wrath to assuage,
  Not ours his sins to assoil.
His challenge must be met,
  His haughtiness brought low.
On guard! The lists are set.
  Stand fast! The trumpets blow.

So stand that none shall flinch
  From the last sacrifice,
A life for every inch,
  For every yard its price.
See – our twin banners dance,
  Linked till the long day's close –
The Fleur-de-lis of France
  Beside the English Rose.

With these to guard her gates
  Against the foeman's power,
Undaunted, Freedom waits
  The issue of the hour.
Her knights are in the field,
  His blade each warrior draws.
Their pride – a stainless shield –
  Their strength – a righteous cause.

F. W. D. BENDALL

Front-Line Lyrics (1918). Taken out of context, this poem might seem civilian work at the start of the war. The enemy spring offensive broke on 21 March 1918, making a German victory seem all too likely: Colonel Bendall, a senior, experienced soldier, knowing that every inch would have to be fought for, stresses chivalry and the righteousness of the cause, avoiding realistic detail.
  Title: To the uttermost.

(194) 'The Soul of a Nation'

The little things of which we lately chattered —
  The dearth of taxis or the dawn of spring:
Themes we discussed as though they really mattered,
  Like rationed meat or raiders on the wing; —

How thin it seems today, this vacant prattle,
  Drowned by the thunder rolling in the West,
Voice of the great arbitrament of battle
  That puts our temper to the final test.

Thither our eyes are turned, our hearts are straining,
  Where those we love, whose courage laughs at fear,
Amid the storm of steel around them raining,
  Go to their death for all we hold most dear.

New-born of this supremest hour of trial,
  In quiet confidence shall be our strength,
Fixed on a faith that will not take denial
  Nor doubt that we have found our soul at length.

O England, staunch of nerve and strong of sinew,
  Best when you face the odds and stand at bay,
Now show a watching world what stuff is in you!
  Now make your soldiers proud of you today!

OWEN SEAMAN

Dated 28 March 1918. *Punch*, 3 April 1918. *From the Home Front* (1918). One of
many poems in the press in April about the military crisis. Seaman's verse was rarely
as serious as this, although *Punch* under his editorship was strongly pro-war.
  Title: also the title of a patriotic 1915 sermon by the Bishop of London, an
outspoken supporter of the war.

(195) April 1918

You, whose forebodings have been all fulfilled,
You who have heard the bell, seen the boy stand
Holding the flimsy message in his hand
While through your heart the fiery question thrilled
'Wounded or killed, which, which?' – and it was 'Killed' –
And in a kind of trance have read it, numb
But conscious that the dreaded hour was come,
No dream this dream wherewith your blood was chilled –
Oh brothers in calamity, unknown
Companions in the order of black loss,
Lift up your hearts, for you are not alone,
And let our sombre hosts together bring
Their sorrows to the shadow of the Cross
And learn the fellowship of suffering.

H. C. BRADBY

Sonnets (1918). Bradby's eldest son had been killed at Arras, April 1917.

(196) The Romancing Poet

Granted that you write verse,
Much better verse than I,
(Which isn't saying much!)
I wish you would refrain
From making glad romance
Of this most hideous war.
It has no glamour,
    Save man's courage,
    His indomitable spirit,
    His forgetfulness of self!

If you have words –
 Fit words, I mean,
Not your usual stock-in-trade,
 Of tags and *clichés*
 To hymn such greatness,
 Use them.
 But have you?
 Anyone can babble.
If you must wax descriptive,
Do get the background right,
 A little right!
The blood, the filth, the horrors,
Suffering on such a scale,
That you and I, try as we may,
 Can only faintly vision it.
Don't make a pretty song about it!
 It is an insult to the men,
 Doomed to be crucified each day,
 For us at home!
Abstain too, if you can,
From bidding us to plume ourselves
For being of the self-same breed
 As these heroic souls,
With the obvious implication,
We have the right to take the credit,
 Vicarious credit,
 For their immortal deeds!
 What next?
 It is an outrage!
 We are not glory-snatchers!

HELEN HAMILTON

Dated April 1918. *Napoo! A Book of War Bêtes-Noires* (1918), a collection of satirical
verses aimed at patriotic poets, 'old men', 'Prussians' and other wartime targets.

(197) 'In the Gallery Where the Fat Men Go'

'GREAT PICTURES OF THE SOMME OFFENSIVE, DAY BY DAY. THE ACTUAL FIGHTING.' See Omnibus and Underground Notices, April 1918

They are showing how we lie
With our bodies run dry:
The attitudes we take
When impaled upon a stake.
These and other things they show
In the gallery where the fat men go.

In the gallery where the fat men go
They're exhibiting our guts
Horse-betrampled in the ruts;
And Private Tommy Spout,
With his eye gouged out;
And Jimmy spitting blood;
And Sergeant lying so
That he's drowning in the mud,
In the gallery where the fat men go.

They adjust their pince-nez
In the gentle urban way, –
And they plant their feet tight
For to get a clearer sight.
They stand playing with their thumbs,
With their shaven cheeks aglow.
For the Terror never comes,
And the worms and the woe.
For they never hear the drums
Drumming Death dead-slow,
In the gallery where the fat men go.

If the gallery where the fat men go
Were in flames around their feet,
Or were sucking through the mud:
If they heard the guns beat
Like a pulse through the blood:
If the lice were in their hair,
And the scabs were on their tongue,
And the rats were smiling there,
Padding softly through the dung,
Would they fix the pince-nez
In the gentle urban way,
Would the pictures still be hung
In the gallery where the fat men go?

LOUIS GOLDING

Cambridge Magazine, 18 May 1918. *Sorrow of War* (1919). Originally entitled 'Offensive'.

(198) Joining-up

No, not for you the glamour of emprise,
Poor driven lad with terror in your eyes.

No dream of wounds and medals and renown
Called you like Love from your drab Northern town.

No haunting fife, dizzily shrill and sweet,
Came lilting drunkenly down your dingy street.

You will not change, with a swift catch of pride,
In the cold hut among the leers and oaths,
Out of your suit of frayed civilian clothes,
Into the haze of khaki they provide.

Like a trapped animal you crouch and choke
In the packed carriage where the veterans smoke
And tell such pitiless tales of Over There,
They stop your heart dead short and freeze your hair.

Your body's like a flower on a snapt stalk,
Your head hangs from your neck as blank as chalk.

What horrors haunt you, head upon your breast!
... O but you'll die as bravely as the rest!

LOUIS GOLDING

Undated. *Sorrow of War* (1919).

(199) The Tide

To The Royal Naval Division
April, 1918

This is a last year's map;
   I know it all so well,
Stream and gully and trench and sap,
   Hamel and all that hell;
See where the old lines wind;
   It seems but yesterday
We left them many a league behind
   And put the map away.

'Never again,' we said,
   'Shall we sit in the Kentish Caves;
Never again will the night-mules tread
   Over the Beaucourt graves;
They shall have Peace,' we dreamed –
   'Peace and the quiet sun,'
And over the hills the French folk streamed
   To live in the land we won.

But the Bosch has Beaucourt now;
  It is all as it used to be —
Airmen peppering Thiepval brow,
  Death at the Danger Tree;
The tired men bring their tools
  And dig in the old holes there;
The great shells spout in the Ancre pools,
  The lights go up from Serre.

And the regiment came, they say,
  Back to the selfsame land
And fought like men in the same old way
  Where the cookers used to stand;
And I know not what they thought
  As they passed the Puisieux Road,
And over the ground where Freyberg fought
  The tide of the grey men flowed.

But I think they did not grieve,
  Though they left by the old Bosch line
Many a cross they loathed to leave,
  Many a mate of mine;
I know that their eyes were brave,
  I know that their lips were stern,
For these went back at the seventh wave,
  But they wait for the tide to turn.

A. P. HERBERT

Punch, 8 May 1918. *The Bomber Gipsy* (May 1918). Cf. (*163*). By April 1918 the
Germans had recaptured many of the villages they had lost during the Somme fighting,
including Beaucourt, Beaumont Hamel and Serre along the Ancre valley. Bernard
Freyberg, a famous commander in both world wars, had been among the survivors
at Beaucourt.

(200) Dawn on the Somme

Last night rain fell over the scarred plateau,
And now from the dark horizon, dazzling, flies
Arrow on fire-plumed arrow to the skies,
Shot from the bright arc of Apollo's bow;
And from the wild and writhen waste below,
From flashing pools and mounds lit one by one,
Oh, is it mist, or are these companies
Of morning heroes who arise, arise
With thrusting arms, with limbs and hair aglow,
Toward the risen god, upon whose brow
Burns the gold laurel of all victories,
Hero and heroes' god, th' invincible Sun?

ROBERT NICHOLS

Dated late spring 1918. *Aurelia and Other Poems* (1920). The words *flashing* and *morning*
were suggested by Sassoon, who liked the poem.

   morning heroes: Sir Arthur Bliss – himself wounded and gassed in 1917 – used this
phrase as the title of his war oratorio (1930), in which this poem, Owen's 'Spring
Offensive' and passages from Homer and Whitman are sung or recited.

(201) Consequences

I met a poet down in Bois d'Arval.
He said, 'I want to find a stoat.'
                          'But why
A stoat? A stoat of all things? Aren't there birds
Fitter for singing of, and flowers and such-like? –
I know a place, among the feet of the trees
That reach up where the aeroplanes drone by
Like painted dragonflies; and there's a pool,
A little brown pool – you must be careful though;
He gassed it yesterday – the stuff hangs still.

Cowslips and violets, like stars in a purple sky,
And a blue flower I've never seen before,
Grow thick among the pale anemones –
Little spirits of the pool, afraid
Of all the incomprehensible noise we make.
All day long the birds, over and under
And in among the interminable moan
Of shells, sing and are happy and build and love;
And one old cuckoo calls the livelong while,
Monotonously, amazingly, serene.
And halfway down the side, by the shell-hole,
My servant saw two deer this very day;
And there are pheasant somewhere – damn these mosquitoes –
Pheasant, or so they say. What more d'ye want?'
But still his wild eyes stared about, and, 'Stoats,'
He said, 'Why aren't there stoats? I want to see
A small lean stoat, with its teeth fast in the neck
Of a squealing rabbit, feet on its quivering chest,
Sucking, sucking blood, red blood, live blood –
God! Why is the sky so aching blue, and the trees
Green with spring and all alive with song,
When just out there crazed men unendingly
In bloody filth unspeakable deal out
Unpurposed, fatuous, unheroic death
To men of their own sort?
                    Once I knew
That man, if not much better, was still no worse
In futile cruelty and self-destruction
Than "Merciful Mother Nature" whence he sprang,
And kept myself from going mad with thought
Of all the blood on her hands, the strife in her eyes.

But now – curse these skies, these everlasting birds!
Stoats are the beasts I want.'
                         Then he went on.
A 5-9 passed me shortly after that;
I have not seen him since. – Damn these mosquitoes.

HENRY L. SIMPSON

Dated Bois d'Arval, May 1918. *Moods and Tenses* (1919). Simpson's early war poems
are entirely conventional, but his style and attitude changed after he had been in battle.
He was killed in August 1918.
   5–9: 5.9 calibre shell.

(202) Greater Love

Red lips are not so red
   As the stained stones kissed by the English dead.
Kindness of wooed and wooer
Seems shame to their love pure.
O Love, your eyes lose lure
   When I behold eyes blinded in my stead!

Your slender attitude
   Trembles not exquisite like limbs knife-skewed,
Rolling and rolling there
Where God seems not to care;
Till the fierce Love they bear
   Cramps them in death's extreme decrepitude.

Your voice sings not so soft, –
   Though even as wind murmuring through raftered loft, –
Your dear voice is not dear,
Gentle, and evening clear,
As theirs whom none now hear,
   Now earth has stopped their piteous mouths that coughed.

Heart, you were never hot,
   Nor large, nor full like hearts made great with shot;
And though your hand be pale,
Paler are all which trail
Your cross through flame and hail:
   Weep, you may weep, for you may touch them not.

WILFRED OWEN

Probably written late March or early April 1918, Ripon. *Art and Letters*, spring 1920. *Poems* (1920). Initially a Swinburnian, Decadent love poem: later drafts add the Christ allusions. Early reviewers often rated this and 'Apologia' (but never the modern favourite, 'Dulce et Decorum Est') as Owen's most perceptive work, but he listed it as 'Doubtful' when he planned a book of poems at Ripon: the notion of redemptive sacrifice had come to seem a 'distorted view', easily exploited by propagandists.

   Title: John 15:13.

   blinded in my stead: a popular wartime painting, 'Blinded for You' by R. Caton Woodville, showed a soldier clutching his eyes.

   God ... care: cf. Matthew 27:46.

   cross: originally 'Rifles', which can be carried in a 'trail' position.

   touch them not: John 20:15–17, but cf. also (*146*), (*148*), (*164*), (*183*), (*188*).

(203) Strange Meeting

It seemed that out of battle I escaped
Down some profound dull tunnel, long since scooped
Through granites which titanic wars had groined.
Yet also there encumbered sleepers groaned,
Too fast in thought or death to be bestirred.
Then, as I probed them, one sprang up, and stared
With piteous recognition in fixed eyes,
Lifting distressful hands, as if to bless.
And by his smile, I knew that sullen hall,
By his dead smile I knew we stood in Hell.
With a thousand pains that vision's face was grained;
Yet no blood reached there from the upper ground,
And no guns thumped, or down the flues made moan.
'Strange friend,' I said, 'here is no cause to mourn.'

'None,' said the other, 'save the undone years,
The hopelessness. Whatever hope is yours,
Was my life also; I went hunting wild
After the wildest beauty in the world,
Which lies not calm in eyes, or braided hair,
But mocks the steady running of the hour,
And if it grieves, grieves richlier than here.
For by my glee might many men have laughed,
And of my weeping something had been left,
Which must die now. I mean the truth untold,
The pity of war, the pity war distilled.
Now men will go content with what we spoiled,
Or, discontent, boil bloody, and be spilled.
They will be swift with swiftness of the tigress,
None will break ranks, though nations trek from progress.
Courage was mine, and I had mystery,
Wisdom was mine, and I had mastery;
To miss the march of this retreating world
Into vain citadels that are not walled.
Then, when much blood had clogged their chariot-wheels
I would go up and wash them from sweet wells,
Even with truths that lie too deep for taint.
I would have poured my spirit without stint
But not through wounds; not on the cess of war.
Foreheads of men have bled where no wounds were.
I am the enemy you killed, my friend.
I knew you in this dark; for so you frowned
Yesterday through me as you jabbed and killed.
I parried; but my hands were loath and cold.
Let us sleep now ...'

WILFRED OWEN

1918

Written March–May 1918, Ripon. *Wheels*, 1919. *Poems* (1920). A poem of unrelieved *hopelessness*. Owen's first, worst memory of the front was of a captured dugout where he and his men had almost been buried alive, a horror that must often have recurred in his shellshock nightmares. As Edmund Blunden noted, the poem is 'a dream only a stage further on than the actuality of the crowded dugouts'. But it is also a very literary vision, Owen's farewell to poetry, with echoes of Homer, the Bible, Dante, Spenser, Shelley, Keats, Tennyson and many others. Acutely aware of the crisis at the front, he foresees his own likely death, expects his poetry to achieve nothing and – unlike most of the war's poets – faces up to the full implications of killing.

Now men will go ... : this prophecy of totalitarianism owes much to Bertrand Russell, *Justice in War-Time* (1916), a book Sassoon would have recommended.

Foreheads of men: cf. Christ's agony (Luke 22:44) – the soldier is no longer a redeemer.

I am the enemy: Jon Silkin preferred Owen's earlier, more political version, 'I was a German conscript and your friend'.

(204) Insensibility

I

Happy are men who yet before they are killed
Can let their veins run cold.
Whom no compassion fleers
Or makes their feet
Sore on the alleys cobbled with their brothers.
The front line withers,
But they are troops who fade, not flowers
For poets' tearful fooling:
Men, gaps for filling:
Losses who might have fought
Longer; but no one bothers.

II

And some cease feeling
Even themselves or for themselves.
Dullness best solves
The tease and doubt of shelling,
And Chance's strange arithmetic
Comes simpler than the reckoning of their shilling.
They keep no check on armies' decimation.

III

Happy are these who lose imagination:
They have enough to carry with ammunition.
Their spirit drags no pack,
Their old wounds save with cold can not more ache.
Having seen all things red,
Their eyes are rid
Of the hurt of the colour of blood for ever.
And terror's first constriction over,
Their hearts remain small-drawn.
Their senses in some scorching cautery of battle
Now long since ironed,
Can laugh among the dying, unconcerned.

IV

Happy the soldier home, with not a notion
How somewhere, every dawn, some men attack,
And many sighs are drained.
Happy the lad whose mind was never trained:
His days are worth forgetting more than not.
He sings along the march
Which we march taciturn, because of dusk,
The long, forlorn, relentless trend
From larger day to huger night.

V

We wise, who with a thought besmirch
Blood over all our soul,
How should we see our task
But through his blunt and lashless eyes?
Alive, he is not vital overmuch;
Dying, not mortal overmuch;
Nor sad, nor proud,
Nor curious at all.
He cannot tell
Old men's placidity from his.

VI

But cursed are dullards whom no cannon stuns,
That they should be as stones;
Wretched are they, and mean
With paucity that never was simplicity.
By choice they made themselves immune
To pity and whatever moans in man
Before the last sea and the hapless stars;
Whatever mourns when many leave these shores;
Whatever shares
The eternal reciprocity of tears.

WILFRED OWEN

Probably written March–May 1918, Ripon. *Athenaeum*, 16 January 1920. *Poems* (1920). A Pindaric ode, modelled on Wordsworth's 'Intimations of Immortality', another poem about the loss of imagination. 'The enormity of the present Battle numbs me', Owen wrote to his mother during the March offensive. Numbness, *insensibility*, was essential protection if poets and officers (*we wise*) were to do their duty (Owen describes writing war poems as his 'duty towards War' in a February 1918 letter). But the poem ends with a Shelleyan curse against civilian *dullards* who choose to be insensible to pity.

(205) The Send-off

Down the close, darkening lanes they sang their way
To the siding-shed,
And lined the train with faces grimly gay.

Their breasts were stuck all white with wreath and spray
As men's are, dead.

Dull porters watched them, and a casual tramp
Stood staring hard,
Sorry to miss them from the upland camp.

Then, unmoved, signals nodded, and a lamp
Winked to the guard.

So secretly, like wrongs hushed-up, they went.
They were not ours:
We never heard to which front these were sent.

Nor there if they yet mock what women meant
Who gave them flowers.

Shall they return to beatings of great bells
In wild train-loads?
A few, a few, too few for drums and yells,

May creep back, silent, to village wells
Up half-known roads.

WILFRED OWEN

Written April–May 1918, Ripon. *Poems* (1920). John Bayley notes the poem's universality: it 'seems both to contain and transcend all the muted terrors to which this century has since accustomed us – trains of deportees, hidden outrage, guilt, the desire not to know' (*Spectator*, 4 October 1963).

(206) Futility

Move him into the sun –
Gently its touch awoke him once,
At home, whispering of fields half-sown.
Always it woke him, even in France,
Until this morning and this snow.
If anything might rouse him now
The kind old sun will know.

Think how it wakes the seeds –
Woke once the clays of a cold star.
Are limbs, so dear-achieved, are sides
Full-nerved, still warm, too hard to stir?
Was it for this the clay grew tall?
– O what made fatuous sunbeams toil
To break earth's sleep at all?

WILFRED OWEN

Written April–May 1918, Ripon. *Nation*, 15 June 1918 (text as above). *Poems* (1920).
One of Owen's men did die from exposure near Serre in January 1917.

(207) Testament

For the last time I say – War is not glorious,
Though lads march out superb and fall victorious, –
Scrapping like demons, suffering like slaves,
And crowned by peace, the sunlight on their graves.

You swear we crush The Beast: I say we fight
Because men lost their landmarks in the night,
And met in gloom to grapple, stab, and kill,
Yelling the fetish-names of Good and Ill
That have been shamed in history.
                                    O my heart,
Be still; you have cried your cry; you have played your part.

SIEGFRIED SASSOON

Found among Sassoon's May 1918 letters to Ottoline Morrell (University of Texas).
Apparently written that month on the boat to France. The military crisis had destroyed
hopes of ending the war by negotiation: Sassoon's protest was finished.

(208) I Stood with the Dead

I stood with the Dead, so forsaken and still:
When dawn was grey I stood with the Dead.
And my slow heart said, 'You must kill, you must kill:
Soldier, soldier, morning is red.'

On the shapes of the slain in their crumpled disgrace
I stared for a while through the thin cold rain ...
'O lad that I loved, there is rain on your face,
And your eyes are blurred and sick like the plain.'

I stood with the Dead ... They were dead; they were dead;
My heart and my head beat a march of dismay:
And gusts of the wind came dulled by the guns.
'Fall in!' I shouted; 'Fall in for your pay!'

SIEGFRIED SASSOON

Written in France, 18 June 1918. *Nation*, 13 July 1918 – by chance, the day a head
wound brought Sassoon's career as a soldier to an end at last. *Picture Show* (1919).

(209) The Guns in Kent

Though I live, as is meant,
   Very near, very near
Happiness, joy, and content,
   And things as they were,

Yet you see what it is:
   When you talk of your Dead,
   I can't sleep in bed.

I am not languid or tired,
   But young, and I wear
Pretty clothes, pretty hats, and a band
   At night in my hair.

But I think as an old woman thinks,
   That life isn't much,
That on each of my pleasures is writ
   'Mustn't touch. Mustn't touch.'

And my eyes from the star
   I withdraw, and my face from the flower.
This isn't my hour. I withdraw
   My life out of this hour.

For there comes very faint, very far,
   As such voices are,
A sound I can hear. That I hear
   Every night with my ear.

And the window shakes at my head
   Over and over,
And each little spring in my bed
   Twangs with its brother.

And there thumps at the heart of the Hill,
 On the house-wall – and runs
In the grass at the foot of the trees,
 The Reminder. The guns.

ENID BAGNOLD

Nation, 20 July 1918. Printed in an editorial column as a reply to Sassoon. Gunfire from the front could often be heard in southern England.

(210) To You in France

Dear, now before the daylight fades away
I wish that I could come and talk to you
A little while, and tell you just a few
Small things that make me happy in my day.
I want to tell you of the perfect scent
Of these red roses I have picked, and how
An organ's playing in the street just now,
And how this sunny afternoon I went

Into the park, and how the children played;
So that at all times in this bloody war,
When you must kill to live, and have to see
Things you hold best on this green earth betrayed,
You will remember you are fighting for
This little world of dear small things, and me.

HELEN DIRCKS

Undated. *Finding* (1918).

(211) 'When the Vision dies ...'

When the Vision dies in the dust of the market-place,
When the Light is dim,
When you lift up your eyes and cannot behold his face,
When your heart is far from him,

Know this is your War; in this loneliest hour you ride
Down the Roads he knew;
Though he comes no more at night he will kneel at your side,
For comfort to dream with you.

MAY WEDDERBURN CANAAN

Undated. *The Splendid Days* (1919).

(212) A Death–Bed

'This is the State above the Law.
    The State exists for the State alone.'
*[This is a gland at the back of the jaw,
    And an answering lump by the collarbone.]*

Some die shouting in gas or fire;
    Some die silent, by shell and shot.
Some die desperate, caught on the wire;
    Some die suddenly. This will not.

'Regis suprema voluntas lex'
    [It will follow the regular course of – throats.]
Some die pinned by the broken decks,
    Some die sobbing between the boats.

Some die eloquent, pressed to death
　　By the sliding trench as their friends can hear.
Some die wholly in half a breath.
　　Some – give trouble for half a year.

'There is neither Evil nor Good in life
　　Except as the needs of the State ordain.'
[Since it is rather too late for the knife,
　　All we can do is to mask the pain.]

Some die saintly in faith and hope –
　　One died thus in a prison-yard –
Some die broken by rape or the rope;
　　Some die easily. This dies hard.

'I will dash to pieces who bar my way.
　　Woe to the traitor! Woe to the weak!'
[Let him write what he wishes to say.
　　It tires him out if he tries to speak.]

Some die quietly. Some abound
　　In loud self-pity. Others spread
Bad morale through the cots around ...
　　This is a type that is better dead.

'The war was forced on me by my foes.
　　All that I sought was the right to live.'
[Don't be afraid of a triple dose;
　　The pain will neutralize half we give.

Here are the needles. See that he dies
  While the effects of the drug endure …
What is the question he asks with his eyes? –
  Yes, All-Highest, to God, be sure.]

RUDYARD KIPLING

Written 1918, when it was rumoured that the Kaiser was dying of throat cancer. *The Years Between* (1919). Perhaps Kipling's most bitter poem. He dreaded getting cancer himself.
  'Regis … lex': 'The will of the King is the supreme law'.

(213) *from* Epitaphs

A servant

We were together since the War began.
He was my servant – and the better man.

A son

My son was killed while laughing at some jest. I would I knew
What it was, and it might serve me in a time when jests are few.

An only son

I have slain none except my Mother. She
(Blessing her slayer) died of grief for me.

The coward

I could not look on Death, which being known,
Men led me to him, blindfold and alone.

The beginner

On the first hour of my first day
   In the front trench I fell.
(Children in boxes at a play
   Stand up to watch it well.)

Batteries out of ammunition

If any mourn us in the workshop, say
We died because the shift kept holiday.

Common form

If any question why we died,
Tell them, because our fathers lied.

A dead statesman

I could not dig: I dared not rob:
Therefore I lied to please the mob.

Unknown female corpse

Headless, lacking foot and hand,
Horrible I come to land.
I beseech all women's sons
Know I was a mother once.

RUDYARD KIPLING

Written April 1918 and later. *The Years Between* (1919). Nine of thirty-one epitaphs, described by Kipling as 'naked cribs of the Greek Anthology'.

   A son: Kipling chose to believe his son had died smiling, firing at a German machine gun – the reality had been very different.

   The beginner: another oblique reference to John Kipling, who died during his first tour of the trenches.

   Batteries ... : strikes at home were bitterly resented by soldiers.

   Common form: modern readers might assume this is an attack on 'old men' and their patriotic rhetoric, but in fact Kipling is once again condemning the pre-war government for underestimating the danger from Germany.

(214) Haig is Moving

August 1918

 Haig is moving!
Three plain words are all that matter,
Mid the gossip and the chatter,
Hopes in speeches, fears in papers,
Pessimistic froth and vapours –
 Haig is moving!

 Haig is moving!
We can turn from German scheming,
From humanitarian dreaming,
From assertions, contradictions,
Twisted facts and solemn fictions –
 Haig is moving!

 Haig is moving!
All the weary idle phrases,
Empty blamings, empty praises,
Here's an end to their recital,
There is only one thing vital –
 Haig is moving!

 Haig is moving!
He is moving, he is gaining,
And the whole hushed world is straining,
Straining, yearning, for the vision
Of the doom and the decision –
 Haig is Moving!

ARTHUR CONAN DOYLE

Dated August 1918. *The Guards Came Through* (1919). Douglas Haig, British
Commander-in-Chief, launched his successful counter-offensive on 8 August. Doyle
had been writing a detailed history of the war in France and Flanders for several years:
for him, as for the nation, Haig's advance was a huge relief after months of anxiety.

German scheming ... humanitarian dreaming: there had been tentative German peace
moves in 1917 and pressure at home for negotiations.

contradictions ... fictions: in an acrimonious parliamentary debate in May 1918, Lloyd
George had used a mass of statistics to deny that he had lied about British strength at
the front.

(215) Spring Offensive

Halted against the shade of a last hill,
They fed, and, lying easy, were at ease
And, finding comfortable chests and knees,
Carelessly slept. But many there stood still
To face the stark, blank sky beyond the ridge,
Knowing their feet had come to the end of the world.

Marvelling they stood, and watched the long grass swirled
By the May breeze, murmurous with wasp and midge,
For though the summer oozed into their veins
Like an injected drug for their bodies' pains,
Sharp on their souls hung the imminent line of grass,
Fearfully flashed the sky's mysterious glass.

Hour after hour they ponder the warm field –
And the far valley behind, where the buttercup
Had blessed with gold their slow boots coming up,
Where even the little brambles would not yield,
But clutched and clung to them like sorrowing hands;
They breathe like trees unstirred.

Till like a cold gust thrills the little word
At which each body and its soul begird
And tighten them for battle. No alarms
Of bugles, no high flags, no clamorous haste –
Only a lift and flare of eyes that faced
The sun, like a friend with whom their love is done.
O larger shone that smile against the sun, –
Mightier than his whose bounty these have spurned.

So, soon they topped the hill, and raced together
Over an open stretch of herb and heather
Exposed. And instantly the whole sky burned
With fury against them; earth set sudden cups
In thousands for their blood; and the green slope
Chasmed and steepened sheer to infinite space.

Of them who running on that last high place
Leapt to swift unseen bullets, or went up
On the hot blast and fury of hell's upsurge,
Or plunged and fell away past this world's verge,
Some say God caught them even before they fell.

But what say such as from existence' brink
Ventured but drave too swift to sink,
The few who rushed in the body to enter hell,
And there out-fiending all its fiends and flames
With superhuman inhumanities,
Long-famous glories, immemorial shames –
And crawling slowly back, have by degrees
Regained cool peaceful air in wonder –
Why speak not they of comrades that went under?

WILFRED OWEN

Owen's last poem, written August–September 1918. *Poems* (1920). Different editions
have different wordings in places: Owen never had time to write a final draft. The last
stanza, added in pencil to the manuscript, may have been written in October after he
had been in action on the Hindenburg Line, where he won the MC for inflicting
'considerable losses' on the enemy. His final question may be the last line of poetry
written before the Armistice by any soldier on active service. The poem is loosely based
on an experience in April 1917: among other changes, the month becomes May, the
traditional time for poetic visions. A nature poem with echoes of Keats and other
Romantics, but with a difference: the offensive is against the spring as well as in it,
and when the men reject nature's blessing, sky and earth answer with deadly fury.
   high place: in the Old Testament, a place of human sacrifice.

(216) Hospital Sanctuary

When you have lost your all in a world's upheaval,
Suffered and prayed, and found your prayers were vain,
When love is dead, and hope has no renewal –
These need you still; come back to them again.

When the sad days bring you the loss of all ambition,
And pride is gone that gave you strength to bear,
When dreams are shattered, and broken is all decision –
Turn you to these, dependent on your care.

They too have fathomed the depths of human anguish,
Seen all that counted flung like chaff away;
The dim abodes of pain wherein they languish
Offer that peace for which at last you pray.

VERA BRITTAIN

Dated September 1918. *Poems of the War and After* (1934). Brittain worked as a nurse during the war. Her fiancé, brother and two close friends all died in the war.

(217) 'No Annexations'

'No annexations?' We agree!
　We did not draw the sword for gain,
But to keep little nations free;
　And surely, surely, it is plain
　That land and loot we must disdain,
Who only fight for liberty.

But, still – we cannot well restore
　To the grim Teuton's iron yoke
The countries that he ruled before,
　Rebind on liberated folk
　The cruel fetters that we broke,
The grievous burden that they bore.

Of course it happens – as we know –
　That 'German East' has fertile soil
Where corn and cotton crops will grow,
　That Togoland is rich in oil,
　That natives can be made to toil
For wages white men count too low.

That many a wealthy diamond mine
   Makes South-West Africa a prize,
That river-dam and railway line
   (A profitable enterprise)
   May make a paying paradise
Of Bagdad and of Palestine.

However, this is by the way;
   We do not fight for things like these
But to destroy a despot's sway,
   To guard our ancient liberties:
   We cannot help it if it please
The Gods to make the process pay.

We cannot help it if our Fate
   Decree that war in Freedom's name
Shall handsomely remunerate
   Our ruling classes. 'Twas the same
   In earlier days – we always came
Not to annex, but liberate.

W. N. EWER

Satire and Sentiment (1918). As attention begins to turn to post-war settlements, the socialist Ewer mocks imperial hypocrisy. Since at least 1917, left-wingers – and Sassoon – had suspected that the government had become more interested in taking colonies than in liberating Belgium.

(218) Justice

October 1918

Across a world where all men grieve
And grieving strive the more,
The great days range like tides and leave
Our dead on every shore.
Heavy the load we undergo,
And our own hands prepare,
If we have parley with the foe,
The load our sons must bear.

Before we loose the word
    That bids new worlds to birth,
Needs must we loosen first the sword
    Of Justice upon earth;
Or else all else is vain
    Since life on earth began,
And the spent world sinks back again
    Hopeless of God and Man.

A people and their King
    Through ancient sin grown strong,
Because they feared no reckoning
    Would set no bound to wrong;
But now their hour is past,
    And we who bore it find
Evil Incarnate held at last
    To answer to mankind.

THE WINTER OF THE WORLD

For agony and spoil
   Of nations beat to dust,
For poisoned air and tortured soil
   And cold, commanded lust,
And every secret woe
   The shuddering waters saw –
Willed and fulfilled by high and low –
   Let them relearn the Law.

That when the dooms are read,
   Not high nor low shall say: –
'My haughty or my humble head
   Has saved me in this day.'
That, till the end of time,
   Their remnant shall recall
Their fathers' old, confederate crime
   Availed them not at all.

That neither schools nor priests,
   Nor Kings may build again
A people with the heart of beasts
   Made wise concerning men.
Whereby our dead shall sleep
   In honour, unbetrayed,
And we in faith and honour keep
   That peace for which they paid.

RUDYARD KIPLING

The Times, 24 October 1918. *The Years Between* (1919). Syndicated in 200 newspapers worldwide, and reprinted as a broadsheet, January 1919, bordered with the names of places destroyed by enemy action. Like Ewer, his political opposite, Kipling was consistent in his politics.

sword / Of Justice: a 1914–15 recruiting slogan ('Take up the Sword of Justice'); cf. Matthew 10:34.

the Law: cf. 'lesser breeds without the Law' ('Recessional', 1897), a reference to Germany.

beasts: in a June 1915 speech, Kipling said the world was divided into 'human beings and Germans'.

(219) The Beasts in Gray

Whether it last for the Seven Years,
Or whether it end in a day,
Peoples of Earth, let us swear an oath:
'No truce with the Beasts in Gray!'

They do not feel as we feel,
Or speak the speech that we speak;
Their god is the naked Steel,
Their law is 'Death to the weak.'
All that our Peoples cherish
They mock, blaspheming the Lord ...
'Who draws the sword, he shall perish,'
Saith God, 'by the sword.'

Wherefore, O free-born Peoples –
Though it last for a year and a day –
This let us vow in the name of our God:
'No truce with the Beasts in Gray!'

They have neither honour nor ruth;
They mock, in the name of Might,
At justice, mercy and truth,
At pity and tears and Right.
There is never a bestial vision
Conceivéd of madman's brain
That they have not wrought with precision
Into some engine of pain.

Wherefore, Peoples Unflinching,
Whatever their puppets say,
Hold to the bond for your children's sake:
'No truce with the Beasts in Gray!'

When they fawn, when they whine, when they howl –
Remember the desolate lands,
And the shameless deeds and the foul:
The stumps that were children's hands;
The things in the seas – your brothers,
Murdered, and murdered again;
The gutted things that were mothers,
The tortured things that were men.

Remembering these, Free Peoples,
By the God of your Fathers, slay!
Let the sword decide what the sword began
'No truce with the Beasts in Gray!'

GILBERT FRANKAU

Daily Mail, 1 November 1918. Poetical Works II (1923). Frankau's obsessive hatred of
Germany became notorious after the war: he even resigned from a club when John
Galsworthy brought a German to dine there.
  Beasts: as an ardent Kiplingite, Frankau uses Kipling's word (218).
  Gray: the colour of German uniforms.

(220) 'They Have Come into Their Kingdom'

Time was we feared the Dead, alas!
  In the incredible days long gone,
The patient dead beneath the grass,
  Lying alone, dreaming alone.

But now the Dead have come alive,
  Gayer and brighter than the Quick.
Laughing and radiant they arrive,
  To lift the mortal world grown sick.

Time was we feared some churchyard thing
　　That passed when life was low and chill,
These are not ghosts, fleet as a wing,
　　With wonderful young eyes laughing still.

And now our shadows are made bright
　　For the beloved faces gay,
These stars upon our blackest night,
　　With whom 'tis always Day – and May.

Oh, we are in the night and cold,
　　And they are warm in the great sun,
Who slipped so soon our mortal hold,
　　So light, so quick the young feet run.

Now to the Kingdom of the Young
　　We reach out of the rain and dark,
Hearing far off the children's song,
　　Blithe as the lark, fresh as the lark.

KATHARINE TYNAN

Spectator, 9 November 1918.
　Title: presumably an echo of Luke 18:16–17 ('Suffer the little children to come unto me ... for of such is the kingdom of God'). Tynan's many war poems often emphasize how young most soldiers were.

(221) Victory

Finished – this body's agony, soul's strain,
Forced wrong of man to man – can these be finished,
And beauty keep the dying woods again,
And peace at sundown be no more diminished?

Where are those ghastly shapes, hatred and fear,
Cruelty and lust, that even our great-hearted
Have armed as comrades many a dreadful year?
Were they but dreams, thus utterly departed?

Dreams were they, and are gone. And gone youth's glamour,
And gone is questing youth from countless houses.
O you in England, hark to the bells' clamour,
And hear them ask (those dead), if victory rouses
Grief alone, and say: Remembering you
Our love and labour shall make earth anew.

GEOFFREY FABER

Dated 'On the march in Belgium, 11 November 1918'. *The Buried Stream* (1941).
The hope in the last line, strongly felt by many soldiers, was to grow into bitter
disillusion during the next decade.

(222) The Armistice

In an Office, in Paris

The news came through over the telephone:
All the terms had been signed: the War was won:
And all the fighting and the agony,
And all the labour of the years were done.
One girl clicked sudden at her typewriter
And whispered, 'Jerry's safe', and sat and stared:
One said, 'It's over, over, it's the end:
The War is over: ended': and a third,
'I can't remember life without the war'.
And one came in and said, 'Look here, they say
We can all go at five to celebrate,
As long as two stay on, just for today.'

It was quite quiet in the big empty room
Among the typewriters and little piles
Of index cards: one said, 'We'd better just
Finish the day's reports and do the files.'
And said, 'It's awf'lly like *Recessional*,
Now when the tumult has all died away.'
The other said, 'Thank God we saw it through;
I wonder what they'll do at home today.'
And said, 'You know it will be quiet tonight
Up at the Front: first time in all these years,
And no one will be killed there any more',
And stopped, to hide her tears.
She said, 'I've told you; he was killed in June.'
The other said, 'My dear, I know; I know ...
It's over for me too ... My Man was killed,
Wounded ... and died ... at Ypres ... three years ago ...
And he's my Man, and I want him,' she said,
And knew that peace could not give back her Dead.

MAY WEDDERBURN CANNAN

The Splendid Days (1919). Cannan, working in Paris for MI5, had the terms of the Armistice dictated to her over the phone. 'Across the table G. lifted her glass to me and said "Absent". I did not know her story nor she mine, but I drank to my friends who were dead and to my friends who, wounded, imprisoned, battered, shaken, exhausted, were alive in a new, and a terrible world' (*Grey Ghosts and Voices*, 136).

Recessional: the famous poem by Kipling, whom Cannan greatly admired.

(223) *from* **Any Soldier to His Son**

What did I do, sonny, in the Great World War? —
Well, I learned to peel potatoes and to scrub the barrack floor.

[...]
So I learned to live and lump-it in the lovely land of war,
Where all the face of nature seems a monstrous septic sore,
Where the bowels of earth hang open, like the guts of something slain,
And the rot and wreck of everything are churned and churned again;
Where all is done in darkness and where all is still in day,
Where living men are buried and the dead unburied lay;
Where men inhabit holes like rats, and only rats live there
Where cottage stood and castle once in days before La Guerre;
Where endless files of soldiers thread the everlasting way,
By endless miles of duckboards, through endless walls of clay;
Where life is one hard labour, and a soldier gets his rest
When they leave him in the daisies with a puncture in his chest;
Where still the lark in summer pours her warble from the skies,
And underneath, unheeding, lie the blank, upstaring eyes.

And I read the Blighty papers, where the warriors of the pen
Tell of 'Christmas in the Trenches' and 'The Spirit of our Men';
And I saved the choicest morsels and I read them to my chum,
And he muttered, as he cracked a louse and wiped it off his thumb:
'May a thousand chats from Belgium crawl their fingers as they write;
May they dream they're not exempted till they faint with mortal fright;
May the fattest rats in Dickebusch race over them in bed;
May the lies they've written choke them like a gas cloud till they're dead;
May the horror and the torture and the things they never tell
(For they only write to order) be reserved for them in Hell!'

You'd like to be a soldier and go to France some day?
By all the dead in Delville Wood, by all the nights I lay
Between our line and Fritz's before they brought me in;
By this old wood-and-leather stump, that once was flesh and skin:
By all the lads who crossed with me but never crossed again,
By all the prayers their mothers and their sweethearts prayed in vain,
Before the things that were that day should ever more befall
May God in common pity destroy us one and all!

GEORGE WILLIS

Extracts from a 90-line poem published anonymously in the *Nation*, 22 November 1918 (very early for such angry writing). Another soldier soon wrote in to praise the poem's truthfulness (*Nation*, 14 December). *Any Soldier to His Son* (1919).
  chats: army slang for lice.

(224) The Smells of Home

I shut the door and left behind
    The reek of wounds – the cries
Of 'Sister! Sister! Go steady, Sister,' –
    The hateful sight of flies
That come like mourners dressed in black,
    And will not be thrust aside,
But over the sheets come prying back
    To a hand where blood has dried.

A scented slap of morning wind
    Came suddenly as I stood,
The grim things of the ward shut out
    By a panel or two of wood.
O wind! Can it be the meadows of France
    That you come whistling through?
For these are the smells of my own country
    You carry along with you.

THE WINTER OF THE WORLD

The breath of ferns and pale marsh-flowers,
  Of meadowsweet and phlox,
Drowsed apricot, of gorse that flames
  In the purple shadow of rocks,
The warm, hewn fragrance of red fir,
  And (smell of heart's desire!)
Blue incense from the peat that smoulders
  Upon an English fire.

The chilly sweetness of drenched things
  At morning when the sky
Shows yellow behind a bird's dark wings
  And threads of mist go by.
Strange air blows cold from another world,
  The still fields shine like glass,
A minute goes like a thousand years,
  And there are pearls in the grass.

O wind! Can it be the meadows of France
  That you come sighing through?
For these are the things of my own country
  Whose scent you bring with you.
Dawn on the bog, and burning peat,
  A wild sea tattered with foam,
Red heather on the eternal hills –
  These are the smells of home.

ROSALEEN GRAVES

Spectator, 30 November 1918. By Robert Graves's sister.

270

(225) The Use of War

When the dark cloud of war burst on the stricken world,
Men said, to solace others and themselves, that from this evil
Good would come; that warring mankind, ennobled by endeavour
And the hardships and dangers of the war, would come
To a higher level of thought and action. But has that been?
It is true that men have suffered, and have known how fear,
Black foe to human reason, brings bondage on the soul.
Have they learned aught else? The brave have been brave,
The pure have been pure, and the generous have laid down their lives.
But all those others, neither generous nor pure of heart,
Neither brave nor clear of brain, have they altered?
What good has come to them? Who knows?
Not you, nor I, nor all the busy scribes of England.

H. F. Constantine

English Review, November 1918.

(226) Memorial Tablet

Squire nagged and bullied till I went to fight,
(Under Lord Derby's scheme). I died in hell –
(They called it Passchendaele). My wound was slight,
And I was hobbling back; and then a shell
Burst slick upon the duckboards: so I fell
Into the bottomless mud, and lost the light.

At sermon-time, while Squire is in his pew,
He gives my gilded name a thoughtful stare;
For, though low down upon the list, I'm there;
'*In proud and glorious memory*' ... that's my due.
Two bleeding years I fought in France, for Squire:
I suffered anguish that he's never guessed.
Once I came home on leave: and then went west ...
What greater glory could a man desire?

SIEGFRIED SASSOON

Dated November 1918. *Nation and Athenaeum*, 8 February 1919, with a different ending. *Picture Show* (1919). Now that the war is over, Sassoon can return to satire. *Lord Derby's scheme*: a 1915 recruiting scheme.

(227) Afterwards

Oh, my beloved, shall you and I
Ever be young again, be young again?
The people that were resigned said to me
– Peace will come and you will lie
Under the larches up in Sheer,
Sleeping,
And eating strawberries and cream and cakes –
    O cakes, O cakes, O cakes, from Fuller's!
And quite forgetting there's a train to town,
Plotting in an afternoon the new curves for the world.

And peace came. And lying in Sheer
I look round at the corpses of the larches
Whom they slew to make pit-props
For mining the coal for the great armies.
And think, a pit-prop cannot move in the wind,
Nor have red manes hanging in spring from its branches,
And sap making the warm air sweet.

Though you planted it out on the hill again it would be dead.
And if these years have made you into a pit-prop,
To carry the twisting galleries of the world's reconstruction
(Where you may thank God, I suppose
That they set you the sole stay of a nasty corner)
What use is it to you? What use
To have your body lying here
In Sheer, underneath the larches?

MARGARET POSTGATE

Poems (1918).
  Fuller's: a chain of tea shops.

(228) Hymn to Death, 1914 and On

'Danse macabre' death –
'Dried-guts' death.

They clatter, girn, mow –
femur rattles skull –
epiphyses shriek, grate –
Brain
a shrunk pea,
quintessential lusts –
rattles,
rattles, rattles
rattles.
O the 'bones', the wonderful 'bones'
(God's the 'darkey')

Toes out, click heels – March!
Evert backbone – March!
Breast-bone out – March!
Shoulder-blades well drawn back –
Thumbs to trouser-seams –
hold chin firm – March!
March! March!
March!

'Danse macabre' death –
'Dried-guts' death

'Hi there –
take your wired toes out o' me ribs.'

They clatter, girn, mow –
pea-brains rattle,
rattle, rattle,
rattle.

* * *

My sweetheart's bouquet at this ball
the sweet skull of this lover –
(he went to the war).

JOHN RODKER

Egoist, November–December 1918. Modernist satire by a conscientious objector.
  girn: show the teeth in a snarl or grin.
  femur: thigh bone.
  epiphyses: ends of bones.
  darkey: God is like a black percussion player on the 'bones' (cf. also Ezekiel 37:4).
  Thumbs to trouser-seams: the position of a soldier's hands when he comes to attention.
  ball: the Dance of Death (*danse macabre*).

1919-30

Promising a 'fit country for heroes to live in', Lloyd George had won an enormous electoral victory for his Coalition in December 1918, but the new government was dominated by Conservatives, many of whom were determined that Germany should be made to pay. The 1919 Treaty of Versailles that officially ended the war contributed to the post-war mood of disenchantment: John Maynard Keynes's best-selling pamphlet, *The Economic Consequences of the Peace*, was widely influential, with its arguments that the treaty was unjust and potentially disastrous for Germany.

Disillusion with the treaty was matched by disillusion at home, where the country was far from being fit for heroes. Women poets in particular wrote movingly about the predicaments of ordinary people. Arrangements for demobilizing the armed forces, widely seen as unfair, led to rioting, and the return of soldiers to an exhausted economy inevitably created social and economic disturbance. Industrial unrest almost culminated in a general strike in 1921 and actually did so in 1926. The contrast between wartime sacrifice and post-war unemployment became a subject for many satirical, angry poems.

However, the market for most war writing, especially poetry, rapidly disappeared. The first selections of poems by Owen and Rosenberg were published in 1920 and 1922 respectively, but neither book sold widely. Several poets, notably Ivor Gurney and Edmund Blunden, wrote their best work about the war in the 1920s, but Gurney's poems from that decade were to remain unpublished for many years. People wanted to forget: there were other things to worry about, and new social freedoms to enjoy. Only at the annual Armistice Day services, with their two-minute silence, did the whole country bring together its complex memories of suffering and bereavement.

It was almost a decade before interest in the war revived. At the end of the 1920s there was a burst of writing, almost all of it in prose. Most of these 'war books' were harshly critical, representing the fighting as hideous and futile; some critics deplored them, but they established a 'myth', a way of thinking about the conflict, that has persisted ever since. At about the same time, a series of diplomatic initiatives by France, Germany and others briefly gave hope that the nations of Europe might never take up arms against each other again. But that hope soon faded under the deepening shadow of another world war.

(229) Everyone Sang

Everyone suddenly burst out singing;
And I was filled with such delight
As prisoned birds must find in freedom,
Winging wildly across the white
Orchards and dark-green fields; on – on – and out of sight.

Everyone's voice was suddenly lifted;
And beauty came like the setting sun:
My heart was shaken with tears; and horror
Drifted away ... O, but Everyone
Was a bird; and the song was wordless; the singing will never be done.

SIEGFRIED SASSOON

Written April 1919. *Picture Show* (1919). Composed 'in a few minutes ... Its rather free form was spontaneous ... it was essentially an expression of release, and signified a thankfulness for liberation from the war years which came to the surface with the advent of spring ... The singing that would "never be done" was the Social Revolution which I believed to be at hand' (*Siegfried's Journey*, 140–1).

(230) Envoie

How shall I say goodbye to you, wonderful, terrible days,
If I should live to live and leave 'neath an alien soil
You, my men, who taught me to walk with a smile in the ways
Of the valley of shadows, taught me to know you and love you, and toil

Glad in the glory of fellowship, happy in misery, strong
In the strength that laughs at its weakness, laughs at its
   sorrows and fears,
Facing the world that was not too kind with a jest and a song?
What can the world hold afterwards worthy of laughter or tears?

EDWARD DE STEIN

The Poets in Picardy (1919).

(231) Unloading Ambulance Train

Into the siding very wearily
She comes again:
Singing her endless song so drearily,
The midnight winds sink down to drift the rain.

So she comes home once more.

Is it an ancient chanty
Won from some classic shore?
The stretcher-bearers stand
Two on either hand.
They bend and lift and raise
Where the doors open wide
With yellow light ablaze.
Into the dark outside
Each stretcher passes. Here
(As if each on his bier
With sorrow they were bringing)
Is peace, and a low singing.
The ambulances unload,
Move on and take the road.
Under the stars alone
Each stretcher passes out.

And the ambulances' moan
And the checker's distant shout
All round to the old sound
Of the last chanty singing.
And the dark seamen swinging.
Far off some classic shore ...

So she comes home once more.

CAROLA OMAN

The Menin Road (1919).

(232) Ambulance Train 30

A. T. 30 lies in the siding.
Above her cold grey clouds lie, silver-long as she.
Like a great battleship that never saw defeat
She dreams: while the pale day dies down
Behind the harbour town,
Beautiful, complete
And unimpassioned as the long grey sea.

A. T. 30 lies in the siding.
Gone are her red crosses – the sick that were her own.
Like a great battleship that never saw defeat
She waits, while the pale day dies down
Behind the harbour town,
Beautiful, complete...
And the Occupying Army boards her for Cologne.

CAROLA OMAN

Westminster Gazette, 6 May 1919. *The Menin Road* (1919).

(233) The Last Salute

We pass and leave you lying. No need
    for rhetoric, for funeral music, for
    melancholy bugle calls. No need for
    tears now, no need for regret.
We took our risk with you; you died
    and we live. We take your noble
    gifts, salute for the last time those
    lines of pitiable crosses, those solitary
    mounds, those unknown graves and
    turn to live our lives out as we may.
Which of us were the fortunate who
    can tell? For you there is silence
    and the cold twilight drooping in
    awful desolation over those
    motionless lands. For us sunlight and
    the sound of women's voices, song
    and hope and laughter, despair,
    gaiety, love – life.
Lost terrible silent comrades, we, who
    might have died, salute you.

RICHARD ALDINGTON

A prose-poem, dated London, 1919. *Anglo-French Review*, May 1919. *The Love of
Myrrhine and Konallis* (1926). Aldington left the army in February 1919.
    we ... salute you: an ambivalent echo of the salute of Roman gladiators ('We, who
are about to die, salute you').

(234) Gethsemane

The Garden called Gethsemane
   In Picardy it was,
And there the people came to see
   The English soldiers pass.
We used to pass – we used to pass
   Or halt, as it might be,
And ship our masks in case of gas
   Beyond Gethsemane.

The Garden called Gethsemane,
   It held a pretty lass,
But all the time she talked to me
   I prayed my cup might pass.
The officer sat on the chair,
   The men lay on the grass,
And all the time we halted there
   I prayed my cup might pass –

It didn't pass – it didn't pass –
   It didn't pass from me.
I drank it when we met the gas
   Beyond Gethsemane.

RUDYARD KIPLING

The Years Between (1919), a book Kipling originally intended to call *Gethsemane*, the title conveying both the agony and the necessity of war (cf. Matthew 26:39).

(235) Peace

June 28th 1919

From the tennis lawn you can hear the guns going,
  Twenty miles away,
Telling the people of the home counties
  That the peace was signed today.
Tonight there'll be feasting in the city;
  They will drink deep and eat –
Keep peace the way you planned you would keep it
  (If we got the Boche beat).
Oh, your plan and your word, they are broken,
  For you neither dine nor dance;
And there's no peace so quiet, so lasting,
  As the peace you keep in France.

You'll be needing no Covenant of Nations
  To hold your peace intact.
It does not hang on the close guarding
  Of a frail and wordy pact.
When ours screams, shattered and driven,
  Dust down the storming years,
Yours will stand stark, like a grey fortress,
  Blind to the storm's tears.

Our peace ... your peace ... I see neither.
  They are a dream, and a dream.
I only see you laughing on the tennis lawn;
  And brown and alive you seem,
As you stoop over the tall red foxglove,
  (It flowers again this year)
And imprison within a freckled bell
  A bee, wild with fear ...

***

Oh, you cannot hear the noisy guns going:
  You sleep too far away.
It is nothing to you, who have your own peace,
  That our peace was signed today.

ROSE MACAULAY

Three Days (1919). The Treaty of Versailles was signed on 28 June 1919.

(236) Dead and Buried

I have borne my cross through Flanders,
  Through the broken heart of France,
I have borne it through the deserts of the East;
  I have wandered, faint and longing,
  Through the human hosts that, thronging,
Swarmed to glut their grinning idols with a feast.

I was crucified in Cambrai,
  And again outside Bapaume;
I was scourged for miles along the Albert Road,
  I was driven, pierced and bleeding,
  With a million maggots feeding
On the body that I carried as my load.

I have craved a cup of water,
  Just a drop to quench my thirst,
As the routed armies ran to keep the pace;
  But no soldier made reply
  As the maddened hosts swept by,
And a sweating straggler kicked me in the face.

There's no ecstasy of torture
That the devils e'er devised,
That my soul has not endured unto the last;
As I bore my cross of sorrow,
For the glory of tomorrow,
Through the wilderness of battles that is past.

Yet my heart was still unbroken,
And my hope was still unquenched,
Till I bore my cross to Paris through the crowd.
Soldiers pierced me on the Aisne,
But 'twas by the river Seine
That the statesmen brake my legs and made my shroud.

There they wrapped my mangled body
In fine linen of fair words,
With the perfume of a sweetly scented lie,
And they laid it in the tomb
Of the golden-mirrored room,
'Mid the many-fountained Garden of Versailles.

With a thousand scraps of paper
They made fast the open door,
And the wise men of the Council saw it sealed.
With the seal of subtle lying
They made certain of my dying,
Lest the torment of the peoples should be healed.

Then they set a guard of soldiers
Night and day beside the Tomb,
Where the Body of the Prince of Peace is laid,
And the captains of the nations
Keep the sentries to their stations,
Lest the statesman's trust from Satan be betrayed.

For it isn't steel and iron
That men use to kill their God,
But the poison of a smooth and slimy tongue.
Steel and iron tear the body,
But it's oily sham and shoddy
That have trampled down God's *Spirit* in the dung.

G. A. STUDDERT KENNEDY

The Unutterable Beauty (1927). The speaker is both an unknown soldier and Christ, 'Crucified, dead and buried'. For Kennedy, a brave chaplain profoundly moved by soldiers' sacrifices, post-war idealism soon gave way to disgust at the 'realpolitik' of the peace conference.

golden-mirrored room: cf. William Orpen's official painting, showing the politicians dwarfed by the ornate Hall of Mirrors at Versailles.

scraps of paper: an ironic contrast between the negotiations and the original 'scrap of paper', as the German Chancellor had called it in 1914, the treaty by which Britain had felt obliged to defend Belgian neutrality.

(237) The Lament of the Demobilised

'Four years,' some say consolingly. 'Oh well,
What's that? You're young. And then it must have been
A very fine experience for you!'
And they forget
How others stayed behind and just got on –
Got on the better since we were away.
And we came home and found
They had achieved, and men revered their names,
But never mentioned ours;

And no one talked heroics now, and we
Must just go back and start again once more.
'You threw four years into the melting-pot –
Did you indeed!' these others cry. 'Oh well,
The more fool you!'
And we're beginning to agree with them.

VERA BRITTAIN

Dated Oxford, 1919. In the anthology *Oxford Poetry* (1920). *Poems of the War and After* (1934).
    more fool you: a new note in the war's poetry. Demobilized volunteers had great difficulty finding employment.

(238) Women Demobilised

July 1919

Now must we go again back to the world
Full of grey ghosts and voices of men dying,
And in the rain the sounding of Last Posts,
And Lovers' crying –
Back to the old, back to the empty world.

Now are put by the bugles and the drums,
And the worn spurs, and the great swords they carried,
Now are we made most lonely, proudly, theirs,
The men we married:
Under the dome the long roll of the drums.

Now are the Fallen happy and sleep sound,
Now, in the end, to us is come the paying,
These who return will find the love they spend,
But we are praying
Love of our Lovers fallen who sleep sound.

Now in our hearts abides always our war,
Time brings, to us, no day for our forgetting,
Never for us is folded War away,
Dawn or sun setting,
Now in our hearts abides always our war.

MAY WEDDERBURN CANNAN

The Splendid Days (1919). July 1919 brought official peace celebrations, but Cannan's fiancé, though surviving the war, had died in February in the great influenza epidemic. Like Brittain (*237*), she noticed 'that curious hostility to those who had "been in it" ' (*Grey Ghosts and Voices*, 148 – her autobiography takes its title from this poem).

(239) Paris, 1919

Tune up with the dance of sorrow,
'Tis a measure we all can tread,
Tune up with the dance of sorrow,
We dance on the graves of the dead.

Tune up with the dance of sorrow,
Let the fountain of laughter flow,
We bankrupts may lightly borrow
And carry our loot to the show.

Tune up with the music of sorrow,
Tango and Jazz and song,
We'll be sodden and stiff tomorrow,
But the night of the grave is long.

MARY STUDD

Poems (1932). The ironical dancing rhythms suggest the emerging hedonism of what was soon to be known as the Jazz Age.

(240) The Cenotaph

September 1919

Not yet will those measureless fields be green again
Where only yesterday the wild sweet blood of wonderful youth was shed;
There is a grave whose earth must hold too long, too deep a stain,
Though for ever over it we may speak as proudly as we may tread.
But here, where the watchers by lonely hearths from the thrust of an
    inward sword have more slowly bled,
We shall build the Cenotaph: Victory, winged, with Peace, winged too,
    at the column's head.
And over the stairway, at the foot – oh! here, leave desolate, passionate
    hands to spread
Violets, roses, and laurel, with the small, sweet, twinkling country things
Speaking so wistfully of other Springs,
From the little gardens of little places where son or sweetheart was
    born and bred.
In splendid sleep, with a thousand brothers
    To lovers – to mothers
    Here, too, lies he:
Under the purple, the green, the red,
It is all young life: it must break some women's hearts to see
Such a brave, gay coverlet to such a bed!
Only, when all is done and said,
God is not mocked and neither are the dead.
For this will stand in our Market-place –
    Who'll sell, who'll buy?

(Will you or I
Lie each to each with the better grace?)
While looking into every busy whore's and huckster's face
As they drive their bargains, is the Face
Of God: and some young, piteous, murdered face.

CHARLOTTE MEW

The Farmer's Bride (2nd edn, 1921). A wood and plaster version of the famous Cenotaph in London was unveiled in July 1919, but Mew is imagining any one of the hundreds of memorials that were being planned and built in provincial towns, often in market places among the traders.
    God is not mocked: Galatians 6:7.

(241) The Women to the Men Returned

You cannot speak to us nor we reply:
You learnt a different language where men die,
Are mutilated, maddened, blinded, torn
To tatters of red flesh, mown down like corn,
Crucified, starved, tormented. Oh! forgive
Us, who whilst all men died could bear to live
Happy – almost, excited, glad – almost,
Extravagantly, counting not the cost –
The cost *you* paid in silence. Now speech is vain,
We cannot understand nor you explain
Your passion and your anguish; we are deaf
And blind to all save customary grief.
How shall our foolish consolations reach
Trouble which lies so deeper far than speech?

It ruffles not the surface – dark it lies,
Hid from all eyes, but mostly from *our* eyes,
Which though they wept for sons and lovers dead
(Our *own* sons, our *own* lovers) have not *bled*
Tears – have not wept such drops of blood and flame,
They must have saved the world for very shame.
Forgive us, then, for all our useless tears,
And for our courage and patience all those years.
Oh! you can love us still, laugh with us, smile,
But in your haunted spirits all the while,
Tortured and throbbing like a nerve laid bare,
Lie sleepless memories we dare not share.
Your secret thought – what is it? We do not know;
Never such gulf divorced you from the foe
As now divides us, for how may you tell
What Hell is to us who only read of Hell?
Your souls elude us in some lonely place
Uncomforted, beings of another race.
Have you our flesh – our flesh and blood become?
You cannot answer us – you are dumb, you are dumb!

MARGARET SACKVILLE

English Review, July 1920.

(242) The Superfluous Woman

Ghosts crying down the vistas of the years,
Recalling words
Whose echoes long have died;
And kind moss grown
Over the sharp and blood-bespattered stones
Which cut our feet upon the ancient ways.

* * *

But who will look for my coming?

Long busy days where many meet and part;
Crowded aside
Remembered hours of hope;
And city streets
Grown dark and hot with eager multitudes
Hurrying homeward whither respite waits.

* * *

But who will seek me at nightfall?

Light fading where the chimneys cut the sky;
Footsteps that pass,
Nor tarry at my door.
And far away,
Behind the row of crosses, shadows black
Stretch out long arms before the smouldering sun.

* * *

But who will give me my children?

VERA BRITTAIN

Dated July 1920. *Poems of the War and After* (1934). Cf. (*157*).

(243) Haunted

Gulp down your wine, old friends of mine,
Roar through the darkness, stamp and sing
And lay ghost hands on everything,
But leave the noonday's warm sunshine
To living lads for mirth and wine.

I meet you suddenly down the street,
Strangers assume your phantom faces,
You grin at me from daylight places,
Dead, long dead, I'm ashamed to greet
Dead men down the morning street.

ROBERT GRAVES

Country Sentiment (1920). Graves's nerves never entirely recovered from his war experiences.

(244) *from* Hugh Selwyn Mauberley

[...]

IV

These fought in any case,
and some believing,
        pro domo, in any case ...

Some quick to arm,
some for adventure,
some from fear of weakness,
some from fear of censure,
some for love of slaughter, in imagination,
learning later ...
some in fear, learning love of slaughter;

Died some, pro patria,
    non 'dulce' non 'et decor' ...
walked eye-deep in hell
believing in old men's lies, then unbelieving
came home, home to a lie,
home to many deceits,
home to old lies and new infamy;
usury age-old and age-thick
and liars in public places.

Daring as never before, wastage as never before.
Young blood and high blood,
fair cheeks, and fine bodies;

fortitude as never before

frankness as never before,
disillusions as never told in the old days,
hysterias, trench confessions,
laughter out of dead bellies.

V

There died a myriad,
And of the best, among them,
For an old bitch gone in the teeth,
For a botched civilization,

Charm, smiling at the good mouth,
Quick eyes gone under earth's lid,

For two gross of broken statues,
For a few thousand battered books.
[...]

EZRA POUND

Hugh Selwyn Mauberley (1920). Pound called the complete seventeen-part poem 'a farewell to London' (he moved to Paris in 1920, abandoning his attempt to modernize English poetry). These two sections, dispassionately listing British motives and reducing the war itself to a few cynical lines, are a famous expression of post-war disillusion.

(245) Wars and Rumours: 1920

Blood, hatred, appetite and apathy,
  The sodden many and the struggling strong,
  Who care not now though for another wrong
Another myriad innocents should die.
At candid savagery or oily lie,
  We laugh, or, turning, join the noisy throng
  Which buries the dead with gluttony and song.
Suppose this very evening from on high
Broke on the world that unexampled flame
  The choir-thronged sky, and Thou, descending, Lord;
What agony of horror, fear, and shame,
  For those who knew and wearied of Thy word,
  I dare not even think, who am confest
Idle, malignant, lustful as the rest.

J. C. SQUIRE

Poems in One Volume (1926).

(246) Two Years After

We thought when we sat in the soup, old man, with the curling flames
  all round,
We thought if we didn't get scorched or choked or buried or boiled or
  drowned,
We thought to the end of our days on earth we should live like kings
  uncrowned.

We thought if we ever came home alive they would fall on our necks
  half mad,
And turn their hearts for us inside out and load us with all they had;
That nothing would be too good for us, since nothing was then too
  bad.

We thought, and the thought of it warmed us up, and gave us strength
  anew,
And carried us on till the task was done; we thought – but it wasn't
  true,
For it isn't much cop down here, old man; how is it up there with you?

GEORGE WILLIS

A Ballad of Four Brothers (1921).

(247) 'And There Was a Great Calm'

(On the Signing of the Armistice, 11 November 1918)

I

There had been years of Passion – scorching, cold,
And much Despair, and Anger heaving high,
Care whitely watching, Sorrows manifold,
Among the young, among the weak and old,
And the pensive Spirit of Pity whispered, 'Why?'

II

Men had not paused to answer. Foes distraught
Pierced the thinned peoples in a brute-like blindness,
Philosophies that sages long had taught,
And Selflessness, were as an unknown thought,
And 'Hell!' and 'Shell!' were yapped at Lovingkindness.

III

The feeble folk at home had grown full-used
To 'dug-outs,' 'snipers,' 'Huns,' from the war-adept
In the mornings heard, and at evetides perused;
To day-dreamt men in millions, when they mused –
To nightmare-men in millions when they slept.

IV

Waking to wish existence timeless, null,
Sirius they watched above where armies fell;
He seemed to check his flapping when, in the lull
Of night a boom came thencewise, like the dull
Plunge of a stone dropped into some deep well.

V

So, when old hopes that earth was bettering slowly
Were dead and damned, there sounded 'War is done!'
One morrow. Said the bereft, and meek, and lowly,
'Will men some day be given to grace? yea, wholly,
And in good sooth, as our dreams used to run?'

VI

Breathless they paused. Out there men raised their glance
To where had stood those poplars lank and lopped,
As they had raised it through the four years' dance
Of Death in the now familiar flats of France;
And murmured, 'Strange, this! How? All firing stopped?'

VII

Aye; all was hushed. The about-to-fire fired not,
The aimed-at moved away in trance-lipped song.
One checkless regiment slung a clinching shot
And turned. The Spirit of Irony smirked out, 'What?
Spoil peradventures woven of Rage and Wrong?'

VIII

Thenceforth no flying fires inflamed the gray,
No hurtlings shook the dewdrop from the thorn,
No moan perplexed the mute bird on the spray;
Worn horses mused: 'We are not whipped today';
No weft-winged engines blurred the moon's thin horn.

IX

Calm fell. From Heaven distilled a clemency;
There was peace on earth, and silence in the sky;
Some could, some could not, shake off misery:
The Sinister Spirit sneered: 'It had to be!'
And again the Spirit of Pity whispered, 'Why?'

THOMAS HARDY

The Times, 11 November 1920. *Late Lyrics and Earlier* (1922). Commissioned by *The Times* for an illustrated supplement on the day of the unveiling of the permanent Cenotaph in Whitehall and the burial of the Unknown Warrior. But the paper disapproved of the poem's sentiments: 'when Mr Hardy makes pity ask why this misery had, and has, to be, the answer is clear ... plain duty forbade the free peoples of the earth, and forbade us, above all others, to renounce all justice and all right'.
    Title: Mark 4:39.
    Spirit of Pity: the Spirit of the Pities and the Spirits Ironic and Sinister comment on the Napoleonic Wars in Hardy's *The Dynastss*.

(248) Armistice Day, 1921

The hush begins. Nothing is heard
Save the arrested taxis throbbing
And here and there an ignorant bird
And here a sentimental woman sobbing.

The statesman bares and bows his head
Before the solemn monument;
His lips, paying duty to the dead
In silence, are more than ever eloquent.

But ere the sacred silence breaks
And taxis hurry on again,
A faint and distant voice awakes,
Speaking the mind of a million absent men:

'Mourn not for us. Our better luck
At least has given us peace and rest.
We struggled when our moment struck
But now we understand that death knew best.

'Would we be as our brothers are
Whose barrel-organs charm the town?
Ours was a better dodge by far –
We got *our* pensions in a lump sum down.

'We, out of all, have had our pay,
There is no poverty where we lie:
The graveyard has no quarter-day,
The space is narrow but the rent not high.

'No empty stomach here is found:
Unless some cheated worm complain
You hear no grumbling underground:
Oh, never, never wish us back again!

'Mourn not for us, but rather we
Will meet upon this solemn day
And in our greater liberty
Keep silent for you, a little while, and pray.'

EDWARD SHANKS

The Shadowgraph (1925).

(249) Trench Poets

I knew a man, he was my chum,
But he grew blacker every day,
And would not brush the flies away,
Nor blanch however fierce the hum
Of passing shells; I used to read,
To rouse him, random things from Donne;
Like 'Get with child a mandrake-root,'
But you can tell he was far gone,
For he lay gaping, mackerel-eyed,
And stiff and senseless as a post
Even when that old poet cried
'I long to talk with some old lover's ghost.'

I tried the Elegies one day,
But he, because he heard me say
'What needst thou have more covering than a man?'
Grinned nastily, and so I knew
The worms had got his brains at last.
There was one thing that I might do
To starve the worms; I racked my head
For healthy things and quoted *Maud*.
His grin got worse and I could see
He laughed at passion's purity.
He stank so badly, though we were great chums
I had to leave him; then rats ate his thumbs.

EDGELL RICKWORD

Behind the Eyes (1921). The quotations are from Donne's often licentious love poems ('Song', 'Love's Deity', 'Elegie XIX: Going to Bed'). By contrast, Tennyson's *Maud* tells the story of a chaste, unsuccessful relationship, ending with the hero's enlistment.

(250) War and Peace

In sodden trenches I have heard men speak,
Though numb and wretched, wise and witty things;
And loved them for the stubbornness that clings
Longest to laughter when Death's pulleys creak;

And seeing cool nurses move on tireless feet
To do abominable things with grace,
Deemed them sweet sisters in that haunted place
Where, with child's voices, strong men howl or bleat.

Yet now those men lay stubborn courage by,
Riding dull-eyed and silent in the train
To old men's stools; or sell gay-coloured socks
And listen fearfully for Death; so I
Love the low-laughing girls, who now again
Go daintily, in thin and flowery frocks.

EDGELL RICKWORD

Behind the Eyes (1921).

(251) Moonrise over Battlefield

After the fallen sun the wind was sad
like violins behind immense old walls.
Trees were musicians swaying round the bed
of a woman in gloomy halls.

In privacy of music she made ready
with comb and silver dust and fard;
under her silken vest her little belly
shone like a bladder of sweet lard.

She drifted with the grand air of a punk
on Heaven's streets soliciting white saints;
then lay in bright communion on a cloud-bank
as one who near extreme of pleasure faints.

Then I thought, standing in the ruined trench,
(all round, dead Boche white-shirted lay like sheep),
'Why does this damned entrancing bitch
seek lovers only among them that sleep?'

EDGELL RICKWORD

Invocation to Angels (1928).
   punk: prostitute (archaic).

(252) Billet

O, but the racked clear tired strained frames we had!
Tumbling in the new billet on to straw bed,
Dead asleep in eye shutting. Waking as sudden
To a golden and azure roof, a golden ratcheted
Lovely web of blue seen and blue shut, and cobwebs and tiles,
And grey wood dusty with time. June's girlish kindest smiles.
Rest at last and no danger for another week, a seven-day week.

But one Private took on himself a Company's heart to speak,
'I wish to bloody hell I was just going to Brewery – surely
To work all day (in Stroud) and be free at tea-time – allowed
Resting when one wanted, and a joke in season,
To change clothes and take a girl to Horsepool's turning,
Or drink a pint at 'Travellers Rest', and find no cloud.
Then God and man and war and Gloucestershire would have a reason,
But I get no good in France, getting killed, cleaning off mud.'
He spoke the heart of all of us – the hidden thought burning, unturning.

IVOR GURNEY

Completed by 1919. *Collected Poems* (1982). Gurney's 1919–25 war poems –
observant, humorous, unrhetorical – recall with passionate sympathy the ordinary
soldiers he had known, giving an unrivalled insight into their lives and longings. His
style, its eccentric rhythms, rhymes and syntax presumably influenced by Hopkins,
becomes as original as the work of many Modernists: in some ways he deserves the
title he proudly gave himself, 'First War Poet'.

(253) Of Grandcourt

Through miles of mud we travelled, and by sick valleys –
The Valley of Death at last – most evil alleys,
To Grandcourt trenches reserve – and the hell's name it did deserve.
Rain there was – tired and weak I was, glad for an end.
But one spoke to me – one I liked well as friend,
'Let's volunteer for the Front Line – many others won't.
I'll volunteer, it's better being there than here.'
But I had seen too many ditches and stood too long
Feeling my feet freeze, and my shoulders ache with the strong
Pull of equipment, and too much use of pain and strain.
Beside, he was Lance Corporal and might be full Corporal
Before the next straw resting might come again,
Before the next billet should hum with talk and song.
Stars looked as well from second as from first line holes.

There were fatigues for change, and a thought less danger –
But five or six there were followed Army with their souls
Took five days dripping rain without let or finish again –
With dysentery and bodies of heroic ghouls.
Till at last their hearts feared nothing of the brazen anger,
(Perhaps of death little) but once more again to drop on straw bed-serving,
And to have heaven of dry feeling after the damps and fouls.

IVOR GURNEY

Probably written 1919–22. *Collected Poems* (1982).

(254) The Silent One

Who died on the wires, and hung there, one of two –
Who for his hours of life had chattered through
Infinite lovely chatter of Bucks accent:
Yet faced unbroken wires; stepped over, and went
A noble fool, faithful to his stripes – and ended.
But I weak, hungry, and willing only for the chance
Of line – to fight in the line, lay down under unbroken
Wires, and saw the flashes and kept unshaken,
Till the politest voice – a finicking accent, said:
'Do you think you might crawl through there: there's a hole.'
Darkness, shot at: I smiled, as politely replied –
'I'm afraid not, Sir.' There was no hole no way to be seen
Nothing but chance of death, after tearing of clothes.

Kept flat, and watched the darkness, hearing bullets whizzing –
And thought of music – and swore deep heart's deep oaths
(Polite to God) and retreated and came on again,
Again retreated – and a second time faced the screen.

IVOR GURNEY

Probably written 1919–22. *Poems* (1954). The individuality of Gurney's soldiers is often conveyed through his frequent use of place names (like Edward Thomas, whom he admired, he loved maps and landscapes and was a prodigious walker) and through direct speech, here his own voice, *polite* but firmly unheroic, and the officer's, *finicking* and comical.

    stripes: chevrons on the sleeve – two for a corporal, three for a sergeant.

(255) Strange Hells

There are strange hells within the minds war made
Not so often, not so humiliatingly afraid
As one would have expected – the racket and fear guns made.
One hell the Gloucester soldiers they quite put out;
Their first bombardment, when in combined black shout
Of fury, guns aligned, they ducked lower their heads
And sang with diaphragms fixed beyond all dreads,
That tin and stretched-wire tinkle, that blither of tune:
'Après la guerre fini', till hell all had come down,
Twelve-inch, six-inch, and eighteen pounders hammering hell's thunders.

Where are they now, on state-doles, or showing shop-patterns
Or walking town to town sore in borrowed tatters
Or begged. Some civic routine one never learns.
The heart burns – but has to keep out of face how heart burns.

IVOR GURNEY

Probably written 1919–22. *Poems* (1954).

(256) Riez Bailleul

Behind the line there mending reserve posts, looking
On the cabbage fields with other men carefully tending cooking;
Hearing the boiling; and being sick of body and heart,
Too sick for anything but hoping that all might depart –
We back in England again, and white roads to walk on,
Eastwards to hill-steeps, or see meadows good to talk on.
Grey Flanders sky over all and a heaviness felt
On the sense that no working or dreaming would any way melt ...
This is not happy thought, but a glimpse most strangely
Forced from the past, to hide this pain and work myself free
From present things. The parapet, the grey look-out, the making
Of a peasantry, by dread war, harried and set on shaking;
A hundred things of age, and of carefulness,
Spoiling; a farmer's treasure perhaps soon a wilderness.

IVOR GURNEY

Collected Poems (1982). Written late 1922 at Barnwood House, the mental hospital where Gurney began his long, miserable years of confinement. Memories of his own and other people's wartime suffering still help to free him from the pain of *present things*.

(257) The Bohemians

Certain people would not clean their buttons,
Nor polish buckles after latest fashions,
Preferred their hair long, putties comfortable,
Barely escaping hanging, indeed hardly able;
In Bridge and smoking without army cautions
Spending hours that sped like evil for quickness,
(While others burnished brasses, earned promotions).

These were those ones who jested in the trench,
While others argued of army ways, and wrenched
What little soul they had still further from shape,
And died off one by one, or became officers.
Without the first of dream, the ghost of notions
Of ever becoming soldiers, or smart and neat,
Surprised as ever to find the army capable
Of sounding 'Lights out' to break a game of Bridge,
As to fear candles would set a barn alight:
In Artois or Picardy they lie – free of useless fashions.

IVOR GURNEY

Written 1922–25. *Poems* (1954). A rare description of unsoldierly soldiers, men like
Gurney himself, unable to *wrench* their souls out of shape to fit in with army ways.
At an inspection in 1917 a sergeant-major explained to a colonel who had noticed
the state of Gurney's brasses, 'A good man, sir, quite all right ... but he's a musician
and doesn't seem able to keep himself clean' (*War Letters*, 126).

   officers: Gurney's lack of respect for officers, whom he rarely even mentions, may have
been typical of many privates – very unlike the intense feelings many officers had for
their men – cf. (*164*).

(258) War Books

What did they expect of our toil and extreme
Hunger – the perfect drawing of a heart's dream?
Did they look for a book of wrought art's perfection,
Who promised no reading, nor praise, nor publication?
Out of the heart's sickness the spirit wrote
For delight, or to escape hunger, or of war's worst anger,
When the guns died to silence and men would gather sense
Somehow together, and find this was life indeed,
And praise another's nobleness, or to Cotswold get hence.
There we wrote – Corbie Ridge – or in Gonnehem at rest –
Or Fauquissart – our world's death songs, ever the best.

One made sorrows' praise passing the church where silence
Opened for the long quivering strokes of the bell –
Another wrote all soldiers' praise, and of France and night's stars,
Served his guns, got immortality, and died well.
But Ypres played another trick with its danger on me,
Kept still the needing and loving-of-action body,
Gave no candles, and nearly killed me twice as well,
And no souvenirs, though I risked my life in the stuck tanks.
Yet there was praise of Ypres, love came sweet in hospital,
And old Flanders went under to long ages of plays' thought in my pages.

IVOR GURNEY

Written 1922–25. *Poems* (1954). By the early 1920s the public had lost interest in war poetry, and critics tended to be dismissive about it.
  to Cotswold get hence: to dream, or in Gurney's case to write, about the Cotswold hills.
  One: possibly Owen ('What passing bells').
  Another: probably Edward Thomas.
  love came sweet: Gurney fell in love with a nurse in 1917.

(259) Elegy in a Country Churchyard

The men that worked for England
They have their graves at home:
And bees and birds of England
About the cross can roam.

But they that fought for England,
Following a falling star,
Alas, alas for England
They have their graves afar.

And they that rule in England,
In stately conclave met,
Alas, alas for England
They have no graves as yet.

G. K. CHESTERTON

The Ballad of St Barbara (1922). The last stanza is aimed at the Prime Minister, Lloyd George, and Lord Reading, a Jewish financier, both of whom had been implicated in the 1911 Marconi scandal, regarded by Chesterton as an establishment–Jewish conspiracy. When Lloyd George appointed Reading to accompany him to the peace conference, Chesterton believed they were betraying the ordinary patriotic soldier.

(260) The English Graves

Were I that wandering citizen whose city is the world,
I would not weep for all that fell before the flags were furled;
I would not let one murmur mar the trumpets volleying forth
How God grew weary of the kings, and the cold hell in the north.
But we whose hearts are homing birds have heavier thoughts of home,
Though the great eagles burn with gold on Paris or on Rome,
Who stand beside our dead and stare, like seers at an eclipse,
At the riddle of the island tale and the twilight of the ships.

For these were simple men that loved with hands and feet and eyes,
Whose souls were humbled to the hills and narrowed to the skies,
The hundred little lands within one little land that lie,
Where Severn seeks the sunset isles or Sussex scales the sky.

And what is theirs, though banners blow on Warsaw risen again,
Or ancient laughter walks in gold through the vineyards of Lorraine,
Their dead are marked on English stones, their loves on English trees,
How little is the prize they win, how mean a coin for these –
How small a shrivelled laurel-leaf lies crumpled here and curled:
They died to save their country and they only saved the world.

G. K. CHESTERTON

The *Ballad of St Barbara* (1922). Patriotism for Chesterton was always localized (in one of the *hundred little lands within one little land*) – he detested all forms of internationalism.

(261) My People

Because through five red years of war most ruthless,
    Armed in a quarrel they most surely did not seek,
Challenged in their honour and slandered by the truthless
    My people made them strong to help the weak;

Because where still unbroken, perfect in devotion,
    Faithful to the last man, the old first army died,
Thousands after thousands from home and over ocean
    Inherited the spirit of their pride;

Because when their foeman in his fleeting triumph vaunted,
    Prisoned in the pest-camp or frozen where they bled,
Cowed by no disaster, starved but still undaunted,
    My people never flinched nor bowed the head;

Because men rough and simple but great of heart and tender,
    Kindly to each other though rude of speech and free,
Fronted hell well knowing for us was no surrender
    And grimly held their backs towards the sea;

Because the mould that shaped them failed not at the casting,
    And steadfast as their own oaks endured the island-bred;
Love be their portion and their glory everlasting,
    And Britain, keep us worthy of thy dead!

RENNELL RODD

Trentaremi (1923).

(262) War Graves

(After the Lacedæmonian)

Tell the Professors, you that pass us by,
They taught Political Economy,
And here, obedient to its laws, we lie.

GODFREY ELTON

Years of Peace (1925). A cynical variation on Simonides – cf. (*23 note*).

(263) The Survivor

I found him in department CO 10.
Three rows of medals, DSO, CB,
Brown, handsome, fearless, born to handle men:
Brushed, buttoned, spurred. Whom did I wish to see?

'Men you can't send for, General,' I said,
'How great soever your expense of ink;
Men you've forgotten; the unribboned dead
Who fell because you were too brave to think.'

GODFREY ELTON

Years of Peace (1925). Probably derived from Sassoon's 1917 poem, 'The General'. Elton's 1925 novel, *The Testament of Dominic Burleigh*, questions traditional notions of heroism.

(264) Two Minutes' Silence (Armistice Day, 1925)

Not mine this year
To keep the silence that I hold so dear,
Since I shall be with you,
My little son too small to understand
Or to keep still,
Being only two.
So, though I take your hand,
And bring you to the grassy, wind-swept hill,
Where I stand and am quiet,
Your baby words
Will chatter still of the cows and trees and birds.

They will not mind.
They loved the country, and children, and sun, and wind.
My little lad,
They gave their life to keep you safe and glad,
That you might grow – a heritage, a trust,
A man to play the game when they are dust.

TERESA HOOLEY

Songs of All Seasons (1927). Not all 1920s poems were cynical – cf. (*261*).

(265) On Passing the New Menin Gate

Who will remember, passing through this Gate,
The unheroic Dead who fed the guns?
Who shall absolve the foulness of their fate, –
Those doomed, conscripted, unvictorious ones?
   Crudely renewed, the Salient holds its own.
   Paid are its dim defenders by this pomp;
   Paid, with a pile of peace-complacent stone,
   The armies who endured that sullen swamp.

Here was the world's worst wound. And here with pride
'Their name liveth for ever,' the Gateway claims.
Was ever an immolation so belied
As these intolerably nameless names?
Well might the Dead who struggled in the slime
Rise and deride this sepulchre of crime.

SIEGFRIED SASSOON

Written 1927–28. *The Heart's Journey* (1928). The new gate, a triumphal arch, was opened in July 1927 as a memorial to the battles of Ypres; it bears the names of 54,889 British soldiers whose bodies were never found.

(266) Zero

O rosy red, O torrent splendour
   Staining all the Orient gloom,
O celestial work of wonder –
   A million mornings in one bloom!

What, does the artist of creation
   Try some new plethora of flame,
For his eye's fresh fascination?
   Has the old cosmic fire grown tame?

In what subnatural strange awaking
  Is this body, which seems mine?
These feet towards that blood-burst making,
  These ears which thunder, these hands which twine

On grotesque iron? Icy-clear
  The air of a mortal day shocks sense,
My shaking men pant after me here.
  The acid vapours hovering dense,

The fury whizzing in dozens down,
  The clattering rafters, clods calcined,
The blood in the flints and the trackway brown –
  I see I am clothed and in my right mind;

The dawn but hangs behind the goal.
  What is that artist's joy to me?
Here limps poor Jock with a gash in the poll,
  His red blood now is the red I see,

The swooning white of him, and that red!
  These bombs in boxes, the craunch of shells,
The second-hand flitting round; ahead!
  It's plain we were born for this, naught else.

EDMUND BLUNDEN

Masks of Time (1925). For the costly attack at Hamel, 3 September 1916, see Blunden's *Undertones of War*, IX (where he never mentions that he won the MC that day). His wartime poems, with their simple juxtapositions of war and nature – cf. *(139)*, *(140)* – are less complex than his post-war work, where war becomes an attack on his beloved pastoral landscape and the literary tradition that had enshrined it; traditional metres are strained; and poetic language, often describing very unpoetic subjects, is set ironically against colloquial speech.

    Title: later 'Come On, My Lucky Lads', an encouragement shouted by Sgt Frank Worley at the start – zero hour – of the attack.

  I am clothed ... mind: Mark 5:15.

  gash in the poll: head wound.

(267) At Senlis Once

O how comely it was and how reviving,
When with clay and with death no longer striving
   Down firm roads we came to houses
   With women chattering and green grass thriving.

Now though rains in a cataract descended,
We could glow, with our tribulation ended –
   Count not days, the present only
   Was thought of, how could it ever be expended?

Clad so cleanly, this remnant of poor wretches
Picked up life like the hens in orchard ditches,
   Gazed on the mill-sails, heard the church-bell,
   Found an honest glass all manner of riches.

How they crowded the barn with lusty laughter,
Hailed the pierrots and shook each shadowy rafter,
   Even could ridicule their own sufferings,
   Sang as though nothing but joy came after!

EDMUND BLUNDEN

Masks of Time (1925). Blunden's battalion was withdrawn to Senlis for a day or two after the Hamel attack.
   O how ... reviving: Milton, *Samson Agonistes*, 1268.

(268) The Zonnebeke Road

Morning, if this late withered light can claim
Some kindred with that merry flame
Which the young day was wont to fling through space!
Agony stares from each gray face.
And yet the day is come; stand down! stand down!
Your hands unclasp from rifles while you can,
The frost has pierced them to the bended bone?
Why, see old Stevens there, that iron man,
Melting the ice to shave his grotesque chin:
Go ask him, shall we win?
I never liked this bay, some foolish fear
Caught me the first time that I came in here;
That dugout fallen in awakes, perhaps,
Some formless haunting of some corpse's chaps.
True, and wherever we have held the line,
There were such corners, seeming-saturnine
For no good cause.
          Now where Haymarket starts,
That is no place for soldiers with weak hearts;
The minenwerfers have it to the inch.
Look, how the snow-dust whisks along the road,
Piteous and silly; the stones themselves must flinch
In this east wind; the low sky like a load
Hangs over – a dead-weight. But what a pain
Must gnaw where its clay cheek
Crushes the shell-chopped trees that fang the plain –
The ice-bound throat gulps out a gargoyle shriek.

The wretched wire before the village line
Rattles like rusty brambles or dead bine,
And then the daylight oozes into dun;
Black pillars, those are trees where roadways run.
Even Ypres now would warm our souls; fond fool,
Our tour's but one night old, seven more to cool!
O screaming dumbness, O dull clashing death,
Shreds of dead grass and willows, homes and men,
Watch as you will, men clench their chattering teeth
And freeze you back with that one hope, disdain.

EDMUND BLUNDEN

Masks of Time (1925). A memory of trenches at Potijze, near Ypres, January 1917, in the bitter weather also recorded by Owen (*206*) and many others.
  minenwerfers: trench mortars.

(269) Rural Economy 1917

There was winter in those woods,
  And still it was July:
There were Thule solitudes
  With thousands huddling nigh;
There the fox had left his den,
The scraped holes hid not stoats but men.

To these woods the rumour teemed
  Of peace five miles away;
In sight, hills hovered, houses gleamed
  Where last perhaps we lay
Till the cockerels bawled bright morning and
The hours of life slipped the slack hand.

In sight, life's farms sent forth their gear;
  Here rakes and ploughs lay still;
Yet, save some curious clods, all here
  Was raked and ploughed with a will.
The sower was the ploughman too,
And iron seeds broadcast he threw.

What husbandry could outdo this?
  With flesh and blood he fed
The planted iron that nought amiss
  Grew thick and swift and red,
And in a night though ne'er so cold
Those acres bristled a hundredfold.

Why, even the wood as well as field
  This ruseful farmer knew
Could be reduced to plough and tilled,
  And if he planned, he'd do;
The field and wood, all bone-fed loam,
Shot up a roaring harvest-home.

EDMUND BLUNDEN

Nation and Athenaeum, 4 November 1922. *Undertones of War* (1928). The stanza form is that of William Cowper's 'The Castaway', the story of a sailor drowned in a storm while his ship is nearby but unable to help. The soldiers are within sight of peace, yet beyond rescue; they are absorbed into the cold earth as fertilizer for a harvest of fire.

Thule: in north Greenland, a legendary end of the world.

(270) Vlamertinghe: Passing the Chateau, July 1917

'And all her silken flanks with garlands drest' –
But we are coming to the sacrifice.
Must those have flowers who are not yet gone West?
May those have flowers who live with death and lice?
This must be the floweriest place
That earth allows; the queenly face
Of the proud mansion borrows grace for grace
Spite of those brute guns lowing at the skies.

Bold great daisies, golden lights,
Bubbling roses' pinks and whites –
Such a gay carpet! poppies by the million;
Such damask! such vermilion!
But if you ask me, mate, the choice of colour
Is scarcely right; this red should have been much duller.

EDMUND BLUNDEN

Undertones of War (1928). Metre and sonnet struggle to keep their shape, and poetic language is challenged by the last two lines. The allusions are to Keats, 'Ode to a Grecian Urn': the garlanded heifer 'lowing at the skies' and the crowd arriving ('Who are these coming to the sacrifice?').

(271) Pillbox

Just see what's happening, Worley! – Worley rose
And round the angled doorway thrust his nose
And Serjeant Hoad went too to snuff the air.
Then war brought down his fist, and missed the pair!
Yet Hoad was scratched by a splinter, the blood came,
And out burst terrors that he'd striven to tame,
A good man, Hoad, for weeks. *I'm blown to bits*,
He groans, he screams. *Come, Bluffer, where's your wits?*
Says Worley, *Bluffer, you've a blighty, man!*
All in the pillbox urged him, here began
His freedom: *Think of Eastbourne and your dad.*
The poor man lay at length and brief and mad
Flung out his cry of doom; soon ebbed and dumb
He yielded. Worley with a tot of rum
And shouting in his face could not restore him.
The ship of Charon over channel bore him.
All marvelled even on that most deathly day
To see this life so spirited away.

EDMUND BLUNDEN

Masks of Time (1925). Describes an incident near Ypres, September 1917
(*Undertones*, XXIII).

(272) Report on Experience

I have been young, and now am not too old;
And I have seen the righteous forsaken,
His health, his honour and his quality taken.
This is not what we were formerly told.

I have seen a green country, useful to the race,
Knocked silly with guns and mines, its villages vanished,
Even the last rat and last kestrel banished –
   God bless us all, this was peculiar grace.

I knew Seraphina; Nature gave her hue,
Glance, sympathy, note, like one from Eden.
I saw her smile warp, heard her lyric deaden;
   She turned to harlotry; – this I took to be new.

Say what you will, our God sees how they run.
These disillusions are His curious proving
That He loves humanity and will go on loving;
   Over there are faith, life, virtue in the sun.

EDMUND BLUNDEN

Near and Far (1929). According to Christopher Ricks this was Blunden's 'best' poem
(*Larkin at Sixty*, 1982, ed. A. Thwaite, 129). Blunden himself said it was
'"Unpremeditated", & almost thrown away'.

   I have ... forsaken: 'I have been young, and now am old; yet I have not seen the
righteous forsaken' (Psalm 37:25).

   Seraphina: presumably beauty personified (Blunden may have been reading Dickens:
the verse from the psalm is alluded to in a paragraph in *Martin Chuzzlewit*, XIII, which
the poem seems to echo; and in 'Mrs Lirriper's Lodgings' (*Christmas Stories*) Seraphina is
'the most beautiful creature that ever was seen ... she had a delicious voice, and she was
delicious altogether').

(273) Memories

'The eradication of memories of the Great War' –
Socialist Government Organ

The Socialist Government speaks:

Though all the Dead were all forgot
  And razed were every tomb,
The Worm – the Worm that dieth not
  Compels Us to our doom.
Though all which once was England stands
  Subservient to Our will,
The Dead of whom we washed Our hands,
  They have observance still.

We laid no finger to Their load.
  We multiplied Their woes.
We used Their dearly-opened road
  To traffic with Their foes:
And yet to Them men turn their eyes,
  To Them are vows renewed
Of Faith, Obedience, Sacrifice,
  Honour and Fortitude!

Which things must perish. But Our hour
  Comes not by staves or swords
So much as, subtly, through the power
  Of small corroding words.
No need to make the plot more plain
  By any open thrust;
But – see Their memory is slain
  Long ere Their bones are dust!

Wisely, but yearly, filch some wreath –
Lay some proud rite aside –
And daily tarnish with Our breath
The ends for which They died.
Distract, deride, decry, confuse –
(Or – if it serve Us – pray!)
So presently We break the use
And meaning of Their day!

RUDYARD KIPLING

Daily Telegraph, 3 November 1930. Also published in pamphlet form as *The Day of the Dead* (1930). *Rudyard Kipling's Verse: Inclusive Edition* (1933). The spirit of internationalism in the late 1920s left Kipling out of step with the times. The memories he wants kept are those of the dead (who still deserve honour), the Labour government (which had told foreign officials they need not observe Armistice Day), and socialists (who had not supported the war effort). Two years later, in 'The Storm Cone', he was forecasting the next war with Germany.
  the Worm: Mark 9:48.

BIOGRAPHICAL
NOTES

Army ranks and abbreviations (principal ranks up to battalion commander:

Private (Pte): Private soldiers are often referred to as 'Tommies' (from a probably fictitious Thomas Atkins). Non-Commissioned Officers (NCOs): Lance-Corporal (L/Cpl), Corporal (Cpl), Sergeant (Sgt). Officers: Second Lieutenant (2/Lt), Lieutenant (Lt) – the two junior ranks, known as subalterns, often commanding platoons. Captain (Capt), often commanding a company; Major (Maj); Lieutenant-Colonel (Lt-Col), often the Commanding Officer (CO) of a battalion.

Other abbreviations
BEF   British Expeditionary Force (the army in France and Flanders)
CBE   Commander of the Order of the British Empire
CH   Companion of Honour
CMG   Companion of the Order of St Michael and St George
DBE   Dame Commander of the Order of the British Empire
DSO   Distinguished Service Order
Ed.   Educated
MC   Military Cross, the most usual gallantry award for junior officers
OM   Order of Merit
OTC   Officer Training Corps
Regt   Regiment
VAD   Voluntary Aid Detachment (for nursing)

Aldington, Richard (1892–1962). One of Pound's Imagist poets. Married another Imagist, the American poet HD (Hilda Dolittle), 1913. Literary editor of the Modernist magazine, *The Egoist* (while he was at the front, T. S. Eliot stood in for him). Volunteered, 1914, but was rejected for medical reasons; worked as secretary to F. M. Hueffer (Ford). Conscripted into the ranks, Devonshire Regt, May 1916. To France, December 1916, with poems by Flint and Manning in his pack. To England for officer training, July 1917. 2/Lt, Royal Sussex Regt, November. France again from April 1918 as signals officer: Acting Capt, October. In the final battles, including the Sambre canal crossing. Diagnosed as neurasthenic. Many books, including the semi-autobiographical novel *Death of a Hero* (1929), a savage attack on wartime values.

Arkwright, John Stanhope (1872–1954). Ed. Eton and Oxford. Barrister, publisher; MP for Hereford, 1900–12. Knighted, 1934.

Bagnold, Enid (1889–1981). Novelist, playwright, poet. Served as a nurse in France and London during the war. CBE, 1976.

Bainbrigge, Philip (1891–1918). Ed. Eton and Cambridge. Taught classics at Shrewsbury School, 1913–17. 2/Lt, Lancashire Fusiliers, November 1917. Close friend of Scott Moncrieff, through whom he met Owen in Scarborough before going out to France, early 1918. Killed in action, September.

Begbie, Harold (1871–1929). Son of a clergyman. Journalist, popular writer on religious and social topics. Many books, including verse on the Boer War, a biography of General Booth of the Salvation Army, and *The Vindication of Great Britain* (1916). The *Daily Chronicle* sent him to America in 1914 to report on public opinion and speak for the Allied cause.

Bendall, Frederic William Duffield (1882–1953). Classical scholar, Cambridge. Schoolmaster and officer in the Territorials before the war. Lt-Col, London Regt, September 1914. Commanded British troops, Khartoum, 1915; Malta, Gallipoli, France, Passchendaele (wounded). CMG and Colonel, 1918. Later an inspector of schools. Director of army education, 1940–42.

Betham-Edwards, Matilda Barbara (1836–1919). Socialist. Many books. Travelled widely in France, where she was esteemed for her studies of peasant agriculture. France's wartime sufferings moved her to write her patriotic *War Poems* (1917) and an account of the German occupation of Alsace (1916).

Binyon, Laurence (1869–1943). Ed. St Paul's and Oxford. On the staff of the British Museum, 1893–1933. His 'For the Fallen' (*The Times*, 21 September 1914), the most well-known consolatory poem of the war, was set to music by Elgar; its two most famous lines are quoted on many war memorials. Worked as medical orderly in France, 1915–16. Reported for the Red Cross on British work for French wounded, 1917. CH, 1932.

Blunden, Edmund (1896–1974). Brought up in rural Kent. Ed. Christ's Hospital and, after the war, Oxford. Due to go up to Oxford in 1915, but instead became 2/Lt, Royal Sussex Regt. Western Front, May 1916 to February 1918, an unusually long period. In some of the worst fighting: Ancre, Ypres, Passchendaele. MC, 1916. Published several small collections of pastoral verse, 1916, and wrote many war poems in 1917, almost all lost in the trenches. With few exceptions, his surviving war poems were written after 1918. Professor, Tokyo, 1924–27. Fellow, Merton College, Oxford, 1931–44. Often wrote about the war's poetry, rarely if ever mentioning his own. Close friend of Sassoon after the war. Edited Owen (1931) and Gurney (1954). His *Undertones of War* (1928) is a superb record of war experience.

Borden, Mary (1886–1968). Daughter of a Chicago millionaire. Ed. at home and Vassar College. Married Douglas Turner, British missionary in India, 1908. After travelling extensively, settled in London: novelist, suffragette, literary hostess, British citizen. In 1914 volunteered to serve with the French Red Cross; from early 1915 financed, directed and nursed in her own 100-bed field hospital for French wounded, keeping it as near the line as possible and enduring many horrors with tireless energy and courage.

Divorced, 1918; married General Edward Spears, the key liaison officer between British and French forces. Gertrude Stein described her as 'very Chicago'. *The Forbidden Zone* (1929), written during the war, contains prose sketches and five long poems about the Somme and French soldiers.

Bradby, Henry Christopher (1868–1947). Son of a Haileybury headmaster. Ed. Rugby and Oxford. Taught at Rugby, 1892–1929: housemaster of School Field, 1910–25, where he succeeded Brooke's father (and Brooke himself, who was acting housemaster for a term in 1910 after his father's death).

Brice, Beatrix [Beatrix Brice-Miller] (1877–1959). Served as a nurse during the war: awarded the Royal Red Cross, 1920. Said to be the originator of the Albert Hall commemoration of the original BEF, December 1917. Compiled three books on the Ypres battlefields, 1925–29. According to her *Times* obituary, the 'ruling purpose' of her life after the war was to ensure that the nation remembered its debt to the professional army of 1914.

Bridges, Robert (1844–1930). Ed. Eton and Oxford. Poet Laureate, 1913–30. Deeply moved by Belgium's resistance, he wrote to *The Times*, 2 September 1914, that the war was a struggle between Good and Evil – but he composed few 'official' war poems. Invited to compile a book for soldiers and the bereaved, he produced *The Spirit of Man* (1915), a well-received anthology of prose and verse from all periods, designed to show literature's highest values. After the war, he retracted some of his wartime statements and called for forgiveness and reconciliation. He was appalled by the 1919 peace treaty, and was attacked in Parliament by Horatio Bottomley for not writing a poem in praise of it. OM, 1929.

Brittain, Vera Mary (1893–1970). Left Oxford to become a VAD nurse, 1915, serving in London, Malta, France. Her fiancé Roland Leighton was killed in 1915, two close friends in 1917, and her brother Edward, on the Italian Front, in 1918. Her 1914–18 poems are largely elegiac and documentary, and do not show the anger at the war that is the dominant note of the poetry she wrote after she returned to Oxford in 1919 to complete her studies. She was active in feminism and peace work from the 1920s onwards, and became a pacifist in 1937. Her *Testament of Youth* (1933) was one of the most successful 'war books' of its time.

Brooke, Rupert (1887–1915). Son of a Rugby housemaster. Ed. Rugby and Cambridge. Fellow, King's College, from 1913. His pre-war poetry shows his scholarly knowledge of Jacobean literature. Leader of the Georgian poets, atheist, Fabian socialist, scorner of convention, some-time Decadent – not the typical public-school patriot he is still often made out to be. Enlisted August 1914: Sub-Lt, Royal Naval Division. The sight of refugees and burning houses during the retreat from Antwerp in October gave him his sudden, intense conviction that the Allied cause was just. Died of blood poisoning, 23 April 1915, on the way to Gallipoli, and rapidly became a national icon.

Burton, Claude Edward Coleman Hamilton (1869– ?). As 'Touchstone' in the *Daily*

Mail and 'CEB' in the *Evening News*, published an average of 300 poems a year for over forty years. His 1915 book of war poems is dedicated to Lord Northcliffe, 'my chief and friend for nearly nineteen years'.

Cannan, May Wedderburn (1893–1973). Daughter of the Secretary, Oxford University Press. Admirer of Kipling: like him, believed the pre-war Liberal government had increased the risk of conflict by dismissing early warnings about Germany. Became a VAD nurse, 1911, among general preparations for a possible war. Nurse in France during the war, then helped to produce propaganda at the Press. In 1918 worked for MI5 in Paris and became engaged to Bevil Quiller-Couch, 'Q''s son, who died of influenza in 1919 after serving in the army throughout the war.

Chesterton, Gilbert Keith (1874–1936). A famous literary figure in pre-war London. Saw himself as a patriot on the side of ordinary people against capitalism and socialism. Opposed to the establishment press and international finance, but also to Prussia. Editor of the *New Witness* in succession to his brother, when the latter enlisted.

Coates, Florence Earle (1850–1927). Born in Philadelphia into an aristocratic American family. Ed. private schools and in France and Belgium. Several volumes of traditionalist poetry. Knew and was encouraged by Matthew Arnold. Elected poet laureate of Pennsylvania. Described in the October 1914 *Poetry Review* (with the magazine's typical flattery) as 'the leading living poet' of the USA. In Paris and England, summer 1914; while waiting to return home, she sent several poems to British periodicals, deploring war but strongly supporting the Allied cause.

Constantine, H. F. Described as a Major in the *English Review*, which published several of his poems in 1918, but the *Army List* contains no one of this name and rank. Pseudonym?

Coulson, Leslie (1889–1916). Journalist before the war. Enlisted in the ranks, London Regt, preferring not to seek a commission. Wounded, Gallipoli. Sgt. In the Somme advance, 1st July 1916. Killed in action, October.

Crawshay-Williams, Eliot (1879–1962). Ed. Malvern, Eton and Oxford. 2/Lt, Royal Field Artillery, 1900; served in India. Worked briefly with Edward Marsh as secretary to Winston Churchill, then became Liberal MP for Leicester, 1910–13, and parliamentary secretary to Lloyd George, but had to resign when his marriage collapsed. Returned to the army. CO, 1 Leicestershires, Egypt and Sinai, 1915–17. Lt-Col, Northern Command, 1918–20. Loathed the war. Later wrote plays, novels, film scripts.

Dartford, Richard Charles Gordon (1895–1988). Born in Lisbon, where his parents lived. Ed. Haileybury. Due to go up to Oxford, October 1914, but took a commission in the London Regt. Near-fatal wound, Loos, September 1915: a bullet went right through his head, damaging his jaw. Near-complete recovery after eight months' sick leave in England and Portugal. Brigade Intelligence Officer, France, June–November

1916. Capt, July. Liaison Officer, Portuguese Expeditionary Force. MC, 1918. Oxford after the war. Major, Intelligence Corps, 1940–45.

de la Mare, Walter (1873–1956). Ed. St Paul's Cathedral choir school. Left at sixteen to work for an oil company, but after eight tedious years a government grant and later a civil list pension enabled him to be a full-time writer of poems, short stories, essays. Worked for Ministry of Food, 1917–18. CH, 1948. OM, 1953.

de Stein, Edward (1887–1965). Ed. Eton and Oxford. Succeeded father as chairman of a tobacco firm, 1911. King's Royal Rifle Corps, 1914–18. Major. Merchant banker after the war, founding his own firm. President, Gallaher Ltd, 1928 to late 1950s. During Second World War, director of finance, raw materials, Ministry of Supply. Chaired Red Cross finance committee, 1949–63. Knighted, 1946.

Dircks, Helen. Two books of verse, 1918 and 1920. The composer Frank Bridge tried setting 'To You in France' to music, but did not complete the score.

Dobell, Eva (1867–1963). Worked as a nurse during the war and corresponded with prisoners. Her poems record admiration and sympathy for soldiers in hospital.

Doyle, Arthur Conan (1859–1930). Creator of Sherlock Holmes. Served as qualified doctor during the South African war. Knighted, 1902. Volunteered again as doctor, 1914, but too old to be accepted; instead, worked as military correspondent and historian, writing a detailed six-volume account of the fighting as events unfolded. His son died of wounds and influenza, 1918.

Drinkwater, John (1882–1937). Left Oxford High School aged fifteen and worked as an insurance clerk, hating it, until he and Barry Jackson founded the Pilgrim Players, 1907, and the Birmingham Repertory Theatre, 1913, where he became general manager. Unfit for military service. Nine volumes of verse and many plays. Founder-contributor, *Georgian Poetry*.

Elton, Godfrey (1892–1973). Ed. Rugby, where he heard Brooke lecture, and Oxford. 2/Lt, Hampshire Regt, September 1914. India, the Gulf, Mesopotamia, 1915–16. Wounded and captured, Kut; prisoner in Turkey. Capt. Fellow in modern history, Queen's College, Oxford, 1919–39. Friendly with Monro, Sassoon and others after the war. Unsuccessful Labour parliamentary candidate; much public service for church and state. Baron, 1934.

Ewer, William Norman (1885–1977). Ed. Merchant Taylors' and Cambridge. Worked for the socialist *Daily Herald* from its foundation in 1912. Knew and admired Brooke. Conscientious objector during the war. *Herald* foreign editor, 1919: reported on the peace conference and was bitterly critical of the treaty. Expelled from Communist Party, 1922. His views moderated in later years. CBE, 1954.

Faber, Geoffrey (1889–1961). Ed. Rugby and Oxford. London Regt, 1914–19: France,

Belgium. Capt, 1916. Distinguished publisher: founder, 1921, and president, Faber & Faber. Recruited T. S. Eliot as a director and published many leading writers. Knighted, 1954.

Fletcher, John Gould (1886–1950). Born in Arkansas, son of a wealthy banker. Ed. local schools and Harvard. Settled in London, 1908; met Pound and many other poets and became an Imagist, the first writer from the American south to take up Modernism. His letters and autobiography record he was in London during the war, except for eighteen months in the US from November 1914. Believed in the Allied cause, despite the tone of some of his poems. Returned to Arkansas, 1933.

Flint, Frank Stuart (1885–1960). Brought up in poverty. Left school at thirteen but read voraciously, teaching himself many languages. In 1908, with Hulme and others, and later Pound, began discussing the principles of what was to become Impressionist/ Imagist/Modernist verse. Three books of poetry and many articles, including a brilliant survey of contemporary French poetry (*Poetry Review*, 1912) and the first Imagist manifesto (*Poetry*, 1913). Friend of Aldington, Monro and other poets. Civil servant, Ministry of Labour. Twice almost killed in London air raids. Disqualified from military service by unfitness and his job until late 1917, when he was conscripted into the ranks of the Rifle Brigade for duties, mainly clerical, in England.

Ford, Ford Madox: see Hueffer, Ford Madox.

Ford, S. Gertrude. Ardent pacifist and feminist. Many articles on spirituality and poetry. Edited the *Little Books of Georgian Verse* series for 'Erskine Macdonald' (Galloway Kyle) and contributed poems to Kyle's *Poetry Review*.

Frankau, Gilbert (1884–1952). Left Eton to join his father's cigar business. Travelled round the world, 1912–14. 2/Lt, East Surrey Regt, October 1914. Transferred to Royal Field Artillery, March 1915. Lt and Adjutant, July. Loos, Ypres, Somme. For a year from September 1916, Staff Capt, lent to the Foreign Office and put in charge of film propaganda in Italy, doctoring British newsreels to make them seem more moving and heroic, until the job was abolished. Ordered to rejoin artillery, he pointed out he had never actually been trained as a gunner: his experience had been 'confined entirely to staff duties'. Treated for shellshock and, in March 1918, invalided out of the army. Passionate admirer of Kipling, whom he met in Italy. Novels, poems, memoirs.

Freston, Rex [Hugh Reginald] (1891–1916). Ed. Dulwich and Oxford, where he was reading English when war broke out. 2/Lt, Royal Berkshire Regt, April 1915. To France, December. Killed by a shell, January 1916.

Garrod, Heathcote William (1878–1960). Fellow of Merton College, Oxford, 1904–60. Civil servant, Ministry of Munitions, 1915–18. Oxford Professor of Poetry, 1923–28. Books on the Romantic poets and a major edition of Keats. CBE, 1918.

BIOGRAPHICAL NOTES

Gibson, Wilfrid Wilson (1878–1962). Born in Hexham, Northumberland. Attended several local schools. Prolific full-time poet: early work conventional and romantic, but in 1905 he decided a poet should focus on contemporary social realities, writing about the lives of the rural and industrial working class. Well known by 1912, when he moved to London and got to know Brooke, Monro and many other writers. Founder-contributor, *Georgian Poetry*. Lecture tour, USA, 1917. Volunteered repeatedly but rejected as 'altogether unfit' until October 1917, when he was conscripted into Army Service Corps Motor Transport. Medical Officer's clerk, 1918. Never served abroad, despite many statements to the contrary.

Golding, Louis (1895–1958). Parents, Orthodox Jews, arrived in England from central Europe just before he was born. Ed. Manchester Grammar School and, after the war, Oxford. Unfit for active service, but worked with the YMCA and Friends' Ambulance Unit in Salonika and France. Poems in many wartime periodicals, often fiercely critical of war and right-wing civilian values. Many books, articles, novels.

Graves, Robert von Ranke (1895–1985). Son of a German mother, a fact that caused him some embarrassment in his youth. Ed. Charterhouse and, after the war, Oxford. Due to go up to Oxford, 1914, but took a commission in the Royal Welch Fusiliers. Capt, 1915. In severe fighting on the Western Front, April 1915 to July 1916, when a near-fatal wound left him physically and mentally unfit for further active service. Insisted on returning to the front in late 1916, but soon had to be sent home again. Home duties until 1919. His autobiography, *Goodbye to All That* (1929), describes his war experiences and friendship with his fellow Fusilier, Sassoon. Met and encouraged Owen, 1917–18. Many books: poetry, fiction, criticism, etc. Oxford Professor of Poetry, 1961–66.

Graves, Rosaleen (1894–1989). Sister of Robert, with whom she wrote stories as a child. Nurse during the war, in London and from November 1917 in France. Qualified as a doctor, Oxford, 1927; practice in London and from 1939 Devon, where she continued working into her eighties.

Grenfell, Julian (1888–1915). Eldest son of the Earl of Desborough. Ed. Eton and Oxford. Went through a period of rebellion and self-doubt before the war. Royal Dragoons, 1910: India, South Africa. To France, October 1914; Capt; DSO. Wounded near Ypres, 12 May 1915; died on 26 May, a month after Brooke.

Gurney, Ivor (1890–1937). Son of a Gloucester tailor. Ed. King's School, Gloucester, and Royal College of Music. Began writing verse and setting poems to music, 1912–13. Volunteered but was rejected for poor eyesight, 1914. Pte, Gloucestershire Regt, February 1915. His wartime letters express admiration for the Georgians, especially Gibson and Masefield. Western Front, May 1916, with no home leave, until mildly gassed, September 1917. To hospital near Edinburgh. Despite persistent myth, war service did not send him mad: in fact, it seems to have slowed down symptoms that had begun to show themselves before 1914. They became more pronounced after his return to Britain, perhaps as a result of a hopeless love affair in hospital. Discharged from the army, October 1918. Wrote much of his best poetry in the next few years, but became increasingly eccentric. Confined to asylums from 1922. Over 1,700 poems and fragments survive among his papers, as well as hundreds of musical settings.

Hamilton, Helen. Schoolteacher.

Hardy, Thomas (1840–1928). By 1914 probably the most famous living British writer, deeply admired by many young poets, including Sassoon. A version of his epic drama on the Napoleonic wars, *The Dynasts* (1904–08), was staged early in the war to strengthen public morale. Wrote poems in support of the war effort, but was greatly distressed by the slaughter and the subsequent peace treaty. Always preferred poetry to prose: despite his age, his poetic talents had been at their height since 1912, aroused by his first wife's death in that year.

Herbert, Alan Patrick (1890–1971). Ed. Winchester and Oxford. Joined the ranks, Royal Naval Volunteer Reserve, August 1914. Sub-Lt, early 1915. Gallipoli and Somme with Royal Naval Division. Severely wounded, 1917: invalided out. Much of his wartime verse was humorous, often satirizing the General Staff, but he also wrote a strongly anti-German broadsheet, 'The Seamen's Boycott Song', 1918. His novel, *The Secret Battle* (1919), about a soldier's breakdown and execution for cowardice, was highly acclaimed. Staff of *Punch* from 1924. Many books, plays, musicals. Independent MP for Oxford University, 1935–45. Knighted, 1945. CH, 1970.

Herbertson, Agnes Grozier. Born in Oslo, lived in Cornwall. Novelist, journalist, books for children.

Herschel-Clarke, May. One collection of verse, 1917. Apparently a reviewer and film critic after the war.

Hodgson, William Noel (1893–1916). Son of a bishop. Ed. Durham School and Oxford, where he volunteered, August 1914: 2/Lt, later Lt, Devonshire Regt. MC for bravery at Loos, 1915. As 'Edward Melbourne', contributed prose and poems to the *New Witness* and other periodicals for several years. Killed in the Somme advance, 1 July 1916; his batman was killed while trying to help him.

Hooley, Teresa (1888–1973). Born in Derbyshire. Ed. privately and at Howard College, Bedford.

Horne, Cyril Morton (1887–1916). Working in an American theatre when war broke out, but returned to volunteer. 2/Lt, King's Own Scottish Borderers. France, summer 1915. Capt. Killed at Loos, January 1916, while trying to rescue a wounded soldier in no man's land.

Housman, Alfred Edward (1859–1936). Professor of Latin, Cambridge, 1911–36: brilliant, meticulous scholar. His *A Shropshire Lad* (1896), brief lyrics marked by skilled simplicity of form and diction and a pervasive melancholy, was a major influence on many war poets.

Howard, Geoffrey (1889–1973). Ed. Haileybury and Oxford. Described himself in *Who's Who* as having been a 'Temporary Gentleman', Royal Fusiliers, 1914–18. Served in France. Barrister, 1919. County court judge, 1952–63, and a Master of the Bench, Inner Temple, 1951–68.

Hueffer, Ford Madox [Ford Madox Ford from 1919] (1873–1939). Son of a German father and English mother. Well-known literary figure before 1914 and an important influence on Modernism: Pound thought him the best critic in England. Founder, and briefly editor, *English Review*, 1908. 2/Lt, Welch Regt, 1915. Concussed by shell blast, unconscious for three weeks, Somme, July 1916. Ypres. Pneumonia: invalided out for home duties. Began *Parade's End* (1924–28), four of the greatest novels of the war, in Monro's cottage on the Riviera, 1922.

Hulme, Thomas Ernest (1883–1917). Ed. Newcastle-under-Lyme High School and Cambridge (sent down for idleness and rowdy behaviour). The most influential theorist in the early stages of Modernist poetry and art. Formed a group with Flint and others to discuss ideas, 1908; Pound joined, 1909. Volunteered as Pte, Hon. Artillery Company, the oldest regt in the army, 10 August 1914. To France, December. Neuve Chapelle. Wounded, April 1915; sent to hospital in London. In 1915–16 the *New Age* published seventeen articles by him (signed 'North Staffs') on the conduct of the war, exposing inefficiency and outdated planning but also attacking pacifism. 2/Lt, Royal Marine Artillery, March 1916. Sent to a line of heavy guns on the Belgian coast, May 1917. Blown to pieces by a shell, September.

Kaufman, Herbert (1878–1947). American newspaperman, perhaps resident in London during the war: his war poems are fervently pro-British, and he contributed articles to *The Times* and other British periodicals.

Kendall, Guy (1876–1960). Ed. Eton and Oxford. Taught at Charterhouse, 1902–16, where he ran the Poetry Society – 'one of the few masters who insisted on treating the boys better than they deserved', according to one of the Society's members, Robert Graves (*Goodbye to All That*). Headmaster, University College School, Hampstead, 1916–36.

Kennedy, Geoffrey Anketell Studdert (1883–1928). Ed. Leeds Grammar School and Trinity College, Dublin. Ordained, 1908. Army chaplain, 1915. Three periods at the front, 1916–18, where he risked his life and shared the troops' hardships. In the intervals he worked behind the lines, preaching powerful, unconventional sermons to large congregations. MC, 1917. Known as 'Woodbine Willie' for his ready supply of cigarettes. In 1916–17 began writing painfully honest war verse, treating basic Christian issues in plain language, recognizing both heroism and horrors and seeing Christ not as the Almighty but as the suffering God of love.

Kerr, Robert Watson (1895–1960). Ed. Edinburgh. Journalist before and after the war, writing for *The Scotsman* and other papers. Lt, Tank Corps; badly wounded and awarded MC during the German offensive, March 1918.

Kettle, Thomas Michael (1880–1916). Ed. University College, Dublin. Barrister and journalist, joint editor of *The Nationalist*, an Irish weekly. MP for East Tyrone, 1906, 1910. A compelling speaker and popular public figure. Professor of national economics, Dublin, 1911. Sympathizing with Belgium and believing Britain was for once in the right, joined the Dublin Fusiliers, November 1914, and gave recruiting speeches. To France, July 1916, where he resolved to dedicate the rest of his life to peace. Killed in action, Somme, September.

Kipling, Rudyard (1865–1936). By 1914 perhaps second only to Hardy as the country's most famous author. British difficulties in the South African war convinced him conscription was necessary, and he campaigned for it loudly up to 1914, alienating many readers. The first British and youngest ever writer to receive the Nobel prize for literature, 1907, but he refused all official British honours, preferring to keep his independence. He also refused fees for his 'public' poems. From 1914, devoted himself to writing poems and prose in support of the war effort, continuing his admiration for ordinary Tommies, angrily denouncing inefficiencies and deploring America's neutrality. The death of his only son at Loos, 1915, affected him deeply but increased his hatred of Germany. Composed the standard inscriptions for war cemeteries. One of the instigators of the burial of the Unknown Warrior in Westminster Abbey.

Kitchin, Clifford Henry Benn (1895–1967). Ed. Clifton and Oxford. Volunteered, September 1915. Lt, Warwickshire Regt. France, 1916–18. Crime novels and other books. On the fringes of the Bloomsbury group.

Lee, Joseph (1876–1949). From a poor Dundee family. Left school at fourteen to work in a solicitor's office, then went to sea. Worked for a time as a rancher in Canada. Trained at the Slade School of Art in the 1890s before returning to Dundee as cartoonist, journalist, editor. Pte, Black Watch, 1914. Sgt. Western Front, 1915–16. 2/Lt, King's Royal Rifle Corps, 1917. Captured, late 1917, spending the rest of the war in German prison camps. Two books of war poems, illustrated with his own drawings. Later sub-editor, *News Chronicle*, London.

Leftwich, Joseph (1892–1983). Born in the Netherlands of Polish-Jewish parents; came with them to London, aged six. With Rosenberg, one of the four 'Whitechapel Boys', a group of poor but intellectually very active young artist and thinkers. His 1911 diary is an important source for Rosenberg biography. Socialist and pacifist: would have refused to serve in the army, but was exempt as a Dutch national. Esteemed in Anglo-Jewry as journalist and translator of Yiddish literature.

Letts, Winifred Mabel (1882–1972). Ed. St Anne's, Bromley, and Alexandra College, Dublin. Irish poet, playwright, novelist. Worked for part of the war as masseuse in military and pensions hospitals.

Lyon, Percy Hugh Beverley (1893–1986). Ed. Rugby and Oxford. Capt, Durham Light Infantry. MC, 1917. Wounded and captured, May 1918. Completed his Oxford degree after the war. Taught at Cheltenham, 1921–26; headmaster, Edinburgh Academy, 1926–31, and Rugby, 1931–48, where he is remembered for his tolerance, enthusiasm and good humour.

Lyon, Walter Scott Stuart (1886–1915). Ed. Haileybury, Oxford, Edinburgh. Advocate, 1912. Part-time Lt, Royal Scots, 1913. Mobilized, 4 August 1914. To Belgium, February 1915. Wrote several poems in the trenches, patriotic but hoping for a world without war. Killed near Ypres, May 1915, the first officer in his battalion to be killed in the war.

Macaulay, Rose (1881–1958). Ed. Oxford (High School and University). Six novels by 1914. Nurse and landgirl, 1914–16, then civil servant, War Office. After the war joined Constable publishers and became a distinguished novelist. DBE, 1958.

McCrae, John (1872–1918). Canadian doctor, son of an artillery officer. Qualified at Toronto University, 1898. Part-time soldier before the war; volunteered for service in France, August 1914. Ran a dressing station near the line at Ypres. Promoted Lt-Col and posted to a Canadian hospital in Boulogne, July 1915, working there until his death from pneumonia, January 1918.

Mackintosh, Ewart Alan (1893–1917). Ed. St Paul's and Oxford, where he volunteered: 2/Lt, Seaforth Highlanders, December 1914. To France, July 1915. MC, May 1916. Invalided home with blood poisoning from barbed wire, August. Trained cadets in Cambridge from November. Became engaged, hoped to enter politics after the war. Lt, December. Sent back to trenches, October 1917. Killed at Cambrai, November.

Manning, Frederic (1882–1935). Born in Australia. Settled in England, 1903, becoming a minor literary figure, friendly with Aldington, Pound and others. Despite chronic asthma and several failed attempts to be accepted as an officer, joined as Pte, King's Shropshire Light Infantry, October 1915. To France, August 1916: Guillemont, Serre. L/Cpl. Shellshocked and slightly gassed. Officer training in England, December: 2/Lt, Royal Irish Regt, May 1917. Posted to Ireland, where he was severely reprimanded for heavy drinking: neurasthenia diagnosed. Resigned from the army, February 1918. Achieved little after the war until 1929, when a publisher persuaded him to write what became one of the greatest war novels, *The Middle Parts of Fortune* (1929; expurgated version, *Her Privates We*, 1930).

Masefield, Charles John Beech (1882–1917). First cousin of John Masefield. Joined father's firm of solicitors after leaving school, qualifying in 1905. Novel and two books of verse before the war. 2/Lt, North Staffordshire Regt, January 1915. France, March 1915 to October 1916; long period of leave; France again from May 1917, when he won the MC. Wounded and captured, 1 July: died of wounds next day.

Masefield, John (1878–1967). Unfit for military service, but volunteered as a Red

Cross orderly, 1915: worked devotedly for the wounded in France, but soon had to be sent home exhausted. Took some boats to Gallipoli for ferrying wounded, but arrived as the campaign was ending. Deeply convinced the war was a German crime, he undertook propaganda work, lecturing in America, 1916, and writing a very popular, romanticized account of Gallipoli (1916). After touring the Somme battlefields in 1917 as an unpaid 2/Lt, wrote two books about them and lectured again in America, 1918. Many books: poetry, novels. One of the early Georgians. Poet Laureate, 1930–67.

Mercer, Thomas William (1884–1947). Started work in a grocer's shop aged twelve. Socialist journalist and pacifist. Many war verses in the *Labour Leader*, organ of the radical Independent Labour Party. Later worked and wrote for the co-operative movement. Labour candidate for Moss Side, Manchester, 1919.

Mew, Charlotte (1869–1928). Lived in Bloomsbury with her sister Anne. Stories in the *Yellow Book* and elsewhere, but wrote few poems until 1909. Her most famous poem, 'The Farmer's Bride', attracted attention when it appeared in the *Nation*, 1913. Hardy and others thought she was the finest British woman poet of the time.

Meynell, Alice Christiana Gertrude (1847–1922). Roman Catholic essayist, poet, feminist. Her poems were admired by Tennyson, Ruskin and others. Her sister Elizabeth (Lady Butler) was well known as a painter of battle scenes. One of Alice's seven children, Wilfred, became publisher and conscientious objector, running the *Herald* during the war and founding the Pelican Press, publishing West's *Diary of a Dead Officer*, Postgate's *Poems* and other anti-war books.

Mitchell, Miss G. M.

Monro, Harold Edward (1879–1932). Ed. Radley and Cambridge. Devoted much of his life and small private income to promoting poetry and poets. Founder and editor, *Poetry Review* (1912), *Poetry and Drama* (1913–14), *The Chapbook* (1919–25), publishing articles and poems by Brooke, Pound, Gibson, Flint and many others. Opened his Poetry Bookshop in Bloomsbury, 1912, as a centre for poets. Gibson and Hulme lodged there, 1913–14; Owen attended several of the twice-weekly readings and stayed for ten days, 1915–16. Bookshop publications included all five volumes of *Georgian Poetry*, Pound's *Des imagistes* and first books by Aldington, Mew and Graves. Impending conscription drove Monro to volunteer, June 1916: 2/Lt, Royal Garrison Artillery. Unfit for active service, he was posted to anti-aircraft gun stations in England, hating every moment of it. Desk job, Ministry of Information, 1918, after a breakdown in health. Revived the bookshop after the war.

Nesbit, Edith (1858–1924). Novelist, poet and effectively the inventor of the children's adventure story. Fabian socialist.

Newbolt, Henry (1862–1938). Ed. Clifton, where he knew Haig, and Oxford. Barrister for twelve years. Famous from the 1890s for verse celebrating imperialist, British values. Poems such as 'Vitaï Lampada' ('play up! and play the game!') and 'Clifton Chapel' provided language and imagery for many wartime imitators, sometimes to his regret. Worked in Admiralty and Foreign Office during the war. Much public service. Knighted, 1915. CH, 1922.

Nichols, Robert (1893–1944). Ed. Winchester and, briefly, Oxford (sent down for rowdiness and failing exams). Volunteered, 1914, not revealing he had been under treatment for nervous instability. 2/Lt, Royal Field Artillery. Sent home with neurasthenia after ten days at the front, September 1915; eventually rated 'totally unfit' for officer's duties. Resigned his commission, September 1916. Desk jobs, Ministries of Labour and Information. The war poems in his 1917 book were highly praised, and he became friendly with Sassoon, the Sitwells and Graves. Propaganda work in USA, 1918–19: lectured on Graves, Sassoon, Sorley and other war poets. Professor of English literature, Tokyo, 1921–24.

Norman, Alfred George Bathurst (1898–1918). Surname sometimes given as Bathurst-Norman. Son of a clergyman. Ed. Harrow: left to join the Royal Flying Corps. Commissioned, July 1917. Back injuries after a crash in England, November. Rated fit only for limited flying, but he transferred to the Independent Air Force. Crashed in fog and was killed, November 1918. A 'boy of great literary promise, spiritual, sensitive … loving much and much loved' [Harrow archives].

Oman, Carola (1897–1978). Daughter of Sir Charles Oman, Oxford historian. Close friend of May Cannan. Red Cross nurse, Western Front, 1916–19. Worked for the Red Cross again, 1938–58.

Owen, Everard (1860–1949). Anglican clergyman and classics master at Harrow.

Owen, Wilfred (1893–1918). Brought up to be a devout evangelical. Ed. Birkenhead Institute (an independent school) and Shrewsbury Technical School, where he took the four-year pupil–teacher course. Qualified as elementary school teacher, 1911. Assistant to Vicar of Dunsden, 1911–13, hoping to prepare for university and perhaps the church, but lost his faith and resolved to become a poet. Language tutor in France, 1913–15. Volunteered for officer training, Artists' Rifles, October 1915. 2/Lt, Manchester Regt, June 1916. Serre, Beaumont Hamel, St Quentin, January–April 1917. Shellshocked, April. Sent to Craiglockhart War Hospital, where he met Sassoon in August. Sassoon's encouragement started him writing war poems: all his best work was written between September 1917 and October 1918. Light duties, Scarborough, November; training, Ripon, spring 1918; France again, September. Helped to lead the final breakthrough on the Hindenburg line, October: briefly Acting Capt; awarded MC. Killed on the Sambre canal, 4 November.

Oxenham, John (1852–1941). Born William Arthur Dunkerley, but took the name of a character in Kingsley's *Westward Ho!* Prolific writer of popular verse and fiction, basing his work on a simple, non-sectarian Christianity that stressed the value of suffering. Undoubtedly the best-selling poet of the war: he claimed his little books of verse sold over a million copies.

Penrose, Claude Quayle Lewis (1893–1918). Born in Florida, but apparently British: to England with parents, 1897. Ed. United Services College and Royal Military Academy, Woolwich. 2/Lt, Royal Garrison Artillery, 1913. To France on outbreak of war; remained there until his death except for periods of leave. Neuve Chapelle, Somme and other battles, commanding gun batteries. Major, mentioned in despatches 1917. MC, 1916, and bar, 1918 (for gallantry in the March retreat). Died of wounds, 1918.

Phillips, Stephen (1864–1915). Actor with the Benson company, then lecturer in an army college. By the late 1890s well known as a poet: his verse plays from 1902 were seen as a great hope for the revival of English poetic drama. Editor, *Poetry Review*, 1913–15.

Plowman, Max [Mark] (1883–1941). Worked for his father's brickworks from age sixteen, then literary journalism. Volunteered as medical orderly, December 1914. Applied for commission, September 1915: 2/Lt, W Yorks Regt. Blown up and concussed, January 1917: sent to Bowhill, a Scottish hospital linked to Craiglockhart; treated by Sassoon's doctor, W. H. R. Rivers. Deciding that 'killing man is always killing God', made contact with pacifists, formally resigned from the army and deliberately disobeyed an order, early 1918. Dismissed from the army by court martial: much publicity in left-wing press. A senior War Office official intervened, hoping Plowman could be declared mentally deficient and dealt with kindly, thereby showing the army as humane and pacifists as probably mad. The top expert on shellshock, C. S. Myers, held a medical board but could find no sign of insanity, so the court's decision was upheld, leaving Plowman liable for conscription into the ranks. He refused to serve, risking severe penalties, but the war ended before a decision was reached. Worked with Brittain and others for pacifist organizations after 1918.

Pope, Jessie (1868–1941). Innumerable poems in magazines, children's books and newspapers; also wrote light fiction. War poems in *Daily Mail*, where she alternated with 'Touchstone' [Burton], and *Daily Express*. Owen's 'Dulce et Decorum Est' was originally addressed to her.

Postgate, Margaret [later Dame Margaret Postgate Cole] (1893–1980). Daughter of a Cambridge don. Ed. Roedean and Cambridge, where she became a socialist. Joined the Fabian Society's research department, 1917. Married G. D. H. Cole, the Labour historian, 1918. Many books, including history, politics and twenty-nine detective novels. DBE, 1970.

Pound, Ezra (1885–1972). Born in Idaho. Arrived in London, 1908. Campaigned to reform English poetry, collaborating for a while with Monro but soon falling out with him and many others. Founded 'Imagism', 1912. Befriended Eliot, promoting his work. Admired the courage of British troops but scorned the war itself. Exempt from conscription as an American, he remained in London throughout the war and must sometimes have been sneered at in the streets as a 'shirker'. Eventually decided England was a 'shit-house' and moved to Paris, 1920.

Read, Herbert (1893–1968). Ed. at a school for orphans, Halifax; left to work in a bank, but was able to enter Leeds University, 1912. Studied Nietzsche, discovered Modernist art and Imagism – also joined the OTC. Applied for commission, August 1914: 2/Lt, Yorkshire Regt, January 1915. Wounded, Ypres, March 1916. Began writing poems critical of the war and wartime rhetoric, 1916. Met Pound and Eliot, 1917–18. MC, 1917. Took command of his battalion when its CO was wounded during the German March Offensive, 1918 (see his much-admired prose account, *In Retreat*): awarded DSO. Brother killed, October 1918. Many publications, including a long meditative poem, *The End of a War* (1933). Eminent art critic after the war, and committed pacifist. Knighted, 1953.

Rickword, Edgell (1898–1982). Ed. Colchester Grammar School. Left to join the Artists' Rifles, September 1916. 2/Lt, Royal Berkshire Regt, 1917. MC. Wounded several times, 1918: developed blood poisoning, eventually losing an eye. Admired Sassoon's war poems as the first to deal with war 'in the vocabulary of war'. Literary critic, writing on Symbolism, Eliot, Rosenberg and other subjects in the 1920s, when he also wrote his few war poems. After 1930, turned to political journalism, arguing for a humane form of Marxism.

Robertson, Alexander (1882–1916). Ed. George Watson's College and Edinburgh and Oxford Universities. Lecturer in history, Sheffield, 1914. Volunteered, York and Lancaster Regt, September 1914. Pte, later Cpl. Missing near Serre, 1 July 1916.

Rodd, Rennell (1858–1941). Ed. Haileybury and Oxford. Friendly with Oscar Wilde and the Pre-Raphaelites in the 1880s, but chose to become a diplomat, serving in Germany, Greece, Africa and elsewhere. Knighted, 1899. British ambassador, Rome, 1908–19, playing a key role in the events leading up to Italy joining the Allies in 1915. Helped to found the Keats–Shelley Association in Rome. British delegate, League of Nations, 1921, 1923. MP, 1928–33. Baron Rennell of Rodd, 1933. Over twenty books: classical studies, memoirs, poems.

Rodker, John (1894–1955). Jewish immigrant parents, father a corset-maker in London's East End. Working as clerk in the Customs House, 1911, when he, Leftwich and Simon Winsten invited Rosenberg to join their group of 'Whitechapel Boys'. Faced with conscription, declared himself a conscientious objector: imprisoned, 1917. In 1919 set up his short-lived Ovid Press, publishing Pound's *Hugh Selwyn Mauberley* and work by Eliot, Wyndham Lewis and others. Later played an important part in publishing Joyce and Freud.

Rosenberg, Isaac (1890–1918). Son of poor Lithuanian-Jewish parents who came to England, 1886–88, settling in the East End. Apprenticed to an engraver, 1909. Friend of Rodker and Leftwich. Slade School of Fine Art, 1911: fellow-students included David Bomberg, Mark Gertler, Stanley Spencer, Paul Nash, C. R. W. Nevinson. Made contact with Binyon, who encouraged his poetry. Met Edward Marsh, who bought some of his paintings and introduced him to Pound and others. To South Africa for health reasons, June 1914 to March 1915. Believed it was wrong to join up 'with no patriotic convictions' (some of his minor poems are actually very patriotic), but could not find work. Enlisted in a Bantam battalion (for men of below regulation height), Suffolk Regt, October. Transferred to King's Own Royal Lancaster Regt, early 1916. France, June 1916 until death, except for ten days' leave in 1917, enduring severe discomfort and danger. Missing, 1 April 1918.

Sackville, Lady Margaret (1881–1963). Daughter of 7th Earl de la Warre. Wrote verse from age six, eventually publishing twenty-one volumes of poetry and prose, some for children. President, Poetry Society, before the war. Active supporter of the pacifist Union of Democratic Control, 1914–18. Gave talks and readings in aid of the Red Cross. Lived for much of her life in Edinburgh, where she met Sassoon and almost certainly Owen, 1917.

Sassoon, Siegfried (1886–1967). Ed. Marlborough and Cambridge. Cricket and fox-hunting before the war, but also some verse. Volunteered, Sussex Yeomanry, 3 August 1914. 2/Lt, eventually Capt, Royal Welch Fusiliers, May 1915. To France, November. Friendship with another Fusilier-poet, Graves. MC, Somme, June 1916. Invalided home with trench fever, August; began writing satires. France again, February 1917; shoulder wound, Arras, April. During convalescence in England, composed his protest against the war: might have been court-martialled, but was instead sent to Craiglockhart Hospital for Neurasthenic Officers, near Edinburgh, 20 July. Protest read in House of Commons and printed in *The Times*, 30–31 July. At Craiglockhart composed some of his harshest poems, showing them to his fellow-patient Owen. Decided to return to active service: Ireland, January 1918; Palestine; France, May. Head wound, July, ended his soldiering. After the war worked briefly as literary editor of the socialist *Daily Herald*. Later wrote many poems and memoirs, including his famous Sherston trilogy (1928–36). CBE, 1951.

Scott Moncrieff, Charles (1889–1930). Ed. Winchester and Edinburgh. 2/Lt, King's Own Scottish Borderers, 6 August 1914; Capt, 1915. Severe leg wound (from which he never fully recovered), 1917: invalided out and awarded MC. Job in War Office, 1918. Reviewed Sassoon's war poems as a 'regrettable incident'; Sassoon describes him unfavourably in *Siegfried's Journey*. Fell in love with Owen, to whom he was introduced by Graves, January 1918. The first of his brilliant translations, *The Song of Roland*, was originally dedicated to Owen, 'my master in assonance': both poets delighted in unorthodox rhyming. Lived in Italy after the war, where he translated Proust, his most famous work.

Seaman, Owen (1861–1936). Ed. Shrewsbury and Cambridge. Staff of *Punch*, 1897; editor, 1906–32. Well known for his parodies and political verse. *Punch* prospered during his editorship and reflected his strongly conservative, patriotic views. Knighted, 1914. Temporary officer, London Volunteers, 1916. Baronet, 1933.

Shakespeare, William Goodman (1890–1975). Probably descended from a cousin of the famous Shakespeare. Doctor, trained in London. Volunteered, Royal Army Medical Corps, 1914. Served in France and Belgium throughout the war. Major. Remained in

RAMC after 1918, serving in India and China. Invalided out, 1943, and went into general practice.

Shanks, Edward (1892–1953). Ed. Merchant Taylors' and Cambridge. Artists' Rifles, then 2/Lt, South Lancashire Regt, 1914, but invalided out before serving abroad. Desk job, War Office, 1915–18 (see his satire, *The Old Indispensables*, 1919). One of the leading later Georgians. Squire's assistant editor on the *London Mercury*, 1919–22.

Shaw-Stewart, Patrick (1888–1917). Ed. Eton and Oxford, a contemporary of Grenfell. Classical scholar; fellow of All Souls. Managing director, Baring's, aged twenty-four. Sub-Lt, later Lt-Cdr, Royal Naval Division, 1914, in same battalion as Brooke. Commanded the firing party at Brooke's funeral. Read Herodotus at Gallipoli: his letters show an extensive knowledge of the area's ancient history. Salonica, 1916. Killed in France, 30 December 1917.

Shillito, Edward (1872–1948). Congregational minister in Kent, Hampshire, London. Verse and prose on religious subjects; many newspaper articles.

Simpson, Henry Lamont (1897–1918). Ed. Carlisle Grammar School and Cambridge. 2/Lt, Lancashire Fusiliers, June 1917: Ypres two months later. Wounded, 1918. Killed by a sniper, August 1918.

Sitwell, Edith (1887–1964). Sister of Osbert and Sacheverell, the three famous children of an eccentric baronet. Left home for London, 1913, determined to become a poet. Edited the first British Modernist – or at least modernistic – anthology, *Wheels* (6 volumes, 1916–21): the 1919 volume was dedicated to Owen's memory and contained seven of his poems, bringing him to public attention for the first time. She also prepared the first edition of his poems (1920).

Sitwell, Osbert (1892–1969). Ed. Eton. Became a cavalry officer at his father's wish, 1911, soon transferring to the Grenadier Guards. Experience on the Western Front drove him to start writing poetry seriously. Wounds to his hands near Ypres became septic, 1916: sent home for treatment and light duties. Wrote anti-war satires in the style of his friend Sassoon, 1917–18. Met and befriended Owen, 1918. Left army as Capt, September 1918. A leading 'modern' with his sister and brother in post-war London. Succeeded as 5th Baronet, 1943; CH, 1958.

Sorley, Charles Hamilton (1895–1915). Son of the professor of moral philosophy, Cambridge. Ed. Marlborough. Six months in Germany, early 1914. Returned home to volunteer on outbreak of war: 2/Lt, Suffolk Regt. Loathed wartime rhetoric ('England – I am sick of the sound of the word'). To France, May 1915. Capt, August. Killed by a sniper, Loos, October.

Squire, John Collings (1884–1958). Ed. Blundell's and Cambridge. Founding member, Fabian Society; twice stood unsuccessfully for Parliament. Journalist and parodist. Literary editor, *New Statesman*, 1913; acting editor, 1917–18. Unfit for active service.

Supported the war effort but sympathized with ordinary soldiers and denounced hypocrisy: his satires were among the earliest well-known criticisms of wartime attitudes. Founder-editor, *London Mercury*, 1919–34.

Stewart, John Ebenezer (1889–1918). From a poor background, but went to Glasgow University and became a teacher. Pte, Highland Light Infantry, early in the war. 2/Lt, Border Regt, late 1914. France and Flanders from September 1915. Somme: Thiepval, Beaumont Hamel, 1916. MC, 1917. Wounded, Messines, June 1917. Took over command of a South Staffordshire battalion, April 1918. Killed in heavy fighting, Kemmel, 23 April.

Streets, John William (1885–1916). Derbyshire coal miner from age fourteen. Sent poems to *Poetry Review* before and after 1914. Enlisted, 12 York and Lancaster Regt (Sheffield Pals), 1914. To France, March 1916. Sgt. Fought in the same trenches at Serre where Manning and Owen were to be in action later. Wrote poems there. Acting Sgt. Wounded on first day of the Somme, but went to help a comrade and was never seen again.

Studd, Mary. *Poems* (1932), published in Ireland, seems to be her only book.

Thomas, (Philip) Edward (1878–1917). Ed. St Paul's and Oxford. Full-time writer: reviews, anthologies, books about the countryside. Writing verse by 1913, discussing it with his friend de la Mare, but friendship with the US poet Robert Frost – and perhaps the outbreak of war – finally got him going as a poet. Over 140 poems, 1914–16. Artists' Rifles, July 1915. Cpl and map instructor in camp at Romford, where he may well have taught Owen. 2/Lt, Royal Garrison Artillery, autumn 1916. To France, January 1917. Killed, Arras, 9 April.

Tomlinson, Albert Ernest (1892–1968). Ed. Middlesbrough High School and Cambridge (where he heard Brooke lecture). 2/Lt, S Staffordshire Regt, June 1915. France, March–July. Bomb wound, Mametz, led to blood poisoning: sent home for treatment and for a while had a War Office job. Tried in vain to relinquish his commission. Sent to France again, August 1917. India, 1918.

Tynan, Katharine (1861–1931). Daughter of an Irish farmer. Ed. at a convent in Drogheda. Leading figure in the Celtic Revival: friend of Yeats, Alice Meynell and many others. Philanthropic work and some nursing during war. Two sons on active service. Frequent poems in periodicals, 1914–18. Many books: verse, fiction, autobiography.

Van Beek, Theo (1889–1958). Born South Africa, where he was known as a promising young poet. Moved to Britain, *c.* 1909. Ed. Edinburgh. Lt, Royal Field Artillery: Somme and elsewhere. Recited some of his anti-war poems in London during the war, wearing uniform: severely reprimanded. Poems in journals until the 1930s. [Information from his son, 1984.]

Vernède, Robert Ernest (1875–1917). Son of a solicitor, of Huguenot descent. Ed.

St Paul's (contemporary of Chesterton, a lifelong friend) and Oxford. Settled in the country to write novels. Joined the ranks of the Royal Fusiliers, September 1914, giving his age as thirty-five (he was in fact thirty-nine, over the maximum permitted age at the time). 2/Lt, May 1915. Attached to Rifle Brigade: Ypres, Somme. Wounded, September 1916, but insisted on returning to action at the end of the year. Died of wounds, Easter Sunday, 8 April 1917. Partly because of his literary connections, partly because he was a good example of a patriotic older poet, his war poems and letters became well known. Hated war's horrors, but excluded them from his verse.

Watson, William (1858–1935). After a false start as a romantic poet, turned to political and literary themes. Like many staunch Liberals, he opposed the Boer War but supported Britain's decision in 1914, when he vainly hoped to become 'the real national poet'. Highly regarded earlier in the century, but his lack of sympathy for new writing put his reputation into sharp decline. His patriotic verse, including his eulogy of Lloyd George, *The Man Who Saw* (1917), earned him a knighthood in 1917 and some derision.

Waugh, Alec [Alexander] (1898–1981). Elder brother of Evelyn. Ed. Sherborne and Sandhurst. 2/Lt, later Lt, Dorset Regt, 1917; prisoner of war, 1918. His first novel, *The Loom of Youth* (1917), caused a scandal with its hints of public-school homosexuality. Helped at Monro's Poetry Bookshop after the war. Many books: novels, travel writing, autobiography.

West, Arthur Graeme (1891–1917). Ed. Blundell's and Oxford. Pte, Public Schools Battalion, February 1915. L/Cpl, May. Trenches, winter 1915–16. Officer training, Scotland, April–July 1916. 2/Lt, Oxford and Bucks Light Infantry, August. Hated war by this stage, losing his religious faith and learning pacifism from his friend C. E. M. Joad and from Bertrand Russell's *Justice in War-Time* (Russell's autobiography contains two 1916 letters from West). Almost refused to serve, but could not bring himself to post the letter: returned to France. Acting Capt, February 1917. Killed, 3 April. Extracts from his diary and some poems published as *The Diary of a Dead Officer* (1919), edited by Joad as a pacifist document – but the editing is highly selective: for example, West is described as hopelessly unsoldierly, although he was in fact in the Oxford OTC for four years, sought a commission in the Regular army and commanded a company in 1917. The full truth may never be known.

Whitmell, Mrs Lucy (d. 1917). Her only known poem, widely anthologized during the war, was admired by both civilians and soldiers (including Penrose).

Willis, George. Apparently served in the infantry on the Western Front. Several poems anonymously in the *Nation* soon after the armistice. Published a book on the philosophy of speech (1919) and two small collections of poems.

Wilson, Theodore Perceval Cameron (1888–1918). Son of a clergyman. Schoolmaster at a prep school before the war: taught Monro's son and became a close friend of Monro. Two novels and humorous contributions to periodicals. Pte, Grenadier Guards,

August 1914. 2/Lt, Sherwood Foresters, February 1915. Trenches, 1916. Staff Capt, May 1917. Met and was much impressed by Haig. Trenches again, January 1918. Killed during the retreat, 24 March 1918.

Yeats, William Butler (1865–1939). Eminent Irish poet, playwright, essayist. His *Oxford Book of Modern Verse 1892–1935* (1936) became notorious for its exclusion of Owen and almost all the other war poets on the grounds that 'passive suffering is not a theme for poetry' (Yeats did include Grenfell's 'Into Battle' and Gibson's 'Breakfast').

Young, Francis Brett (1884–1954). Ed. Epsom and Birmingham, where he qualified as a doctor. Royal Army Medical Corps, 1914: served in East Africa. Major. Invalided out with malaria, 1918. His most famous war poem at the time was a patriotic, pantheistic sonnet, 'The Gift' (*The Times*, 31 May 1916). Best-selling novelist after the war.

SOME FURTHER READING

Reference. Two very useful books are Catherine Reilly's *English Poetry of the First World War: A Bibliography* (Prior, 1978) and Ann Powell's *A Deep Cry* (soldier-poets killed in the war: biographical information and some poems, Palladour Books, 1993).

Biography. There are now numerous biographies of most of the leading war poets, as well as of some of the lesser-known figures such as Grenfell, Lee, Monro and Nichols. Details can often be found on the internet. See also A. St John Adcock, *For Remembrance: Soldier Poets Who Have Fallen in the War* (Hodder, 1920); Laurence Housman (ed.), *War Letters of Fallen Englishmen* (Gollancz, 1930); and the *Oxford Dictionary of National Biography*. Personal files for many army officers can be seen in the National Archives at Kew.

Criticism. Academic interest in First World War literature has grown considerably in recent years. Among many helpful studies are:

Bergonzi, Bernard, *Heroes' Twilight: A Study of the Literature of the Great War* (Macmillan, 1965; 2nd edn, 1980)

Das, Santanu, *Touch and Intimacy in First World War Literature* (Cambridge University Press, 2005)

Featherstone, Simon, *War Poetry: An Introductory Reader* (Routledge, 1995)

Fussell, Paul, *The Great War and Modern Memory* (Oxford University Press, 1975)

Graham, Desmond, *The Truth of War: Owen, Rosenberg and Blunden* (Carcanet, 1984)

Hibberd, Dominic (ed.), *Poetry of the First World War: A Casebook* (Macmillan, 1981)

—— *The First World War: Context & Commentary Series* (Macmillan, 1990)

Hynes, Samuel, *A War Imagined: The First World War and English Culture* (Bodley Head, 1990)

Kendall, Tim, *Modern English War Poetry* (Oxford University Press, 2006)

—— (ed.), *The Oxford Handbook of British and Irish War Poetry* (Oxford University Press, 2007)

Kerr, Douglas, *Wilfred Owen's Voices: Language and Community* (Oxford University Press, 1993)

Khan, Nosheen, *Women's Poetry of the First World War* (Harvester Wheatsheaf, 1988)

Lyon, Philippa, *Twentieth-Century War Poetry: A Reader's Guide to Essential Criticism* (Palgrave, 2005)

Marsland, Elizabeth, *The Nation's Cause: French, English and German Poetry of the First World War* (Routledge, 1991)

Parfitt, George, *English Poetry of the First World War: Contexts and Themes* (Harvester Wheatsheaf, 1990)

Ramazani, Jahan, *Poetry of Mourning: The Modern Elegy from Hardy to Heaney* (University of Chicago Press, 1994)

Roucoux, Michel (ed.), *English Literature of the Great War Revisited* (proceedings of a 1986 conference, UFR Clerc Université Picardie, 1989)

Sherry, Vincent (ed.), *The Cambridge Companion to the Literature of the First World War* (Cambridge University Press, 2005)

Silkin, Jon, *Out of Battle: The Poetry of the Great War* (Oxford University Press, 1972)

Todman, Dan, *The Great War: Myth and Memory* (Hambledon and London, 2005)

The War Poets, a new series of booklets edited by Jean Moorcroft Wilson and published by Cecil Woolf, includes studies of Blunden, Monro and Gibson, Sorley, Thomas, T. P. C. Wilson, and a selection of Aldington's war poems.

Literary Societies and Websites: Many of the more famous war poets now have their own societies – the Friends of the Dymock Poets (Brooke, Drinkwater, Gibson, Thomas), the Ivor Gurney Society, the Wilfred Owen Association, the Siegfried Sassoon Fellowship, the Edward Thomas Fellowship and others (see the Alliance of Literary Societies at: www.sndc.demon.co.uk). Most of these organizations have their own websites, journals and newsletters, as well as arranging meetings and expeditions. Other websites are dedicated to individual poets, including Blunden. The War Poets Association (www.warpoets.org) is interested in the poetry of all wars. See www.oucs.ox.ac.uk/ltg/projects/jtap/ for information on the First World War Digital Poetry Archive, to be launched in November 2008, and for access to the existing Wilfred Owen Multimedia Digital Archive, a teaching resource that includes many images of manuscripts, places, people, *The Hydra* and much else.

ACKNOWLEDGEMENTS

This anthology would not have been viable if many agents and publishers had not generously agreed to reduce their copyright fees, in some cases by more than half. We are most grateful to the many private owners of copyrights who have allowed us to include poems at no charge.

We record our thanks to the many people who have so kindly helped us in the preparation of this book, including Timothy d'Arch Smith, Patrick Aylmer, Sarah Bendall, Pam Blevins, Mark Bostridge, Bob Burrows, Max Egremont, Andor Gomme, Richard Graves, Linda Hart, Duff Hart-Davis, Gwen Millan, Jane Potter, John Shakespeare, James Slater, Anne Turner and Ann Wheeler. Tom Coulthard very kindly volunteered to scan and proof-read all the poems and notes. We owe a special debt to three previous anthologists, Anne Harvey, Nosheen Khan and Vivien Noakes. Jeff Cooper provided us with an accurate date for *New Numbers*, Tony Verity explained the subtleties of Athenian particles, and Danny Wigley told us about the blizzard at Romford in March 1916. We are also most grateful to our agent, Andrew Lownie, our editors, Becky Hardie and Andreas Campomar, and our copyright agent, Nicholas Wetton.

Thanks are due to the following for permission to reprint poems: the Estate of Richard Aldington, c/o Rosica Colin Limited, London, for poems by Richard Aldington, © the Estate of Richard Aldington; the children of Enid Bagnold for a poem by Enid Bagnold; the Society of

Authors as the Literary Representative of the Estate of Laurence Binyon for a poem by Laurence Binyon; PFD on behalf of the Estate of Edmund Blunden for poems by Edmund Blunden; Patrick Aylmer for a poem by Mary Borden; Mark Bostridge for poems by Vera Brittain; James Slater for poems by May Wedderburn Cannan; Lord Elton for poems by Godfrey Elton; the University of Arkansas, University Libraries, Special Collections Division, for a poem by John Gould Fletcher; A. P. Watt Ltd on behalf of Timothy D'Arch Smith for poems by Gilbert Frankau; the Warden and Fellows of Merton College Oxford for a poem by Heathcote Garrod; Macmillan, London, for poems by Wilfrid Gibson; Carcanet Press for poems by Robert Graves from *The Complete Poems* (2000); Paul Cooper for a poem by Rosaleen Graves; the Ivor Gurney Trust and Carcanet Press for poems by Ivor Gurney from *Collected Poems* (2004); A. P. Watt Ltd on behalf of the Executors of the Estate of Jocelyn Herbert, M. Y. Herbert and Polly M. V. R. Perkins for poems by A. P. Herbert; the National Federation of Retirement Pensions Associations for poems by Teresa Hooley; David Higham Associates for a poem by Ford Madox Hueffer; Martin Kendall for a poem by Guy Kendall; David Higham Associates for a poem by C. H. B. Kitchin; Kathleen Lee Blackwood and the University of Dundee for poems by Joseph Lee; PFD on behalf of the Estate of Rose Macaulay for poems by Rose Macaulay; the Literary Trustees of Walter de la Mare and the Society of Authors as their representative for a poem by Walter de la Mare from *The Complete Poems of Walter de la Mare* (1975 reprint); the Society of Authors as the Literary Representative of the Estate of John Masefield for a poem by John Masefield; Peter Newbolt for a poem by Henry Newbolt; Anne Charlton for a poem by Robert Nichols; Sir Roy Strong for poems by Carola Oman; the Random House Group for two poems by Wilfred Owen

ACKNOWLEDGEMENTS

from *The Poems of Wilfred Owen*, edited by Jon Stallworthy (Chatto & Windus, 1990); David Higham Associates for poems by Margaret Postgate; Faber & Faber and New Directions Publishing Corporation for *Hugh Selwyn Mauberley, IV* and *V* from *Selected Poems 1908–1969* (Faber & Faber, 1977), © 1926 by Ezra Pound; David Higham Associates for poems by Herbert Read; Carcanet Press for poems by Edgell Rickword from *Collected Poems* (1991); Juliet Boobbyer for a poem by Rennell Rodd; the Barbara Levy Literary Agency and Penguin Group (USA) Inc for poems by Siegfried Sassoon; John Shakespeare for a poem by W. G. Shakespeare; Macmillan, London for a poem by Edward Shanks from *Poems 1912–32* (Macmillan, 1933); David Higham Associates for a poem by Edith Sitwell; David Higham Associates for poems by Osbert Sitwell; the Master and Fellows of Emmanuel College, Cambridge for a poem by A. E. Tomlinson; Peter Waugh for a poem by Alec Waugh; A. P. Watt Ltd on behalf of Gráinne Yeats for a poem by W. B. Yeats from *Collected Poems* (Picador, 1990); David Higham Associates for a poem by Francis Brett Young.

Every effort has been made to trace copyright holders, but in some cases they could not be found. The publishers would be interested to hear from any copyright holders not here acknowledged, and will rectify any omissions brought to their notice at the earliest opportunity.

INDEX OF POETS
AND THEIR POEMS

INDEX OF TITLES
AND FIRST LINES

Titles are listed in *italic*.